Longitudinal Qualitative Research

Longitudinal Qualitative Research

Analyzing Change through Time

Johnny Saldaña

ALTAMIRA
P R E S S

A Division of
ROWMAN & LITTLEFIELD PUBLISHERS, INC.
Walnut Creek • Lanham • New York • Oxford

ALTAMIRA PRESS
A Division of Rowman & Littlefield Publishers, Inc.
1630 North Main Street, #367
Walnut Creek, California 94596
www.altamirapress.com

Rowman & Littlefield Publishers, Inc.
A Member of the Rowman & Littlefield Publishing Group
4501 Forbes Boulevard, Suite 200
Lanham, Maryland 20706

PO Box 317
Oxford
OX2 9RU, UK

British Library Cataloguing in Publication Information Available

Library of Congress Cataloging-in-Publication Data

Saldaña, Johnny.
   Longitudinal qualitative research : analyzing change through time / Johnny Saldaña.
      p. cm.
   Includes bibliographical references and index.
   ISBN 0-7591-0295-3 (hardcover : alk. paper)—ISBN 0-7591-0296-1 (paperback : alk. paper)
      1. Social Sciences—Research. 2. Qualitative research. 3. Longitudinal method.
   I. Title.

H62.S3186 2003
001.4'2—dc21   2002043908

Printed in the United States of America

∞™ The paper used in this publication meets the minimum requirements of American National Standard for Information Sciences—Permanence of Paper for Printed Library Materials, ANSI/NISO Z39.48-1992.

Contents

Acknowledgments

Thanks are extended to:

Tom Barone and Mary Lee Smith, my qualitative research instructors at Arizona State University, for teaching me how to fly while keeping both feet on the ground.

Harry F. Wolcott, whose writings and collegiality strengthen my practice as an artist and scholar.

The National Endowment for the Arts; the Arizona Commission on the Arts; the Arizona State University Department of Theatre, Institute for Studies in the Arts, and Katherine K. Herberger College of Fine Arts; and the International Drama in Education Research Institute for their financial support during various stages of my longitudinal studies.

Erin Dye, Carole S. Miller, and the anonymous reviewers and jurors of this book's prospectus or manuscript for their revision recommendations.

Ted Barrington of QSR International's Research Services for his consultation on NVivo qualitative data analysis software and image contributions to this book.

Mitch Allen, editor, who opened the door and invited me in.

The thirty-two participants profiled in this work, who spent years with me as I observed their changes through time.

Permission to quote from articles published in *Youth Theatre Journal* granted by the American Alliance for Theatre and Education. These articles are as follows. "Teamwork Is Not Just a Word: Factors Disrupting the Development of a Departmental Group of Theatre Teachers" by L. A. McCammon from *Youth Theatre Journal* (vol. 8, no. 3 [1994], pp. 3–9). "A Quantitative Analysis of Children's Responses to Theatre from Probing Questions: A Pilot Study" by Johnny Saldaña from *Youth Theatre Journal* (vol. 3, no. 4 [1989], pp. 7–17). "'Is Theatre Necessary?' Final Exit Interviews with Sixth Grade Participants from the ASU Longitudinal Study" by Johnny Saldaña from *Youth Theatre Journal* (vol. 9 [1995], pp. 14–30). "'Significant differences' in Child Audience Response: Assertions from the ASU Longitudinal Study" by Johnny Saldaña from *Youth Theatre Journal* (vol. 10 [1996], pp. 67–83). "'Survival': A White Teacher's Conception of Drama with Inner-City Hispanic Youth" by Johnny Saldaña from *Youth Theatre Journal* (vol. 11 [1997], pp. 25–46). "Playwriting with Data: Ethnographic Performance Texts" by Johnny Saldaña from *Youth Theatre Journal* (vol. 13 [1999], pp. 60–71). Copyright © American Alliance for Theatre and Education. Reprinted with permission.

Permission to quote from *The Sociology of Social Change* by P. Sztompka granted by Blackwell Publishers. Copyright © 1993 by Blackwell Publishing. Reprinted with permission.

Permission to quote from *Grounding Grounded Theory: Guidelines for Qualitative Inquiry* by Ian Dey granted by Academic Press, an imprint of Elsevier Science. Copyright © 1999 by Elsevier Science. Reprinted with permission.

Permission to quote from "What Is 'Appropriate Practice' at Home and in Child Care? Low-Income Mothers' Views on Preparing Their Children for School" by Holloway et al. from *Early Childhood Research Quarterly* (vol. 10 [1995], pp. 451–473) granted by Elsevier Science. Copyright © 1995 Elsevier Science. Reprinted with permission.

Permission to quote excerpts from *Scared Straight! Twenty Years Later* courtesy of Arnold Shapiro Productions. Copyright © 1999 AIMS Multimedia. Reprinted with permission.

Permission to quote from *42 Up: "Give Me the Child Until He Is Seven and I Will Show You the Man"* edited by Bennett Singer granted by The New Press. Copyright © 1998 by The New Press. Reprinted with permission.

Introduction: Looking toward the Journey

"The longest journey begins with a single step."

—Ancient proverb

Longitudinal Qualitative Research: Analyzing Change through Time is recommended as a supplement to introductory texts in qualitative inquiry or as a handbook for researchers conducting long-term fieldwork. This book outlines basic concepts and recommended questions for analyzing qualitative data collected from longitudinal studies conducted by novice researchers in education and selected social sciences. I describe transferable methods developed from my own and others' research experiences, but I also acknowledge that each study is context-specific and driven by its particular goals, research questions, conceptual framework, methodology, and other matters. I do not discuss statistical procedures for longitudinal quantitative data or fundamental techniques of interviewing, participant observation, or document review, except when they are relevant to longitudinal qualitative data gathering and analysis. This book also does not focus on the theoretical macro- or mezzolevels of social process (Sztompka, 1993), or sociology's mesodomain analysis (Hall, 1995). Instead, it focuses on microlevels of change observed within individual cases or groups of participants.

My primary field of study is theatre education, and my research and publications cover a spectrum of genres in both the traditional quantitative and qualitative paradigms: semantic differential surveys (Saldaña and Otero, 1990), experimental research in drama (Saldaña and Wright, 1996), educational ethnography (Saldaña, 1997), ethnic studies (Saldaña, 1991), ethnographic performance texts (Saldaña, 1998b, 1999, 2001a, at press), confessional tales (Saldaña, 1998a), and longitudinal field experiments (Saldaña, 1993, 1995, 1996). My initial education was that of an artist-educator, not a social scientist. But throughout the past twenty years as a professor, research has become for me a necessary as well as an engaging academic responsibility. Virtually no one outside of theatre education accesses my field's research literature, so several of the examples I profile in this work will be new to most readers. But don't let that deter you from reading further; we share much in common. My on-the-job training was supplemented with concurrent university course work in quantitative and qualitative research methods. At first, I was surprised by how many terms and concepts in the qualitative literature paralleled my own discipline of theatre (e.g., actor, character, role, setting, stage, dramaturgical analysis, ritual, script, vignette, scene, plot, social drama, interaction, conflict, and performance). But then I realized that playwrights and qualitative researchers write for the same purpose: To create a unique, insightful, and engaging text about the human condition.

As I learned the language of scholarship, I discovered that my artistic worldview brought a unique perspective to my research endeavors, data analysis, and writing. I would not presume to label myself an expert in social science or educational research. Nor can I compare this effort to such established titles as Fullan's *The New Meaning of Educational Change* (2001); the decades-long fieldwork projects profiled in Kemper and Royce's *Chronicling Cultures: Long-Term Field Research in Anthropology* (2002); the prolific psychological research on behavioral change; and the voluminous educational literature on school reform. I do not write as the definitive authority; I write as someone who's had particular longitudinal qualitative research experiences and who's reflected on those experiences. I also include excerpts from others' longitudinal qualitative work as illustrative examples of what I consider best practices. Depending on your perspective, I bring to this report either a vision untainted by social science dogma and "educationese," or a foolish and uninformed naïveté. But like a playwright who cannot resist the artistic impulse to create a script, my own artist-researcher impulses drove me to express my thoughts and experiences in this format.

An opportunity arose to pilot test the contents of this book when I guest lectured to a research methods class. The date was just seven weeks after the September 11, 2001, terrorist attacks. Media coverage since that day reflected how we as a nation had "changed" and that things would never be the same again. The students and I put that assertion to task by discussing (i.e., analyzing) systematically how we as individuals and social citizens of America had become "different" in just seven weeks. We brainstormed answers to the sixteen questions for analyzing change that I pose in the upcoming chapters. When class was over, we all left with a sense of order—not only because we had talked about our personal and painful feelings along the way, but because we brought some semblance of order to the chaotic influences and affects[1] of terrorism. We left still pondering the meaning of it all, but it was as if, for just that morning, we were able to able to bring clarity to the confusion of the times.

A juror reading a report from one of my early longitudinal endeavors wrote that my personal research paradigm was "caught between the quantitative and qualitative traditions." Back then, I thought that was criticism. Now, I perceive it as a comfortable location with a broad panoramic view. As epistemological and ontological conflicts among theorists play themselves out on stage, I remain seated in the front row of the theatre, watching, listening, and thinking deeply. I prefer not to perform as one of the methodological orators featured in the spotlight, but as an audience member I am nevertheless an essential participant in the event. My own paradigmatic assumptions and pragmatic ways of making meaning in qualitative inquiry boil down to not a flippant response but a research orientation that suits me: "Whatever works." Rather than explain at this point the theoretical foundations of this work, I will raise them, when needed, throughout. (For the record, my signature perspective is an interpretivist lens with critical and arts-based filters.) My research methods educators and diverse fieldwork experiences have taught me both the rigorous craft and creative art of qualitative research. So, consider this book a primer in longitudinal qualitative research (cf. Taris, 2000). It is intended for fellow newcomers to long-term inquiry, and it is my effort to document my personal learnings from longitudinal study design and data analysis.

Finally, it was difficult to organize this text into discrete subject areas because any main topic or subtopic in research methods can be interwoven with at least two or three others. How can one neatly discuss the coding of qualitative data, for example, without preparatory discussion of or embedded references to various paradigms, change processes, and data analytic software—subjects worthy of their own sections or chapters? I will not jump back and forth idiosyncratically from one topic to another like some playful time traveler, but understand that there will be a few necessary shifts, diversions, and artificial divisions and distributions of content areas as the book proceeds.

CHAPTER ONE

Longitudinal Qualitative Studies, Time, and Change

This chapter reviews three foundation principles of longitudinal qualitative research: length of the study, time, and change. Though "qualitative" is generally an umbrella term for several approaches to and genres of human inquiry, I shall rely on the examples profiled in this chapter and throughout this book to illustrate the paradigm and methods.

When Does a Qualitative Study Become Longitudinal?

Three Examples

A student once asked me to define "longitudinal" and inquired whether a qualitative study's fieldwork should progress through a minimum number of years to be considered longitudinal. I reflected on my own experience and practice for an answer: After two years (1982–1984) of literature review and preliminary research designs to discern how children perceive and respond to theatre; seven years (1984–1991) of fieldwork and interviews with the same group of children viewing theatre events as they progressed from kindergarten through sixth grade; four years (1991–1995) of quantitative and qualitative data analysis of field notes, interview transcripts, and surveys for several published reports; and two and a half years (1995–1997) of follow-up interviews and fieldwork with one of the original participants during his adolescence to discern any residual effects from the initial study; I shook my head and replied facetiously, "Longitudinal means a lonnnnnnnng time." But not all *panel field experiments* (a continuous, experimental treatment condition to

1

the same group of participants in a naturalistic setting over an extended period of time) such as the seven-year Theatre Response Study, as I shall refer
to it, need to be this extensive to qualify as a longi-
tudinal qualitative study.

Longitudinal means a   An *educational ethnography* (naturalistic obser-
lonnnnnnng time   vation of participants' daily culture in a school setting over an extended period of time) I conducted
with Nancy (pseudonym), a teacher participant,
extended off and on through a twenty-month period. This case study tracked
a white novice instructor in an inner-city, grades K–8 magnet school site
from September 1993 through April 1995. Initially, this project began as
nothing more than three interviews across two months in 1993 to gather
Nancy's perceptions of assessment in the drama classroom for an article I was
writing. But after learning more about her difficult teaching environment
and her stories of working with impoverished Hispanic youth, the study
changed focus and extended into 1994 with the development of her thesis, a
journal-based report of her first-year experiences. In 1995, I used my sabbat-
ical to conduct more interviews, accompanied with participant observation
of Nancy's daily classroom work. Unlike the carefully planned Theatre Response Study with its a priori (determined beforehand) research goals and
questions, the Survival Study, as I shall refer to it, emerged as a unique
ethnographic research opportunity that extended longer than originally intended.

Barry (pseudonym), one of the original participants from the Theatre Response Study, was perceived and assessed by the research team as the most
talented individual from the panel by the time he completed sixth grade.
When he entered high school in ninth grade, Barry voluntarily enrolled in
theatre coursework and participated in extracurricular play production activities for four years. From the middle of his sophomore through his senior
years, I observed Barry's development as both an adolescent and as an actor.
We collaborated toward the end of the study to document his *life history* (biography and autobiography) in the form of a one-act play, a most appropriate choice for the presentation and representation of this talented case study
(a "prodigal analysis," according to Cairns and Rodkin [1998]).

Epstein classifies long-term studies into three formats of researcher participation: "continuous research in the same small society over a number of
years; periodic restudies at regular or irregular intervals; and/or returning after a lengthy interval of time has elapsed since the original research"
(2002, 64). The Theatre Response, Survival, and Barry Studies respectively
align with Epstein's formats, in addition to being three genres of qualitative

inquiry: a panel field experiment using qualitative interview data to assess children's aesthetic development; an educational ethnography of a unique school culture; and the life history of one young man's participation in his chosen art form. A qualitative study becomes longitudinal when its fieldwork progresses over a lonnnnnnnng time. All three studies described earlier were labeled "longitudinal," but their fieldwork periods progressed across seven years, twenty months, and two and a half years, respectively. Was one of these fieldwork projects more longitudinal or more qualitative than the others? No. They are just three of many possible models of longitudinal qualitative research.

How Long Is a Longitudinal Qualitative Study?
Is there a required minimum length of fieldwork time for a qualitative study to be considered longitudinal? I can find no consensus or authoritative answer to satisfy multiple disciplines. The *Inventory of Longitudinal Studies in the Social Sciences* (Young, Savola, and Phelps, 1991) establishes a span of at least one year as a criterion for its inclusion of studies. Vogt's *Dictionary of Statistics and Methodology: A Nontechnical Guide for the Social Sciences* describes related terms such as "time-series analysis," "event history analysis," "age effects," "cohort effects," "maturation effects," and "period effects," yet remains nonspecific when defining "longitudinal study": "over time," accompanied with an illustrative example (1999, p. 164). Kelly and McGrath's *On Time and Method* specifies that a longitudinal design has "multiple waves of observations" over "a substantial calendar time—months or years" (1988, p. 135). Schwandt's *Dictionary of Qualitative Inquiry* (2001) does not include longitudinal as a specific entry. Time is briefly mentioned when relevant to such terms as "ethnography" or "participant observation," the latter occurring across a "relatively prolonged period" (186). Stewart states that prolonged fieldwork "has customarily been construed as 12 to 18 months" for ethnographers (1998, p. 68), and some anthropological studies have been multigenerational, achieving up to fifty years of fieldwork in the same site (Kemper and Royce, 2002). Finally, life-course research relies heavily on longitudinal qualitative *and* quantitative data amassed over several generations to describe, explain, and predict human pathways and actions from birth through death (Cairns, Bergman, and Kagan, 1998; Heinz and Krüger, 2001; Lerner et al., 2001; Ruspini, 1999).

I hesitate to set precise parameters around longitudinal because many qualitative studies, regardless of fieldwork length, *are* longitudinal in its broadest sense. Sztompka asserts, "It is impossible to conceive of time without reference to some change. And, vice versa, the idea of change apart from time is simply inconceivable" (1993, p. 41). Qualitative researchers, ethnographers in particular, devote an extensive period of time to the study of people in natural settings. Good ethnography, in fact, assumes long-term field engagement (Wolcott, 1994, p. 178; Stewart, 1998, p. 20). During that time we focus on how people think, feel, and act from moment through moment to capture in-depth perceptions and meanings, to extract stories for narrative inquiry, and to log rich details for individual biography. Additionally, we learn how human actions and participant perspectives might change during the course of a study to reveal temporal-based themes and patterns of human development or social process. For example, in Lister et al.'s three-year study of sixty-four young adults' "transitions to citizenship" in the United Kingdom, qualitative data (derived from interviews and focus groups) with supplemental quantitative data (derived from questionnaires and existing government statistics) were gathered to "illuminate young people's experiences and understandings of the meanings of citizenship and their changing perceptions of themselves as citizens" (2002, p. 1). The study was historically situated to observe their developing political attitudes from the year before through the year after the 2001 general election.

Human actions and participant perspectives might change during the course of a study

If I was forced to specify a minimum length of fieldwork time for a qualitative study to be considered longitudinal *in educational settings*, my experience tells me it should be, at a minimum, nine months. I supervised a qualitative study with a three-month fieldwork period to document theatre teachers' perceptions of newly adopted state standards (Hager et al., 2000) and a second qualitative field experiment with a four-month fieldwork period to assess children's responses to sociopolitical classroom drama (Saldaña, 2000). In the former study, the research team gathered "snapshots" of teachers' perceptions about recent sweeping changes in educational policy, but we did not assess if any significant changes had occurred in the teachers' classroom practice. Had the fieldwork period extended beyond three months, we may have found evidence of change through the course of the academic year. In the latter study, I collected ample evidence of changes in children's knowledge about interpersonal oppression and in girls' sympathetic and empathetic responses; but changes in most children's daily actions to counteract oppression were only occasional. Participating teachers shared with me through interviews that had the treatment and fieldwork period continued through the course of the nine-month academic year, more significant changes might have occurred in the children. Hence, a minimum of nine months of fieldwork is suggested for an educational study to be considered longitudinal, whether the project is ethnographic or a field experiment.

Some qualitative researchers label their studies "longitudinal" solely on the basis of extended time in the field or due to an extended period of time between pre- and postinterviews. And sometimes missing from their methods discussions are (a) considerations of how time interacts and interplays with the collection and analysis of qualitative data, (b) attention to the multiple and possible *types* of changes, and (c) the influences and affects on human actions and participant worldviews. One educational ethnographer may log 100 clock hours of part-time fieldwork at one school setting through the course of a year. Another ethnographer working full time might log the same number of clock hours at the same site within a month. Is a study longitudinal because of its annual breadth ("It's been a *long* year") or its daily depth ("It's been a *long* day")? Or can it be both, as Kidder profiles a teacher's summer and academic year through carefully selected details of daily classroom life in *Among Schoolchildren* (1989)? What is important in the discernment of change: length or amount, months or years, short term or long term, quantity or quality, categories and variables or themes and stories, or various combinations thereof? Admittedly, it depends, because time and thus change are contextual.

> *Time and thus change are contextual*

Conceptions of Time for Longitudinal Qualitative Studies

A discussion of longitudinal qualitative inquiry necessitates a brief discussion of time. You might think it unnecessary to review the obvious, but time may not be as obvious as you or your participants experience it.

Time Constructions

We sometimes read that qualitative data are fluid, a metaphor that evokes movement. An "ocean" of data will be used in this book instead of the more popular metaphor "landscape." The latter suggests a fixed and stable canvas, albeit three dimensional, for positionality. An ocean is an image that suggests vastness and ever-present motion, regardless of depth. Just as water is fluid, so is time. The physical sciences grapple with this concept and its relationship to movement in space. I am not a physicist, yet I marvel at the idea that time is a physically contextual construct. Hawking writes, "In the theory of relativity there is no unique absolute time, but instead each individual has his own personal measure of time that depends on where he is and how he is moving" (1988, p. 33). The existence of time is one of several things that cannot be easily proven by science (the two others being consciousness and the soul). Theoretically, the gravitational magnitude of black holes even dis-torts time. Science fiction has developed fascinat-ing scenarios about human control of the physics of

Just as water is fluid, so is time

time. Whether possible in the future or not, it is in-triguing to ponder the possibilities.

Time is also a cultural construct (Agar, 1994, pp. 63–64; Davies, 1989; Levine, 1997; Lippincott, 1999; Smith and Abrahamson, 1999). Graveline, for example, discusses how the cyclical and ceremonial Aboriginal conceptions of time oppose tradi-tional Western temporal constructions of linearity and chronology (1998, p. 139). American missionaries, accustomed to the tightly fixed arrival and departure schedules of buses and planes, may find themselves in flux with the comparative casualness of Tanzanian transportation. A chartered bus driver, arriving in Dar es Salaam two hours after the prearranged arrival time to pick up missionaries, explained that since material possessions are scarce for him, time is his luxurious commodity, "Time is all I own." Davies (1989) also as-serts how time is gendered and constructed as an instrument of power and control. Her longitudinal qualitative study of forty women over three years examined their movement variations within the labor market and unem-ployment. Their stories of constraining factory conditions illustrate how hegemonic, linear "male time" oppresses, creates dysfunction for women in the workplace, and negatively affects their lives and emotional well-being.

Finally, time is an individually and subjectively interpreted construct (Fla-herty, 1996, 1999; Levine, 1997). Kelly and McGrath assert that people "do not experience time as a smooth linear flow of undifferentiated moments. Rather, they experience time as epochal and phasic in its flow. Different points in time and different periods of time seem to be qualitatively different from one another" (1988, p. 55). What seems an engaging and riveting theatrical per-formance to one audience member can be ponderously slow and boring to an-other. Young adults tell me they admittedly possess short attention spans and expect instant gratification, more so than those of comparable age a few decades ago. If this new generation's conception of time has been shaped by rapid technological bombardment, even their conception of longitudinal may mean an extended number of months rather than years.

Time is no longer linear in the postmodern paradigm; time curves in new and creative chronological forms (Denzin, 2001, pp. 29–30). According to the U.S. National Institutes of Standards and Technology, time is no longer based on the movement of celestial bodies. A second has been redefined as the duration of "an atom of Cesium 133 to tick through exactly

9,192,631,770 resonant cycles after it has been passed through an electro-magnetic field" ("U.S. Unveils," 1999). Technology can now manipulate au-dio and video recordings by speeding the playback slightly, thus reducing a few seconds from the original total time, while keeping voices at their origi-nal pitch and maintaining for the audience the illusion of "real time." Films like *Annie Hall*, *Pulp Fiction*, and *Memento* present their stories in unique and seemingly idiosyncratic blends of past, present, and future. Though tradi-tional narratives have beginnings, middles, and ends, filmmaker Jean-Luc Godard offers an alternative perspective attributed to him, "A story should have a beginning, a middle, and an end—but not necessarily in that order."

Time Is Data
This semiexistential review of time does serve a purpose. It encourages you to sensitize and attune yourself to how a lonnnnnnnng time is not just a prerequisite for a longitudinal qualitative study. In other words, time is data. Levine's (1997) cross-cultural empirical studies of time observed that different countries around the world, and even different cities within the United States, maintain their own cultural tempos and durations of events. Such factors as economics, population, climate, and cultural values shape human agency and interactions on a daily basis, suggesting that the con-textual conditions of a native's geographic location may influence and af-fect the tempos and durations of an individual's and group's changes through time. Put simply, longitudinal qualitative change in Mexico will differ from longitudinal qualitative change in Japan. And since Levine notes that individuals also have their own perceptions, constructions, and applications of time based on personality (e.g., Type A and B), a person's psychological clock may control the tempo, duration, and other dynamics of intraindividual change. Examining such behaviors as speech patterns, waiting, scheduling, and list making provides insight on one's "time ur-gency": "[T]he pace of our lives governs our experience of the passage of time. And how we move through time is, ultimately, the way we live our lives" (p. xix).

Time is data   Analyzing change requires at least two reference points through time, such as "then" and "now," 1996 and 1999, sophomore year and senior year. But a Point A–Point B longitudinal model or a before-and-after chart limits the ability to discern evolutionary processes. In this book, the concept *from-through* rather than *from-to* is used to locate and connect time. "From-to" suggests discrete starting and ending points (*from* kindergarten *to* second grade), which may gloss over details and reduce assertions of change to descriptive statements of stark contrast. "From-through" implies a more temporal-based perspective that details the complexities of the journey. To me, "from-to" generates a product of change; "from-through" outlines the process of change. Likewise and when appropriate, the words "through," "throughout," or "across time" will be used instead of "over time." The latter phrase suggests a sweeping, temporal leap, while the former word choices suggest more processual immersion throughout the course of longitudinal research.

> *"From-to" generates a product of change; "from-through" outlines the process of change*

Conceptions of Change for Longitudinal Qualitative Studies

Like time, change also necessitates a brief discussion to ensure that we are not assuming the obvious.

Defining Change

Much has been written in every discipline about change, but we still seem puzzled by its slippery nature and our attempts to capture it tangibly in our research endeavors, despite the assertion that "[c]hange has substance and form, content and process" (Hargreaves et al., 2001, p. 184). Naisbitt (1982) illustrates this expertly by using basic yet exhaustive content analyses of thousands of daily newspapers to develop his ten initial "megatrends" and provides substantial evidence (both quantitative and qualitative) to support his general observations of change during 1980s' U.S. society. Though he glosses over the specific analytic tactics and strategies he employes, these trends ideas emerged from Naisbitt, as he unabashedly admits, after a lot of reading and reflection—two essential tasks for longitudinal qualitative data analysis.

So, what *is* change? Do we rely on synonyms such as "evolution," "development," "difference," or "process" for further clarification, or are these constructs just as confounding? What about "conversion," "alteration," "variation," "modification," "transformation," or "substitution"? Do we turn to other writers to gather definitions of change such as

- a "succession of differences in time" in persisting entities (Nisbet, 1976, p. 97);
- "observable differences in our experience of the configuration of things" (Fabun, 1967, p. 7);

- "a disturbance in one or more systemic forces that causes changes in other forces, more or less simultaneously" (Kelly and McGrath, 1988, pp. 17–18);
- "*a process, not an event*" of individual and shared meaning (Fullan, 2001, p. 52, emphasis in the original);
- "a continuous unending stream of events . . . [because] life is nothing else but movement, motion, and change" (Sztompka, 1993, p. 9);
- the "reculturing" of a system during its "evolutionary trajectory" (Hargreaves, 2000); or
- a distinct period of "decompartmentalization" and "social fluidity" where "hybrid systems" emerge from "paradisciplinary" dialogue and interaction (Century, 2001).

Clandinin and Connelly (2000, chapter 1) review selected writers and their concepts that have played influential and significant roles in the development of narrative inquiry as it relates to temporality and change. John Dewey suggests a criterion of continuity, Mary Catherine Bateson suggests themes of improvisation and adaptation, Robert Coles suggests the unfolding of a lived life, and Clifford Geertz struggles with the uncertainties of documenting change and the metaphor of watching a parade as an attempt to capture the elusive process. "For Geertz . . . certainty is not a goal, theoretical precision not possible. For Geertz, the anthropologist creates lumbering, shaky, grand contraptions" (Clandinin and Connelly, 2000, p. 9).

The definitions and conceptions outlined earlier may frame our analytic mind-set as we gather, code, and interpret longitudinal qualitative data, but semantics alone will not reconcile the problematic issue. It is not my intent to avoid answering the question: What is change? But an all-purpose response that will satisfy every academic discipline is impossible and impractical to construct for a very simple reason: Since time is contextual, and our social actions and circumstances within it are contextual, change is contextual (Fullan, 1999). Pettigrew (1995) advises that researchers define what change means for each particular longitudinal study at hand and how change is to be observed and inferred—before analysis begins, as analysis proceeds, or after the fact—to examine whether or not it has occurred at all in participants. We do so, however, with the understanding that our systematic attempts are "shaky" at best and are subject to the particular conditions of our particular fields of study. For example, Hallebone, in her typologies for measuring self-identity change in women during five years of psychotherapy, defines the construct for her study, "Stability or change in self-image (or self-identity) for individuals, was judged in relation to congruence between original and present self-image. Self-identity change was considered to be a 'fact' when later self-descriptions indicated respondents had changed categories within the typology constructed at the first interview stage" (1992, p. 10). Counseling's Transtheoretical Model (TTM) acknowledges ten distinct processes of change, derived from empirical study. Some of these processes include client consciousness raising, self-liberation, stimulus control, and dramatic relief. In TTM, "[i]ndividuals engage in or attempt an array of solutions to modify problematic thinking, deficiencies in functioning, problem behaviors, or undesirable affects" (Petrocelli, 2002, pp. 23–24). Labeling and describing these ten processes of change enables counselors to plan appropriate therapies for their clients.

Change is contextual

There are some research projects whose questions have no immediate answers or previous research for guidance. Admittedly, we enter many of our qualitative, naturalistic inquiries with hunches, speculations, and attempts to predict the outcomes along the way. Some studies are germinal in their disciplines by finding patterns never observed before (e.g., the transitional stages in Daniluk's [2001] three-year study of infertile couples adapting to childlessness). There are times, however, when a study's long-term investigation "shatters the myths" of long-held beliefs or finds disconfirming evidence against a previous researcher's work (e.g., Braver and O'Connell's *Divorced Dads: Shattering the Myths* [1998]). Not always do we know what to look for in advance, and sometimes the processes and products of change are so subtle we are unaware of them at first glance. Hence, I feel we should be flexible and allow a definition of change to emerge as a study proceeds and its data are analyzed. Ironically yet fittingly, we should permit ourselves to change our meaning of change as a study progresses.

We should permit ourselves to change our meaning of change as a study progresses

Searching for Change
Societies have always changed and are always changing, yet we seem to have developed a contextually resurgent consciousness of our need to and methods of change as we ended the twentieth century and began the twenty-first century. Bill Maxwell identifies change as "the most important phenomenon of the [twentieth] century" ("Who Are," 1999). A national best-selling book

was Johnson's *Who Moved My Cheese? An Amazing Way to Deal with Change in Your Work and in Your Life* (1998). This simple tale presents seven important lessons on how people can adjust and adapt to and initiate positive changes in their personal circumstances. The recent genre of action research suggests the desire for individuals and community groups to seek empowerment and thus transformation of their practices for the better (Wadsworth, 1997). Even theatre and education, my two fields of study, have adopted major calls to action within the last two decades. The current movements in theatre for social change (Boal, 1995) and critical pedagogy (e.g., hooks's *Teaching to Transgress: Education As the Practice of Freedom* [1994]; Oakes and Lipton's *Teaching to Change the World* [1999]) seek "transformation," "activism," and "liberation" through "progressive" and "revolutionary" acts. Technology has accelerated the tempos of our lives and the rhythms of our interactions, particularly since world knowledge and information doubles every five years, according to modern lore (Pritchett and Pound, n.d., p. 2). Within this particular span of history, we seem more than ever before to question why things are as they are and to ponder the possibilities for social metamorphosis (though individuals living during the Golden Age of Greece, the European Renaissance, and the American Industrial Revolution may have been thinking and feeling the exact same way about their eras).

Just as there is no definitive length of time for a study to be considered longitudinal and no universal definition of change, there are no definitive opinions on change processes and products. One can find several conflicting perspectives in the educational change literature. For example, Lee and Yarger state that narrative inquiry holds great potential in such areas as teacher research to "produce rich, detailed descriptions of how changes occur over time" (1996, p. 34). But Sarason observes, "If anything is incontrovertible in the literature on educational reform, it is how difficult it is to get teachers to change their accustomed beliefs and practices" (1999, p. 62). Institutional change in education and other social organizations, such as government, becomes problematic to document and analyze due to its "disjointed, uncoordinated, and often contradictory" nature (Sikula, 1996, p. xv), despite the assertion that organizations "have a higher capability for change than do individuals and societies" (Cooper, 1998, p. 122). Regardless of the emergent, inspired writings to develop individual critical consciousness for personal empowerment, thus creating a better world, Florence cautions us, "It is hard for people to change behaviors. It is even harder to change attitudes" (1998, p. 140). But with clear goals, proper support systems, and motivated people in place, significant educational change can not only happen, but it can also be positive for all constituencies (Hargreaves et al., 2001). The tempos of change in technology are likened to the speed of Pentium processors, and human social action sometimes matches that speed with an "as-soon-as-possible" mind-set. But in education, "[m]eaningful change is slow: there are always stellar moments, but real change takes time and patience" (Murray, 1998, p. 3).

So how do we reconcile the contradictions? We don't. We acknowledge them as inherent properties of change. Pettigrew's "Longitudinal Field Research on Change: Theory and Practice" (1995) offers rich comments on the complex nature of longitudinal research. This publication appeared after I finished my first longitudinal project, but it confirmed what I had learned experientially, "Explanations of change are bound to be holistic and multifaceted" (p. 94). Pettigrew addresses researchers in organization science, yet his challenges have particular relevance to education and social science. Contrary to grounded theory, he encourages analysts not to gloss over or reduce the conditions of change to a single variable or grand theory:

Contradictions are inherent properties of change

> [The] task is to explore the complex, haphazard, and often contradictory ways that change emerges and to construct a model that allows for an appreciation of conflicting rationalities, objectives, and behaviors. There is an explicit recognition that change is multifaceted, involving political, cultural, incremental, environmental, and structural, as well as rational, dimensions. Power, chance, opportunism, and accident are as influential in shaping outcomes as are designs, negotiated agreements, and master plans. (p. 93)

As long as our analyses of change processes and products take into account multiple rather than singular factors, then we are giving the study of change its proper due.

Take into account multiple rather than singular factors

In my own analytic work, changes in data from one time period through another were both minor and major but, for the most part, readily discernible—to me. It never occurred to me, though, that what I perceived as change might conflict with my participants' perceptions or readers' operating conceptions. Holmes cautions us to attend to our own sociocultural and research orientations, as these may negatively influence and affect our perceptions and analysis of data, particularly our observations about young people. "American fieldworkers may be more apt to emphasize and attend selectively to changes occurring in . . . children's culture. The American value structure places a great deal of emphasis on change, and change is viewed as good" (1998, p. 94). Nisbet (1976) suggests that discerning change is actually an inferential act, successful only to the extent that the researcher can imaginatively yet persuasively express it in an account. These caveats suggest that some type of monitoring is needed for our longitudinal work, lest we claim participant change without supporting evidence.

As I reflect on the data analytic processes used in my own longitudinal work, I had no problems locating change—as my participants or I defined it—for the contexts of my studies. My biggest obstacles were:

1. Managing vast amounts of data;
2. Continuous attunement and sensitivity to many possible types of changes;
3. Determining whether and in what ways these multiple types of changes interrelated with each other;
4. Analyzing how and/or why these changes occurred;
5. Pulling everything together for a coherent report.

The first obstacle, data management, has been addressed by other writers and computer software developers and will be discussed only briefly in this book. It is the last four obstacles that no single text offered guidance for me. I relied on an amalgam of methods ("shamelessly eclectic," as the saying goes) and learned by doing—and redoing and redoing when I erred. But were I to conduct another longitudinal qualitative study, it is the collected contents of this book that I would use as an analytic map to navigate the long journey through time, and they are guidelines I offer to you. Articles and books on longitudinal qualitative studies, due to length restrictions primarily, rarely outline the detailed process of how the data were systematically examined. So what follows are the "nuts and bolts" of it all—the researcher's behind-the-scenes backstage work for analyzing qualitative change through time.

In sum, a longitudinal qualitative study and its appropriate length of fieldwork are what the researcher and intended audience for the final report perceive as appropriate for the study's particular and primary goals. Describing from qualitative data (visual- or language-based records, such as interview transcripts, participant observation field notes, journals, photographs, and documents) what types of participant changes occurred, if any, through an extended period of time, is the basic outcome for a longitudinal qualitative study. Analyzing or interpreting when, how, how much, in what ways, and/or why changes might have occurred or did not occur

The researcher is affected by longitudinal enterprises

through that extended period of time are additional outcomes that rise above the descriptive database. Even the researcher is affected by longitudinal enterprises through personal and professional outcomes, since his or her own journey toward the destination is both processual and developmental.

CHAPTER TWO

Longitudinal Qualitative Research Design

Preparatory design matters for long-term studies begin this chapter, followed by a review of ethical issues. Other technical matters that arise during field-work are then discussed, followed by an examination of trustworthiness issues. Additional research design elements and methods are discussed, when appropriate, in later chapters. Included here are particular introductory topics that relate to paradigm and practice.

Preparation for a Longitudinal Qualitative Study

Imagine you're describing a road trip you took across Arizona, a trip where your journey was determined by careful planning ("After spending two days at the Grand Canyon, I was going to drive to Flagstaff"), unexpected opportunities ("But I discovered there was a pow-wow in Chinle, so I drove there instead"), uncontrollable forces ("The unexpected heavy snowfall closed the highway and delayed me"), detours ("I took a state road instead of the main highway because of construction and drove into the town of Jerome"), and revised plans ("When I saw the red mountains of Sedona, I just had to drive off the interstate for a closer look"). Such is the researcher's journey through a longitudinal qualitative study. Careful planning, unexpected opportunities, uncontrollable forces, detours, and revised plans are part of the fieldwork and data analytic processes. No researcher can accurately predict and rigidly control the future lives of a group of participants, let alone his or her own personal life. So, be prepared, but expect the unexpected.

Be prepared, but expect the unexpected

There are several excellent texts available with recommendations for designing qualitative studies, and you're encouraged to review several of these titles for their strategic methods: Creswell's *Qualitative Inquiry and Research Design: Choosing among Five Traditions* (1998); Glesne's *Becoming Qualitative Researchers: An Introduction* (1999); LeCompte and Preissle's *Ethnography and Qualitative Design in Educational Research* (1993); Marshall and Rossman's *Designing Qualitative Research* (1999); Maxwell's *Qualitative Research Design: An Interactive Approach* (1996); Meloy's *Writing the Qualitative Dissertation: Understanding by Doing* (2001); Patton's *Qualitative Research and Evaluation Methods* (2002); and Rossman and Rallis's *Learning in the Field: An Introduction to Qualitative Research* (1998). The design suggestions in these books apply readily to short- and long-term fieldwork, and there is no need for me to reinvent the wheel by churning out yet another "how-to" chapter. But there are several recommendations I would add to my colleagues' excellent writings, and several longitudinal qualitative research principles that merit discussion.

Longitudinal Qualitative Research Goals and Questions

It is assumed that you are planning a minimum of nine months of fieldwork with an individual or a group of participants, and/or conducting periodic interviews with or observations of them through an extended period of time. Other data collection methods may be part of your design, but the focus here is on the length of the project. If our movement through time is how we live our lives (Levine, 1997), and if time cannot be separated from change (Sztompka, 1993), then we conduct a longitudinal study for two primary purposes: to capture through long-term immersion the depth and breadth of the participants' life experiences, and to capture participant change (if any) through long-term comparative observations of their perceptions and actions.

A research study's goal might focus on how children or adults grow and develop in particular domains (e.g., cognitively, socially, and professionally) and in particular ways through time. The seven-year Theatre Response Study, for example, established its objectives months before fieldwork began and maintained these purposes throughout the project. "Two objectives for this study were: (1) to determine how regularly scheduled classroom drama and frequent theatre viewing experiences affected the way a treatment group interpreted theatre differently than second site groups with no treatment experience; and (2) to observe and document the development of the treatment group's unique perception and response processes to theatre" (Saldaña, 1996, p. 67).

When clear objectives are determined prior to fieldwork or interviews, the research team can maintain its focus on gathering data pertinent to the study of human growth and development (e.g., identity, aging, or teacher expertise). Also remember that the Theatre Response Study was a field experiment with a purposefully administered treatment to child participants. Naturalistic studies do not include deliberate interventions by researchers, but they can still address topics related to growth and development.

Other research studies might focus on how the researcher observes daily life in a particular social setting and, from the analysis of data collected through time, notices change in particular cases or particular cultures. In the Survival Study, I did not go into the field deliberately seeking change in the teacher participant. I looked at and listened to the people in a unique school program to get as much of an understanding of that world as I could. Data were collected through a twenty-month period of time. Change became evident to me only as I reflected on my past experiences observing Nancy and as data analysis proceeded. The ethnographic report's statement of purpose identified what I learned both during fieldwork and after the fact, "This qualitative case study profiles how and why Nancy's conception of educational drama—its philosophy, curriculum, and practice—changed as she worked at Martinez School from September 1993 through May 1995. . . . The central research question guiding this study was: How does Martinez School's Hispanic culture affect Nancy's actions as a white teacher of drama?" (Saldaña, 1997, p. 26) Other longitudinal qualitative studies profiled in this book will provide more examples of longitudinal goals, purposes, objectives, and central research questions.

Though we should always expect the unexpected when we embark on any long-term project, we should also expect the *possibility* of change to occur—never a guarantee. I remember the cautionary advice given by my research mentors when I first ventured into fieldwork, "Be careful: If you go looking for something, you'll find it." What they meant, of course, was not to let my preconceptions, expectations, and biases distort what was "really" happening out there. Sztompka's (1993) sweeping statement that time and change are inseparable is true only to a certain extent. You might not collect enough data to credibly support any assertions of change, you might not be in the field long enough to see change because it may happen later, or there might not be any participant change at all. So, be careful: If you go looking for change, you'll find it. Phrase your a priori research goals, objectives, purposes, and questions in such a way that indicates you're looking for change *if* it occurs. For emergent studies (e.g., ethnographies), remain attuned to possible participant change during fieldwork, data analysis, and reporting.

Expect the possibility *of change*

Establishing Baseline or Core Data

Also critical is laying the foundation for baseline or core data—essential demographics, particular categories, or other descriptive qualitative data for future reference, implied by the research questions or areas of interest that launch the study, to assess any future change. Examples might include initial participant perceptions (attitudes, values, and beliefs), family structures, grades, previous educational experiences or training, income, the setting's environment, population statistics, and so on. Baseline data include what you believe is important and what might become important in the future, based on your particular research agenda. If you enter a study with no a priori focus and are uncertain what will become essential as fieldwork progresses, the best advice I can offer is to observe general participant actions at first. As salient categories or areas emerge, your observational lens can then focus on those issues that surge to the foreground.

Entry interviews, surveys, questionnaires, and "grand tour" observations are just a few of the methods employed to gather baseline or core data for assessing future change—somewhat similar to collecting pretest data. Patton asks participants in an Outward Bound program strategic questions during standardized open-ended interviews at the beginning of, end of, and six months after the event to evaluate possible change:

- Precourse Interview: What changes in yourself do you hope will result from the experience?
- Postcourse Interview: What changes in yourself do you see or feel as a result of the course?
- Six-Month Follow-Up Interview: What kinds of changes in yourself do you see or feel as a result of your participation in the course? (2002, pp. 422–427)

Participant change may not occur as quickly as you would like it to or happen within the time parameters of your study. Wolcott, in a pragmatic discussion on time constraints in ethnography, advises that researchers "might devote special attention to aspects deemed most likely to change. That would maximize the opportunity to track what does change and what does not, with observations conducted over an extended period" (1999, p. 217). Elsewhere, Wolcott advises his students intent on studying change "to direct their attention instead to what can be learned about any social system from its *efforts* to change itself" and "why systems so seemingly dedicated to change usually manage to entrench the status quo" (1994, p. 178). Baseline or core data established early in the study provide testing opportunities for these two guidelines.

A Chronological Archive
I am a notorious pack rat with my materials. My paranoia is such that I save virtually everything because, as I say to myself, "I'll never know when I might need this." That ethic has served me well. I saved all documents generated by or about my participants (e.g., lesson plans, newsletters, performance programs, and surveys) and discovered years later that they contained small but vital nuggets of information I needed for additional data analyses and final reports. Whether in paper filing systems or scanned documents for computer files, begin an organized and carefully indexed archive for the voluminous amounts of field notes, interviews, and artifact data forthcoming, which includes the flexibility to adapt to future space needs and technological advances in software. My recommendation is to file materials first in chronological order (e.g., 1995, 1996, 1997), then in categories and subcategories of need or emergent interest to the particular study, such as

1995, August–December
    Field notes of Barry at Rehearsals and Performances
        The Glass Menagerie
        Scapino!
    Interviews with Barry
        September 17 (after rehearsal)
        October 10 (after *The Glass Menagerie* performance)
    Play Production Programs
        The Glass Menagerie
        Scapino!
1996, January–May
    Interviews with Barry
        January 10 (after rehearsal)
        February 21 (after *The Universal Language* performance)
    Interview with Sandy (mother)
    Interview with Derek (theatre teacher)

In my future recommendations for analysis, I will encourage the comparison of data by time pools first, then by categories. Hence, a chronological indexing system is strongly suggested. If there are multiple participants in your study, each with his or her own data gathered from one-on-one interviews, surveys, or other methods, create a separate file for each case as a category under each year or other major time period.

A chronological indexing system is strongly suggested

State-of-the-Art Technology

During the three longitudinal studies I conducted, my technological tools progressed from DOS to Windows; from DisplayWrite 3 to Word; from 5¼ to 3½ inch disks; from software version 3.1 to new version 6.0; from purple dittos to laser printing; from standard to microcassettes; from hand-held to built-in microphones; from pocket calculators to SPSS (Statistical Package for the Social Sciences); and from handwritten index cards to cut-and-paste word processing. Technological advancement, particularly in computing, progresses rapidly. Though we may not always be up to speed with the latest software programs or possess the maximum amount of hard-drive space available, my recommendation is to begin archiving digital data utilizing whatever equipment, tools, and methods are state of the art (as much as your budget and expertise permit). If you decide to employ a qualitative data software storage and analysis program such as Qualis Research's The Ethnograph or Qualitative Solutions and Research's NVivo or N6 (discussed later on), shop wisely before investing in the product to guarantee that it will meet your particular study's needs and that the data you enter presently will be compatible with future versions. If research team members each contribute to the data corpus and need access to it at various times for reference and analysis, the data should be stored in a shared network system or intranet website with password entry.

No one wants to experience months or years of hard work lost when a computer suddenly and ultimately "crashes" with the only record of your data. Though it may seem overly cautious, save everything generated daily on a computer five times: on the hard drive, on a network storage system, on a back-up floppy disk, as an e-mail attachment, and on printed hard copy—with each data source kept in a separate location. The extra security is worth the huge investment in time you're making to the longitudinal study.

Attrition Contingency Plan

I also recommend that you develop a series of actions to implement in the event that your individual case study or members from your panel become unavailable or withdraw from the study in progress. Some communities and institutions have a highly transient and mobile population. Child participants at a school site will leave when their families change geographic location. Some teacher participants may change jobs and transfer to another school. Some participants may have auto accidents or develop extended illnesses and become inaccessible for a while; some participants may become fatigued by the project and choose to withdraw altogether; and, yes, a few participants may die during the study. All of these happened to various participants in my longitudinal studies—some events were foreseen and some were unexpected.

Though I have never "lost" an individual in a study during a long-term project, I have lost members of panels. At the beginning of the Theatre Response Study in 1984, we purposefully included all kindergarten children (N = 64) enrolled in the school as participants, knowing that by the time they would graduate from sixth grade in 1991, we would have a smaller panel of original members (N = 30) at the site due to family mobility. By the time this panel graduated from high school in 1997, only twelve of those thirty students remained in their district's feeder school for follow-up, and only six of them volunteered or were available to participate in interviews.

The lesson from this attrition record is to start with more participants than you might actually need as a precautionary measure, particularly if a panel will be involved in a study for at least three years. If members are lost during that time, then you'll hopefully have adequate remaining numbers for your study (see Ågren, 1998; Coleman, 2001). If everyone stays, then you'll have additional data to support your analyses and assertions. There seems to be no consensus about an acceptable cut-off point for attrition rates before a study's credibility and trustworthiness become questionable. I cannot prescribe an exact minimum number or a "back-up" percentage with which to begin, since the number of participants needed will vary from study to study. Your own judgment of the possible attrition rate in site-specific contexts is the best call.

Start with more participants than you might actually need

Pilot Studies

If time and resources permit, researchers may wish to consider whether a small-scale and short-term pilot study is worthwhile as a preparatory investigation before the actual longitudinal project begins, particularly if the project will extend across several years (Saldaña and Wright, 1996, p. 126). Data gathering methods can be assessed for their effectiveness and revised as needed. A pilot study also permits opportunities to initiate and refine data management and analytic procedures for the researcher. This is especially important because, in some cases, once particular instrumentation is selected and initiated for data gathering, it becomes a permanent design choice for the longitudinal project (but see the section "Trustworthiness of Longitudinal Qualitative Data" later in this chapter).

Other preparatory matters for a longitudinal study include site and participant selection; permissions processes; research team membership, agreements, and protocol; and choices of methods and instrumentation. These initial and ongoing matters overlap with ethical issues, so this is perhaps the most appropriate point in the book to discuss them.

Ethics and Longitudinal Qualitative Studies

Graue and Walsh note the primary commandment of research, "But first, do no harm" (1998, p. 70). All research, whether short- or long-term, requires the ethical treatment of human participants. Legal as well as ethical obligations arise, particularly with minors. I present an overview of ethical considerations with a focus on youth since many developmental studies are longitudinal in design.[2] Recent publications on research with children address these matters in more detail (Christensen and James, 2000; Fine and Sandstrom, 1988; Graue and Walsh, 1998; Grieg and Taylor, 1999; Holmes, 1998; Lewis and Lindsay, 2000; Zwiers and Morrissette, 1999).

Young Participants

Federal laws in the United States regulate research with people (coldly labeled "human subjects"), especially with those under the age of eighteen. The regulations adopted by the Department of Health and Human Services in 1983 require approval for proposed research by an Institutional Review Board (IRB). Furthermore, the researcher must obtain both the consent of the parents or legal guardians and the assent of the child or adolescent, provided that the research involves only minimal risk (Areen, 1992).

Federal regulations later distinguished between biomedical and behavioral research. As a result, most survey and interview research and most observational studies in public settings were exempted from the regulatory process. When researchers solicit information about sensitive matters, especially if respondents could be identified and subject to civil or criminal liability, or if it damages their financial standing or employability, it is still subject to IRB regulation. In addition to federal laws regulating research with minors, individual states and local institutions may have separate provisions and policies (Areen, 1992).

In addition to obtaining informed consent, common legal and ethical practices include changing all participants' names (including that of an identifying site) to pseudonyms in data records and reports to protect their identity; guaranteeing anonymity, if requested by the participant, by including no identifying references in data or reports; providing participants preliminary and final drafts of the report to review how they are portrayed and to confirm or disconfirm researcher assertions; and maintaining the participants' confidentiality by not discussing or disclosing their personal information to others outside the research team. It is also good ethical practice to note in the final report the steps taken to secure permissions for the study and what the researcher has done to protect the participants.

Masson observes that there "is a close relationship between law and ethics, but not everything that is legal is ethical. Frequently law, when used as a tool of regulation, attempts only to set the minimum ethical standard. The aspirations of ethical practice are higher" (2000, p. 35). While there is a growing interest in involving the voice of the child or adolescent in both research and policy matters concerning them, some research organizations still lag behind in their recognition that those under the age of eighteen can have the same rights as those over eighteen. Lindsay (2000) surveys the ethical codes of several major research organizations including the British Educational Research Association, the American Psychological Association, the British Psychological Society, the Canadian Psychological Association, and the European Federation of Professional Psychologists Association. He finds that while "guidance on research with children is barely addressed as a specific topic" (p. 16), all associations reflected a commitment to respect the dignity of the person, to responsible practice, and to serve the needs of society.

Not everything that is legal is ethical

At the heart of the issue of ethical considerations in research involving children and adolescents are questions of their right to refuse participation and their ability to give informed consent. Opinion seems divided as to what extent children and adolescents should be involved in decisions directly affecting them. I take the stance that young people involved in research *should* be informed of the purpose of the research (in as much as the researcher can, without influencing the results) and *should* be given the right to consent to participate or to withdraw. As Taylor notes, "Giving children a voice in decision making makes them visible and gives them a stake in that process, thereby reducing the chances of their wanting to sabotage it" (2000, p. 32). Some may argue that perhaps adolescents are competent to make informed decisions, but that competence does not extend to very young children. I disagree and cite Masson for support, "Competence, the level of understanding required to make decisions, is directly related to the decision to be taken. Thus children are competent and can decide whether or not to participate in a research study, provided they have sufficient understanding of what participation entails and how participating may affect them. . . . It is children's level of understanding, not their age, which is important" (2000, p. 39). Furthermore, Morse and Richards state that the child's preference to withdraw from a study overrides the parent's preference for the child to participate (2002, p. 206).

Finally, an understanding and presentation of possible short- and long-term affects, even if speculation is the only option, by the researcher should be part of the negotiation process with obtaining the participants' consent. Yates and McLeod (1996) provided a progress report two years into their seven-year study with adolescents. The researchers admirably confessed:

> [T]he open-endedness [of the study] has meant a continuing anxiety, uncertainty and tension about where the research is going and whether the questions and interventions and constructions are appropriate ones. . . . Should we try to gather more information to look at our interviews in context (e.g. from the teachers or school records)? Should we ask the students more about their families? These matters raise both ethical issues about what we are doing to the students, and issues about the standing of the knowledge that our methods are constructing. (pp. 91, 92)

France, Bendelow, and Williams (2000) advise that consent is a process, not an initial act. Participants should be continuously consulted throughout all phases of the longitudinal research enterprise, as well as during data analysis and final reporting stages for review of the researcher's findings, for consent to continue.

Consent is a process

Negotiating and Maintaining Access

School districts and other community agencies have their own procedures for securing permission to conduct research with participants under their care or supervision (though they do not supercede the researcher's IRB procedures). This may mean that the researcher has to develop slightly different versions of a research proposal to satisfy different permission-granting groups. If the research is conducted with individuals in such programs as juvenile detention centers or group homes, the permission-granting process is likely to be long and arduous to satisfy any legal liability the cooperating parties might face. If a researcher wishes to conduct research at a school, for example, the principal as gatekeeper, in addition to a school district, might also be involved in the negotiations. Permission-granting agencies will most likely require signed permission forms from the parents and teachers involved. Signed assent to participate forms or—at the very least—verbal permission, should also be obtained from children or adolescents involved in the research. Figure 2.1 provides an example adapted from Arizona State University's IRB forms of the written text for a minor.

The proposed methods of data gathering can also affect the permissions process. Most institutions will not object to written field notes or audiotape recordings, but photographs and videotape recordings can be problematic since anonymity and confidentiality are virtually impossible to guarantee if faces or other identifying features are not obscured. Capturing still or moving images also places some children at risk, such as those who are illegal aliens, victims of abuse trying to hide from their abuser, children of divorced parents in conflict with custody issues, or juveniles who might be involved in illegal activities. The participant's or parent's preferences for image capturing must be honored by the researcher. Archived photographs or videotapes for data analysis should be stored in a secure location with restricted viewing access and viewed only by research team members. Visual images, whether still or motion, provide some of the richest and most tangible data for assessing changes through time. Ironically, some agencies or permission-granting groups may also require erasure of both audio- and videotapes once transcription or data analysis are complete.

The researcher may find constraints placed on him or her by others not directly involved in the research. For example, there are times when a school's or district's administration may feel uncomfortable with outside researchers interviewing children in individual or focus group settings, especially when

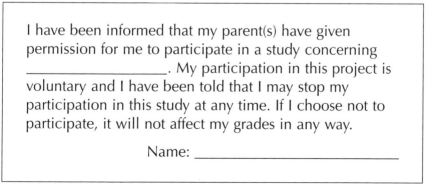

I have been informed that my parent(s) have given permission for me to participate in a study concerning _____. My participation in this project is voluntary and I have been told that I may stop my participation in this study at any time. If I choose not to participate, it will not affect my grades in any way.

Name: _____

Figure 2.1   A permission form for a child's assent to participate in research

the topics deal with potentially problematic issues. In one short-term study (Saldaña, 2000), I explored children's perceptions of oppression in order to generate content for improvisational classroom drama. But the school principal advised me that individual interviews about these sensitive issues were a concern to her. Hence, group talk with the whole class, with the teacher present during the questioning process, was the negotiated interview method for this study, though individual interviews may have provided the security and privacy needed by some children to disclose their personal perceptions of oppression. Individual interviews also would have been the best method of assessing the effectiveness of the field experiment toward the end. But since I was bound by the initial agreement, alternative, "noninvasive" methods of data gathering were employed, such as written stories by students who retold a personal incident of peer cruelty and researcher observations of peer conflict on the playground and peer exclusion in classroom activities.

Long-Term Engagement
There may be many administrators and teachers who will give the researcher virtual carte blanche to work in their schools. In this situation, the researcher must take care not to abuse the generosity of school personnel, especially if the residency or fieldwork will be long term. Frequently, some sort of reciprocal arrangement is negotiated whereby the researcher can provide a service for the school. In the Theatre Response Study, for example, child participants were provided twenty-six theatre-viewing experiences free of charge at their school or in university theatres during the seven-year study. Annual "reality checks" between the school principal and research team members during this project were also conducted at the beginning and end of each year to share any concerns or issues before the next cycle of data gathering.

Child or adolescent participants in a longitudinal study may experience changes in family membership through time. The permissions process and its accompanying paperwork may have to be repeated if new stepparents or guardianship arrangements enter the picture. Likewise, schools may experience changes in leadership or staff across time. A compatible working relationship with one principal may be lost if a new administrator inherits a longitudinal study at his or her site. Researchers should be prepared to inform all new staff of the study's progress to date and, if needed, negotiate any new ways of working that will not affect the integrity of data already collected. IRBs will follow up annually with researchers to monitor progress with a study. Extended longitudinal studies will require reapplication and review after a selected number of years have passed. And since revised or additional data gathering methods may emerge during a longitudinal study, IRBs should be notified of any changes in a project's protocol. Likewise, new federal or local regulations may be legislated, requiring the researcher to stay current and maintain eligibility with new IRB qualifications.

Depending on their duration and magnitude, some longitudinal studies may involve more than one researcher as part of the project, and multiple researchers raise both methodological and ethical issues. Manderson, Kelaher, and Woelz-Stirling, writing on data management procedures for the Australian Longitudinal Study on Women's Health, note that

> [t]echnical and ethical difficulties emerge with respect to access to and interpretation of data when there is more than one investigator, even when there has been close collaboration and a common approach to the collection, management, and use of data. For example, in longitudinal studies that allow for individual follow-up, the assurances of confidentiality that operate in cross-sectional studies cease. A new researcher may be responsible for a new round of data collection. Hence, more than one researcher may need to communicate with a respondent, ask follow-up questions, administer repeat questionnaires, and integrate various data sets. (2001, p. 153)

It is preferable to maintain continuity for participants and to maintain consistency of data gathering by assigning the same researcher or same team members to particular participants or field site throughout a longitudinal study. But when one interviewer or observer must "pass the torch" to another across time, a carefully planned transition process must occur, acquainting the new researcher with the study and the long-term participants to a new member of the research team. Initial agreements to gather data from participants in longitudinal studies should note that there may be changes in research personnel as the project continues, due to the longevity of the design. Hence, participant permission to share interview transcripts, researcher field notes, and other data with qualified research team members should be negotiated and secured initially to maintain the integrity of the study and the continuity of data gathering for analysis.

In the Theatre Response Study, graduate students were employed as research assistants to gather data from children and teachers or assigned fieldwork experiences as part of research coursework. The students were not just available labor but colleagues in the enterprise. Their participation generated more and richer interview and observation data than I could have gathered on my own, plus they brought to the project new perspectives on what was happening and emerging. (By the sixth year of the seven-year study, I was beginning to lose sight of the forest for the trees.) They also brought to the project current knowledge about child development, methodology, and related literature they were reading in other research seminars. Students have made offhand verbal comments or jotted occasional field notes that, unintentionally, inspired or captured an analytic insight that probably never would have occurred to me had I been a lone researcher. The lesson here is to collaborate with and care for all members of the research team, to shoptalk and exchange ideas frequently, to treat research "assistants" as peers, and to value what each one brings to the study.

Agreements should also be contracted between all research team members for use of the data corpus. Each contributor pools his or her field notes into a central repository for comprehensive documentation and data analysis, but each should also understand the terms for his or her access and rights for individual or joint authorship of results. Foster's (2002) longitudinal field research in Mexico has progressed over fifty years. Two generations of colleagues and students, the latter for anthropological training, have participated as researchers on site. Collaboration on this project was never part of Foster's plan for his students, but understandings were outlined nevertheless, "I had a formal, written agreement that spelled out our mutual rights and expectations. All gave me copies of their field notes. If dealing with comparative topics where their data were pertinent, I had permission to cite their findings, with appropriate credit. The data, however, belonged to them and could be used in any way they wished. Students, in turn, had full access to my files with comparable reciprocal rights" (p. 272).

Personal Matters in Long-Term Fieldwork

Fortunately, most naturalistic research in educational settings is relatively low risk for participants. However, the adult researcher and child participant relationship also raises significant power and ethical issues for consideration during all phases of the process (Lewis and Lindsay, 2000; Mienczakowski, 1999; Nicholson, 1999), especially when the child discloses unsolicited personal or family background information (Oakley, 2000; Saldaña, 1998a) or when interviews focus on sensitive topics such as abuse (Bury, Popple, and Barker, 1998).

The longer you engage with participants, the more likely you will become knowledgeable about their personal matters. Through interviews Barry offered me a candid and deep understanding of his artistic and personal worldviews. Concurrent interviews with two of his theatre teachers and his mother provided me additional family information and adult perspectives. I was trusted enough to hear about this young man's troubled past with bullies, drug use (by both him and his parents), an alcoholic father, and early psychological counseling for depression. These honest confessions led me to *believe* I had learned all about Barry's personal issues. And despite a troubled life, his personality and demeanor toward the end of the study suggested that he had grown to become a young man with a positive and optimistic outlook.

It was not until a few months after the two-and-a-half-year fieldwork period concluded that I learned about Barry's attempted suicide during his junior high school years. This information was revealed through one of his teachers who also informed me of his second and most recent suicide attempt after graduation—fortunately, unsuccessful and with no long-term damage. The experience with this study taught me that, despite how much is learned or disclosed to you over a long-term fieldwork period, you will never know everything about your participants and must be careful about assuming you do. We all have deep, dark secrets that we want no one to know—even a trusted researcher who guarantees your anonymity and respects your confidentiality. And no matter how carefully you consider and implement all ethical measures to ensure the safety of your participants, you cannot foresee all possible contingencies and outcomes.

You cannot foresee all possible contingencies and outcomes

The longer you engage with participants, the more likely your own attitude and value and belief systems will conflict with what you see and hear. During my fieldwork periods at elementary and secondary schools for three long-term studies, I observed effective teaching, strong leadership, exciting programming, and contented youth. But I also observed aged and burned-out teachers who verbally humiliated children, perceived outdated and ineffective educational practices, listened to children's worries about their divorcing parents, and saw subtle signs of adolescents who were most likely destined for problems with the law. Personal intervention is a matter of personal choice, but that may unduly influence and affect the natural social setting and actions of participants. Yet, it would be foolish not to acknowledge that the researcher is just as much a part of the social setting as the participants. "But first, do no harm" means an ethical and legal obligation to intervene and report when child-to-child or adult-to-child violence is witnessed at a school site. Purposeful intervention also means acting and responding appropriately when the study is an action research project. I cannot offer any further advice when other types of witnessed conflicts or judgment calls arise. They must all be considered and enacted on a case-by-case basis through careful reflection on your own values and then in documentation in field notes.

Throughout the Longitudinal Qualitative Study

As the longitudinal study proceeds, there are additional factors that play a major role in methodology and method.

Cumulative and Collaborative Field Notes

Some parents measure the growth of their child by having her stand straight against a wall. They then draw a line directly above the top of her head on the wall's surface and write the date or the child's age next to the mark. A series of parallel lines with chronological indicators progress upward, serving as a visual record of how much she has grown across time. The activity may be a delightful ritual for all, but often it is the child who may derive more excitement from it than the parents. The joy, however, does not come just from seeing what her height is presently. The joy comes from seeing how tall she has become—that is, how tall she is now compared to how short she was before.

Field notes for a longitudinal qualitative study should operate in the same way. We keep a written record of what happens each day we conduct fieldwork. Each day's observations are like a progressively upward and dated mark on the wall. But the last and most recent field entry has no "joy" until we devote some reflection time comparing what has happened today with what has happened before. As the study progresses, document not only what you observe on a particular day, but compare how the present day's observations build on, nest with, or connect to what has been previously written. Don't just let your field notes accumulate, make them *cumulative* through time. Spiral back to previous observations of your participants and note any comparative impressions for a more detailed analysis in the future. A biweekly or, at the very least, monthly "maintenance check" of your notes will generate coding, analytic, or theoretical memos (Strauss and Corbin, 1998) for reflection or testing as the study continues. In my own field notes, I frequently take stock in a stream-of-consciousness manner of what seem to be emergent key points and future directions for inquiry or writing. Six months into the thirty-month study with Barry, I noted the following after three interviews with him, two interviews with his theatre teachers, and several observations of rehearsals, performances, and classroom work:

> *Don't just let your field notes accumulate, make them* cumulative

February 6, 1996
    Free-form thinking/thoughts thus far: Was Barry's drug use during junior high years a substitute for the spiritual experience he's now getting from the-

atre? He may have been using them to fit in, to get attention from peers—
something that theatre has now given him in high school. . . . The field
[theatre] has Barry because he was raised that way—he was "destined" to turn
out the way he did because of all the influence around him. (Is this the key
assertion?) I'm still stuck on what the study is "about." It's more than just
"about" one high school actor. It's about a high school actor with a lot of theatre around him as he grew up. It's about giftedness/talent that was nurtured.
What I noted earlier as key themes: "romantic," "destiny," "spirituality," "intuition," "talent," "passion." The spiritual rebirth is a strong metaphor—and
that's one way of finding a theme, a core to this report. But don't discount
"passion." *Emotional Intelligence* legitimizes such feelings. No need to be clinical here—go for social insight. There's spirituality—immersion in the *rasa* of
theatre. He could have been many things but chose theatre because it feels
"right."

If you are one of several research team members conducting fieldwork
for a longitudinal study, or if your work extends over several years (if not
decades) with new team members to be folded into the project in progress,
this also affects how you write your field notes. The audience for your written observations has now become larger, and your documentation should
be clear and detailed enough to acquaint fellow data gatherers and newcomers with what has happened thus far, from your perspective. My aforementioned stream-of-consciousness writing was sufficient for me as the
lone researcher and for you as an example of taking stock. But if you were
to read months or years of field notes written in that manner, I would be
doing a grave disservice to my collaborators and inheritors. Compose your
field notes with a point of view, but also with the understanding that others must make sense of what you've observed. During the first few weeks of
fieldwork, share your field notes with other team members, or a sample
of your field notes (with all participant names or other site-identifying features stricken from them) with someone not involved with the research
study, to receive feedback on your writing clarity and communication. Also
highlight through boldfaced or boxed text those passages you feel are important to or critical about the study for others to know (e.g., a problematic participant, allies, key ways of working on site, major learnings to date,
and so on).

Reflections on Time and Change
Particular attention should be paid to the nature of time and change as
they relate to your study in your field notes (with participant observations

written in the present tense), memos, journal entries, and other written documentation. Whether the research project is a field experiment or naturalistic study, attunement and sensitivity to the nuances of participant differences across time are essential qualities when studying change. Devote some time to reflect on theoretical change processes in your area of research and on how time interacts and interplays with the actions and phenomena you observe. For example, in early field note reflections for the Barry Study, I brainstormed questions related to change for follow-up investigation:

January 4, 1996
How do the home/family and school as social systems influence and affect the student's preferences/interests? What factors made Barry connect so strongly with theatre and performance? Why did others in the longitudinal study not turn out like him? What were some traces in grades K–6 data that can be linked to the present? What were major "turning points" for Barry? What influences has Derek [the theatre teacher] made on Barry? Why does Barry perceive his life thus far as "destiny"?

Learning, teaching, ethnic identity, child development, aging, divorce, smoking, childlessness, and imprisonment are just a few of the longitudinal study subjects illustrated in this book. Research your discipline's literature for qualitative *and* quantitative longitudinal studies (and note that several long-term studies may not have been labeled "longitudinal" by their writers).

Heighten your awareness of time; watch the clock and calendar intensely during fieldwork. Enhance your consciousness of tempos and rhythms by placing your observational focus on the tempo, frequency, and duration of human actions. Observe carefully how short or how long it takes for something to happen. Keep a log of how participants spend their time across time. What actions or categories of activity shift in allocation throughout the study? Spend a day observing exclusively just one of the categories involved with change (described in chapters 4 through 6): increases, decreases, consistencies, idiosyncrasies, and so on. Record the differences—however small—you notice in participants and yourself. When the fatigue of fieldwork sets in and you need a diversion, reflect on your own life and how you yourself have changed through time. Examine your contextual conditions, what has increased, decreased, remained constant or consistent, and so on. Speculate on how and why you got to where you are today, and who and what you are becoming. Enhance your time literacy by reading Levine's *A Geography of Time* (1997). Read studies about current and future sociopolitical trends, and speculate how these observations and fore-casts might possibly influence and affect your participants' futures. Finally, reflect on how you yourself are changing as a researcher during the study. These strategies will fine-tune your senses and perceptions about change.

Reflect on your own life and how you yourself have changed through time

Waves of Longitudinal Qualitative Data Collection

One of your research design choices will concern data gathering methods and the frequency of collection. A *wave* in traditional quantitative research refers to the administration of observations or interviews (generally with standard-ized protocols), surveys, tests, or other data collecting methods to partici-pants during predetermined periods in longitudinal studies, such as once per year across a ten-year period. Some longitudinal qualitative studies have also followed this model, but in ethnographic studies, sustained fieldwork gathers data on a more frequent basis such as daily or weekly across extended periods of time. Continuous rather than infrequent contact provides the qualitative researcher opportunities to observe and reflect on the detailed processes of change, not just its periodic products. Also, more frequent contact enables researcher immediacy to the contextual and intervening conditions and epiphanies in participants' lives. It's as if the qualitative researcher observes human action and gathers data in drops and ripples as well as retrospective waves, permitting deeper analyses of the nuances and subtleties of processual participant change.

There are no fixed formulas, no standardized number of interviews or minimum fieldwork clock hours to determine what constitutes an adequate amount of qualitative data collected across time. But no longi-tudinal study is credible or trustworthy on the basis of prolonged field en-gagement alone (Denzin, 1994, p. 513; Wolcott, 1995, p. 78). Hence, it's not just how long you're in the field—quantity time—it's how and what you observe while you're there—quality time.

If a longitudinal study's design or participant availability permits only oc-casional personal contact, additional data gathering methods and follow-up procedures should be considered. Holloway et al. (1995) followed fourteen mothers over three years to gather their perceptions of school preparation for their children. Only one one- to two-hour semistructured interview was conducted at nine-month intervals with each participant, but "[n]umerous telephone calls were used to stay in touch between interviews," and these conversations provided additional data for analysis. Also, "child care providers were visited and observed when access could be obtained. Each woman was asked to keep a diary documenting the events of at least 2 weekdays and 1 weekend" (p. 455).

One of the most impressive achievements in waves of data collection is a series of artworks: filmmaker Michael Apted's critically acclaimed *Up* documentary series (Singer, 1998). Apted follows and portrays fourteen individual lives at ages seven, fourteen, twenty-one, twenty-eight, thirty-five, and forty-two in separate and successive films. The filmmaker reflects:

> We used the Jesuit saying, "Give me the child until he is seven, and I will show you the man," as a theme, and I think the power of the project is that everybody has a different opinion about whether or not it has any truth. Some find the film depressing because they think the Jesuits were right and nothing alters what is set out at seven; others are more optimistic, for they see evidence of change, of social mobility, with people overcoming obstacles and defying the limitations of their upbringing. For my money, lives can change, but I wonder whether the personality ever does. (pp. 13–14)

One character from the series, Paul, struggles from early childhood to midlife with his low self-confidence. Whether this is indeed an evidentiary through-line that supports Apted's theory, or whether the documentaries purposefully follow-up and focus on this issue during each wave of interviews through carefully edited footage, is for the audience to determine, based on how it interprets Paul's life history, captured in his own words, from a sad little boy at age seven to a happily married man at age forty-two. The *Up* series teaches longitudinal researchers to pursue areas of inquiry that appear to be of emergent importance from early periods of a study for confirmation during later waves of data collection. But we should also be cautious of maintaining allegiance to what we, rather than our participants, perceive as important or salient in their lives. The time in-between waves is an opportunity for a reality check of our research goals and of how the next period of interviews or observations can build on rather than simply replicate the previous data sets.

Another strategy for gathering data in a substantial wave is to follow and observe an embedded yet extended event during the total fieldwork period from the beginning through the end. In the Survival Study, Nancy's script development and direction of a play production with her students took approximately two months during a five-month block of classroom observations. The rehearsal and performance unit became a case-within-a-case wave for focused study across the total twenty-month period of data gathering—a "shortitudinal" research project within a longitudinal design.

A longitudinal qualitative study can also be composed of a series of distinct yet cumulative field experiences. McVea (2001) and her research collaborators conducted a series of separate studies from 1997 to 2001 (with the intent of continuing beyond), all related to smoking among teenagers. Each annual study informed the next year's project and provided additional questions for future research. The first "qualitative, exploratory study" examined tobacco use at one school. "From this we learned that despite the presence of written tobacco policies, this high school was not a 'safe haven' from smoking pressures. . . . The results from our first study raised an interesting question, why didn't schools enforce their no smoking policies?" (2001) The next project addressed that very issue:

> We discovered that administrators found rules difficult to enforce because of the large number of smokers, and the significant resources required to police their behavior. Teachers were concerned that driving students off campus to smoke caused them to miss class, and they feared punitive penalties caused more harm than tobacco use. Students interpreted the lack of enforcement as evidence that the faculty "didn't care" about smoking. Smoking students even commented about how the ability to smoke at school with friends contributed to their habit. (2001)

With these new learnings, the next three simultaneous, mixed-method studies explored nonpunitive, therapeutic actions the schools could take to help teenagers quit smoking. One of these studies followed teen smokers over the course of a year through monthly interviews, "[W]e are finding that peer influences are very powerful in determining whether or not a teen attempts to quit smoking and whether or not they are successful." Future studies evaluated the effectiveness of peer counselors and other smoking cessation services for young people. These carefully designed, sequential projects demonstrate both the rigor and flexibility longitudinal researchers must exhibit with data gathering.

Final Exit Interviews

Toward the end of a longitudinal study, consider the administration of final exit interviews to the participants, if possible or applicable. Questions designed to assess their personal perceptions of differences and change add to the field notes and transcripts collected to date. Participants could be asked to recall and reconstruct, through narratives, the stories of their own experiences during the longitudinal period (Flick, 2002, chapter 9), plus their own predictions about the future. In the following interview excerpt, I asked the adolescent Barry, "What do you want to do after high school?"

> Well, I'm struggling with that right now. College is a very scary thing for me to think about. So my tentative game plan—in fact, there's a couple different ways it could go. I may go to ASU and major in theatre and minor in choral music and then come out and look for a job, look for a place to work as an actor. What I would love to do is to get out of high school, work around the valley for a bit, like, I don't know, just some crap job to get the money, go to New York or Chicago, and try to make it big. You know, every actor's dream: to go to one of the big towns and try to be famous, try to get my big break. And I know that it's not likely that it will ever happen, but there's a part of me—I guess it's the romantic side of me again that says, if I want it bad enough, I'll get it.

Six years after the interview, Barry has not yet achieved his "big break." But he is still being tracked in the event that he does become famous (as he defines fame).

Basic "then and now" inquiry may also yield valuable participant insights about personal change. Kvale astutely asks, "If you want to know how people understand their world and their life, why not talk with them?" (1996, p. 1) As a natural extension to this question, if you want to know how, how much, in what ways, or why people have changed, why not ask them directly? The following is an excerpt from an interview conducted in February 1995, toward the latter months of the Survival Study. Notice how the phrasing of my opening question was too general. Nancy's response led me to clarify what I was searching for. Also notice that after her first example was presented, I continued asking what was different. After two more stories, Nancy began asking herself what had changed:

> I: How do you see yourself as different from when you first got your job way back in 1993? How do you feel that you're changed or different?
> Nancy: Just in general, you mean?
> I: Either as a teacher, as an individual; you know—personally or professionally. What do you notice different about yourself now than when you first began this position?
> Nancy: I think when I first began I was very idealistic. And now I'm more realistic in what I expect from the students. It's really humbling at first. I don't

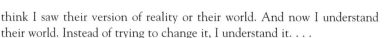

think I saw their version of reality or their world. And now I understand their world. Instead of trying to change it, I understand it. . . .
I: How else are you different or changed here?
Nancy: I think the first year I was just trying to get through. It was a lot to be thrown at as a first-year teacher. And now I think I'm much more—I don't know if it's "relaxed" in the classroom? I still keep moving a lot and doing things, but I'm not going to sit and scream at them to be quiet. I'll just sit there and stare and go, "What are you doing? Well, I'm waiting for you." I think I feel more in control that way, instead of the kids being in control all the time. I feel more in control in a lot of ways. I'm more—what's the word I'm looking for?—confident in what I'm doing. Last year I was always worried about pleasing all the other teachers and doing what they wanted. Now, I'm more like, "Well, *I'm* here for a reason and *I* have my curriculum. And I'm sorry if that doesn't fit in with yours, but *I'm* the specialist in this area [*slight laugh*], you know? Um, what else has changed? Just probably my relationship with the kids.

Questions could also be designed to confirm or disconfirm any assertions, themes, or trends the researcher may have formed as the study progressed. Daniluk reports that in final exit interviews with infertile couples, participants were asked to reflect over the three-year tracking period, "When you think back over the last 3 years, and the process you've gone through in dealing with the permanence of your biological childlessness, how would you describe that process?" (2001, p. 441) This data provided a confirmation "reality check" for the researcher's personal observations of change formulated throughout the study. Participant memory, however, can be faulty, and contributions in retrospective recall should be carefully and critically examined, particularly if the time period recalled extends back several years (Rutter et al., 1998).

Final exit interviews also permit opportunities to "fill in the holes" with additional data that may be missing from the corpus. Sixth-graders, at the conclusion of the Theatre Response Study, were asked to share both their own impressions of theatre plus their parents' views of the art form (whether parents took children to theatre outside of school hours, how much television viewing was permitted at home, and so on). The responses we received provided new insights about the family's influence on the child's value of the art form. The research team had spent seven years gathering the treatment group's perspectives, yet we failed until the final year to inquire about their parents' attitudes toward theatre.

Discerning participant change does not have to resort to second-guesswork on the researcher's part. It can, and should, be a collaborative enterprise. But the outcomes can be unanticipated if you're not careful (Kvale, 1996, p. 156). I was quite stunned one day after I sneered at the limited number of menu choices at a restaurant and my life partner told me in frustration, "You've gotten so picky as you've gotten older, did you know that?" I didn't. It was our conversation over dinner that provided an opportunity for us to jointly remember and reconstruct past incidences of my "pickiness" and to help me realize that, with age, I had become annoyingly fussy about circumstances beyond my control. That discussion heightened my awareness of a bad trait, and as time progressed I made a conscious effort to lessen that habit for the sake of my partner. The same may happen with a participant in your study if you offer him or her what you've observed as change from your perspective, or even if you simply ask him or her, "What has changed about yourself?" Deep reflection on past change sometimes serves as a stimulus for future change.

Deep reflection on past change sometimes serves as a stimulus for future change

Keeping Up with the Literature

Other studies with new methods and findings relevant to a particular longitudinal enterprise may emerge through time as the study progresses. The longitudinal researcher should keep up with the current literature, since selected works may have some bearing on the design, analysis, or interpretation of data from the ongoing study. In the latter years of the Theatre Response Study, an article appeared on the memories of adult audiences recalling their childhood theatre viewing (Deldime and Pigeon, 1989). This research provided a rich component for final exit interviews with Theatre Response participants: Asking children what *they* recalled from seven years of theatre viewing. The results supported the previous article's findings; several of the same response patterns and general categories of recall appeared in the data.

Depending on the length of the study, your own methodological orientation may change as the longitudinal project progresses through time. I originally planned to write up my fieldwork experiences with the adolescent Barry into a traditional, thirty-page, APA-formatted case study report. But during the final year of fieldwork, Denzin's *Interpretive Ethnography: Ethnographic Practices for the Twenty-First Century* (1997) appeared, and his provocative chapter on "Performance Texts" introduced me to the genre of ethnodrama—the scripting of research. It suddenly "clicked" that the most appropriate mode of presentation for and representation of an actor's life history was not an article but a theatrical production (Saldaña, 1998b). So, remain open to new paradigms and methods as the study continues and don't be afraid to change your approach to inquiry midway, because a necessary change in research design due to road-

Your own methodological orientation may change

blocks or unexpected findings might indicate that some type of change has occurred in the participants as well.

"Change is good" is a common adage. But some individuals within the research community may question the credibility and trustworthiness of their peers when they read how methodological changes occurred midway or throughout a long-term study. Hence, here is an appropriate point in the book to discuss these issues.

Trustworthiness of Longitudinal Qualitative Data

A recent longitudinal study on divorce ("Researchers Create," 2000) generated a complicated mathematical formula that incorporates physiological measures such as perspiration and measures of emotional reactions such as anger (extracted from videotaped interviews with participants). The formula, developed by two university psychologists who tracked seventy-nine couples over fourteen years, predicts whether and when married couples would divorce. The news story, of course, had its detractors—even from within the profession, "Some local psychologists and marriage counselors were wary of reducing human relationships to a math problem. 'It's a relationship. It's one's humanity. It's complex, but not that kind of complex,' said Alice Dollinger, an Encino couples therapist for about 15 years. 'My experience says that the overwhelming predictor of an unhealthy, unhappy marriage is a lack of empathy,' which is best measured by human interaction, not mechanical monitors" (p. J2).

Are the tools of the quantitative paradigm to predict divorce valid? There has been a long-standing tension between researchers and clinical therapists over the utility of statistics versus the "real world, in-the-trenches" knowledge accumulated by those in private practice. A therapist working with various married couples over a number of years, and a statistical researcher collecting data from various married couples over a number of years, will each develop a personal paradigm for assessing whether and when marriages will end in divorce. Neither relies exclusively on quantitative or qualitative data, though. It is almost impossible, in fact, to not notice the emotional qualities of humans as you measure the number of times they refer to divorce, or to not be aware of the number of times they refer to divorce as you counsel them through emotional upheaval. Trustworthiness and validity issues in qualitative research have been established but long debated (Lincoln and Guba, 1985; Wolcott, 1990), and it is not my intent to summarize them here. But as it relates to longitudinal inquiry, I cannot help but think: If my marriage were in trouble and I needed professional intervention to help me and my spouse, I'd prefer to see a therapist with years of experiential knowledge to guide us through our troubled times, rather than take a statistical test that might suggest whether or not I should get a divorce.

Changing Paradigms in Midstream

The emergent nature of qualitative research suggests flexibility on the researcher's part. But how does flexibility with types of data and data gathering methods affect the trustworthiness of a longitudinal project, particularly if you realize midway through the study that the initial design choices you've made aren't generating adequate outcomes? If all raw data have been vigilantly maintained, you can always reanalyze what you've collected, but you should also acknowledge that the data collected years ago is all you have with which to work. You enhance the trustworthiness of your longitudinal study if you openly admit that the beginning phase or stage of the data-collection process did not generate as much as you had hoped for and that your analysis is based solely on the available corpus. One of my qualitative research instructors once told my class to rely on the evidentiary warrant and not our memories, "If it's not in your field notes, then it didn't happen."

For example, the first two years of the Theatre Response Study relied on an interview protocol developed and adapted from a quantitative study measuring the response of the young audience (Goldberg, 1977). The child was shown several photographs from the production and asked "What is happening at this moment of the play?" and "What were you thinking or feeling at this moment of the play?" Interview responses were then coded and the results statistically analyzed with the Mann-Whitney U Test. But after two years, I was dissatisfied with the limited amount of data gathered from children as a result of the standardized set of questions posed by the interviewer. I did not want to abandon Goldberg's interview protocol, since I felt that choice would make the next five years of data incomparable to the first two years (this was my positivist rationale at the time). Isaac and Michael, addressing quantitative studies, advised me, "[Once] underway, the longitudinal method does not lend itself to improvements in techniques without losing continuity of the procedures" (1995, p. 51). Yet Menard, also addressing the quantitative longitudinal method, cautioned that repeated measurement systems may damage "internal validity" over time (1991, pp. 38–39). So what was I to do?

The solution was to maintain Goldberg's interview protocol for the rest of the study, but to include an additional repertory of probing questions and questions specifically related to the annual production for the next five years ("Who was the best actor in the production? Why?" "The story of the play you just saw was set in the mid-1800s, but how is the play's story like life today?" and so on). It wasn't until later that the best solution emerged: Discard the quantitative transformation of children's interview responses all together and reanalyze the interview data in a qualitative manner. The statistics told both the study's auditors and me very little about the response of the young audience. The qualitative result was a more descriptive, developmentally rich, new knowledge base that was accessible to a broader readership.

Menard's caveat on repeated measurement systems manifested itself to some degree in the Theatre Response Study. By the fifth year of the project, a few children had memorized the standardized repertory of questions from the protocol and repeated them to the adult interviewer before the session even began. Many of them also knew toward the latter years of the study that the follow-up interview was part of their theatre-viewing experience at school. Though the protocol remained the same for all seven years of the study, the play productions themselves were so varied in content, and the children developed naturally in their cognitive abilities, that their response quality did not "decay" as the study progressed. Indeed, quite the opposite, since most children's responses reflected an enhanced ability to analyze and critique the performance, not just recall it, in follow-up interviews.

Changing Methods in Midstream

What about the trustworthiness of long-term studies that do not employ the same data gathering methods across time? In the Survival Study—an emergent design—1993 data consisted primarily of transcribed interviews with the teacher participant. Data from 1994 were extracted primarily from the teacher's written journal with its reflections on her classroom practice. Data from 1995 consisted of a significant amount of field notes from classroom participant observation in addition to further interviews. Could this mix of data-gathering methods across a twenty-month period generate trustworthy researcher inferences for assessing longitudinal change in the teacher?

Recall that the validity of a longitudinal study may be damaged by "improvements in techniques" over time. But that warning seems more applicable to studies relying on the quantitative paradigm and its accompanying measurement systems to assess change. In most qualitative studies, data gathered from interviews, participant observation field notes, and documents build a collective corpus that permits an interchange and combination of sources for discerning change. Sometimes through interviews the participant may be unaware of his or her own personal growth or development. It is from the researcher as participant observer and analyst that some types of change become more apparent. Documents collected across time may also reveal change when an outside researcher compares and charts the differences between them from one time period through another.

Consistency and purity of qualitative instrumentation are not necessarily essential to prevent "unreliable" or "contaminated" data. What seems more important is evidentiary rigor, whatever data-gathering methods are chosen, coupled with the persuasiveness of the written report. For example, Bullough and Baughman, in their ten-year case study of Kerrie Baughman's teaching career, included "a three-year hiatus" (1997, p. 5) after the initial fieldwork reported in *First-Year Teacher* (Bullough, 1989). But throughout the course of ten years, Bullough estimates, "I have observed Kerrie teach weekly over a total of nearly four years" (p. 6). Despite the three-year gap of direct participant observation, Bullough and Baughman present a persuasive, compelling, and "thick" account of Kerrie's professional life:

> We have included a good deal of data to support our conclusions and to illustrate the points made. We have included what we hope is a sufficient amount to sustain our claims for having made valid, compelling interpretations. Validity and credibility are further enhanced by inclusion of a good deal of information about ourselves and our relationship as it has evolved. We trust that we have provided sufficient evidence of various kinds, gathered through "prolonged engagement," to establish that our findings are credible (see Lincoln and Guba, 1985, p. 301), and that we have established what Polkinghorne (1988) calls "verisimilitude," or results that have the appearance of truth or reality (p. 176). (Bullough and Baughman, 1997, p. 11)

What seems more important is evidentiary rigor

As a second example, Sleeter (1996) with Grant provide a concise and elegant overview of their qualitative methods for a longitudinal study on adolescent perceptions of race, class, and gender. Note that their methods differed slightly during years 1–3 and 4–7:

> Data were collected over a seven-year period. During the first three years, a team of three researchers made one two-week visit and twenty-three other visits lasting two to three days each. Several methods of data collection were used: observations (including shadowing of students), interviews, and questionnaires. A total of 160 hours were spent observing twenty-three junior

high school classrooms. During the last four years, two of the three original researchers maintained the vigil on the student population, periodically visiting the school and interviewing the students and a counselor. Phone calls were also made to the counselor in order to keep up with the students' actions. Interview data were recorded and transcribed for analysis. Research bias was partially controlled by rotating interviewers, having all researchers participate in data analysis, and re-asking the same questions in subsequent interviews. (p. 158)

The emergent nature of qualitative research permits some interchange of different types of data collected through a repertory of methods employed across time. Attunement and sensitivity to the effectiveness or ineffectiveness of one's methods throughout a study are essential. Longitudinal "improvements in techniques" are admirable researcher tactics, not those to be avoided for the sake of traditional reliability or validity. Plus, circumstances in the field setting itself may also necessitate a change of method. Scudder and Colson's (2002) decades of fieldwork in Zambia adjusted to the ever-shifting economic and political conditions of the beleaguered country. The anthropologists noted that "unexpected events bedevil the planning of long term research. . . . [A] rigid research design becomes a handicap over time" (p. 206).

Longitudinal "improvements in techniques" are admirable

Midstream Audits

Also worthy of consideration is a midstream audit of the longitudinal study and its data (Lincoln and Guba, 1985). After the third year of the seven-year Theatre Response Study, the research team assembled outside peer reviewers from the field of theatre for youth to critique the study's progress reports and to offer recommendations as it continued. Though their support and suggestions were helpful and some were implemented in the future, I recall a naïveté from some of those outside the project on the contingencies and "realities" of longitudinal research. This gathering generated fruitful discussion on methodological issues for a discipline in which preexisting longitudinal studies in its professional literature were nonexistent. These audits served both the research team and its auditors, and enhanced the credibility and trustworthiness of future final reports from the research team.

CHAPTER THREE

Longitudinal Qualitative
Data Analysis

This chapter surveys key methods works relevant to longitudinal qualitative data analysis, followed by a discussion of data management and coding. Last is an overview of the sixteen questions proposed for analyzing change through time.

Foundation Principles for Longitudinal
Qualitative Data Analysis

No standardized methods for qualitative data analysis exist, just a repertory of frameworks and techniques advocated in the professional literature. Which methods work "best" depend, of course, on the researcher's methodological orientation, the primary and related research questions of the particular study, and the types of qualitative data collected to answer those questions. Selected writers of qualitative texts offer basic guidelines relevant to longitudinal inquiry. Several of these methods have been particularly useful for my own and others' studies. A brief overview of these works and their principles follows as a cursory and obligatory literature review, of sorts. But it is also an attempt to synthesize relevant longitudinal methodologies and methods to front-load the reader with terms and concepts that play a role in the section "Questions to Guide the Analysis of Longitudinal Qualitative Data" that appears later in this chapter.

Quantitative Support for Longitudinal Qualitative Data
The longitudinal quantitative method has identified such human behavioral change processes as initiation, escalation, reduction, suspension (Menard,

1991, p. 53), continuation, accumulation, reoccurrence (Kelly and McGrath, 1988, p. 81), persistence, delays, cycles, and rhythms (p. 26). Sophisticated statistical procedures can ascertain such phenomena in data as inflection points, trend lines, and feedback loops, though some quantitative researchers admit that almost "no real world system processes operate in neat, one-link-of-the-chain-at-a-time fashion" (p. 40). Numerical data representing various types of changes over time are valuable pieces of information for assessing our long-term economic picture, educational efforts, health and safety programs, national perspectives and opinions, and other areas of public concern. Qualitative researchers should not shun or shy away from statistics, but regard them as one available source of information, if appropriate and available, to support, corroborate, and springboard into qualitative observations of change. Statistics are not neutral; they are open to various interpretations. For example, what did the 1,800 percent increase of American flag sales from Wal-Mart stores after September 11, 2001, suggest ("After the Terror," 2002)? A surge of patriotism may have been the initial reason, but social critics reflected deeper on this phenomenon and interpreted it as a need for community, a need to regain control and assert strength, or a need to mourn for the thousands of lives lost. The American flag, as an artifact, took on various yet significant symbolic meanings for many citizens in this country. And analyzing those meanings, accompanied with the statistical magnitude of sales, adds depth and texture to your observations of change.

Statistics are not neutral

Those still immersed in the tiresome quantitative versus qualitative ("hard" versus "soft") debate might feel that the qualitative paradigm, with its focus on narrative, glosses over or negates the inherent complexity found in numeric representation, reasoning, and analysis. I assert that longitudinal qualitative reasoning is just as complex, if not more so, than quantitative methods. The challenge for qualitative researchers is to rigorously analyze and interpret primarily language-based data records to describe credibly, vividly, and persuasively for readers through appropriate narrative the processes of participant change through time. This entails the sophisticated transformation and integration of observed human interactions in their multiple social contexts into temporal patterns or structures. There is no result-oriented qualitative equivalent to computer software programs for statistical analysis. Hence, the qualitative researcher is not only the data collecting "instrument," he or she is also the "word cruncher."

Proportions As Longitudinal Qualitative Data

Miles and Huberman's *Qualitative Data Analysis* (1994) offers an array of techniques and matrix ideas that are hybrids of both quantitative and qualitative methodologies. The scope and sheer volume of longitudinal data need systematic reduction and management, and the methods outlined by Miles and Huberman offer practical solutions when computer-assisted programs such as N6 (Qualitative Solutions and Research's latest version of NUD*IST [Non-numerical Unstructured Data with powerful processes of Indexing Searching and Theorizing]) are unavailable, inaccessible, or impractical.

Miles and Huberman (1994) advocate, for selected studies, the transformation of qualitative data into proportions as a quantitative tactic for charting category frequency and thus discerning change. For example, when comparing two different cases and their pathways across time (cross-case causal networking analysis), "[i]deally, the low cases would have some of the same *variables* in the same or similar *sequences* as for the high cases, but the *ratings* [quantities] would be different" (p. 233). This tactic was a primary method for discerning both cross-case differences and longitudinal change among the treatment and second-site participants in the seven-year Theatre Response Study. An example of interview data transformed into proportions from that study includes:

Category of Response: References to Production Design (Scenography)

Grade	Treatment Group	Second Site Groups
K	66%	35%
1	14%	2%
2	2%	0%
3	5%	3%
4	2%	0%
5	2%	0%
6	4%	0%

The higher proportions of response during kindergarten signal to the analyst that something different is happening at this grade level than in grades 1–6. And, the higher proportions among the treatment group also suggest different responses from the second-site group. The proportions function as an indicator that something interesting is happening qualitatively and that the next step is to return to the interview transcripts for investigating the differences.

Proportions function as an indicator that something interesting is happening

To some, dependence on quantitative indicators for analyzing qualitative change may be statistically supportive but qualitatively abhorrent. Proportions are merely surface indicators of quantity and, to some degree, quality—much like employing the general mode instead of the precise mean for deducing central tendency. Nevertheless, if a longitudinal study examines the multiple pathways of human action, quantitative strategies for discerning qualitative change should not be perceived as an incompatible methodological mix, but as a complementary or integrated set of procedures (see Wenger, 1999).

Miles and Huberman's (1994) complex prescriptions for time-ordered displays and matrices may seem intimidating at first. But from my own experience, these techniques permit the analyst to locate such phenomena described by the authors as critical incidents, as well as sequences, processes, and flows, along with patterns, themes, and trends through comparison and contrast of qualitative data. But keep in mind that these transformative and reductive methods may potentially sacrifice one of the classic features of ethnographic reporting: thick description. Hence, use proportions as a springboard or supplement to additional analytic schemes and not as the sole measure of change.

Process As Longitudinal Qualitative Data
The comparison of data is the hallmark of generating grounded theory. Strauss and Corbin's *Basics of Qualitative Research* (1998, in particular chapter 11) provides general guidelines for answering some of the primary research questions of selected longitudinal studies. Briefly, grounded theory is the development of a human or social process that is transferable to broader populations and contexts via systematic coding and comparative analysis of qualitative data. Coding—the summative labeling of formative processes—progresses from an inductive and open-ended start, through a more deductive and focused approach, with the purpose of discovering a central category that integrates all previous codes. In my research methods class, students play the board game *Three for All!* to practice grounded theory's basic principles. One reader is given a list of three words or phrases plus what they share in common—for example, "head," "goat," "American" are all types of cheeses. The reader verbally describes each word without referring to the common bond, and listeners must guess the word inductively from the clues provided:

Coding—the summative labeling of formative processes

Reader: This body part has your ears, eyes, nose, mouth, and hair.
Player: Face.
Reader: No, the whole body part above the neck.
Player: Head.
Reader: Correct.

The same is done for the two remaining words. Then the listener recalls all three items and deductively discovers what they share in common, "Types of cheeses!"

Think of the reader's verbal description of each word as a qualitative datum, such as a particular field note entry or interview passage. The word that summarizes the essence of that datum is a code. And when all three codes are compared with each other, the listener attempts to discover what they share in common—how they integrate with each other to create yet another essence at a higher level: a theory, grounded in and emergent from the available data. Now, what if the three codes were action-oriented in nature, such as "digressing," "disagreeing," and "stalling for time"? What's the higher-level process, the "–ing" word at work here, that summarizes yet links all three codes? Unlike the *Three for All!* game, there is no correct answer. I could provide my own deduction as to what these three actions have in common, but it may differ from yours. Such is the nature of interpretive work when we examine human processes through time.

Process, according to Strauss and Corbin, is "a series of evolving sequences of action/interaction that occur through time and space, changing or sometimes remaining the same in response to the situation or context" (1998, p. 165). The authors advise researchers to discern theoretical relevance from what is repeatedly present, notably absent, and/or newly introduced in the data. This search takes into consideration such influences as conditions, consequences, and contingencies (p. 181). A consequence is not the final result defining how change has occurred, but a step in the continuous action/interaction process of participants across time.

Strauss and Corbin (1998) note that change has dimensional properties such as rate, direction, and degree of impact. Change may also occur in "stages and phases" over time, yet "also can be examined in terms of sequences or shifts in the nature of action/interaction" (p. 166). Just as Miles and Huberman (1994) recommend the reduction of qualitative data into matrices for analysis at a glance, Strauss and Corbin suggest miniframeworks or conceptual diagrams developed during coding processes, which collapse the study's multiple codes and categories into a manageable matrix to determine their possible relationships (1998, pp. 140–42) (see fig. 3.1).

Most important to note in the analysis is the search for a central or core category during coding and theory generation, "[A]ll the products of analysis condensed into a few words that seem to explain what 'this research is all about'" (Strauss and Corbin, 1998, p. 146). This theme or abstraction and its properties serve as a through-line of the participants' process in the study, "It must be central; that is, all other major categories can be related to it"

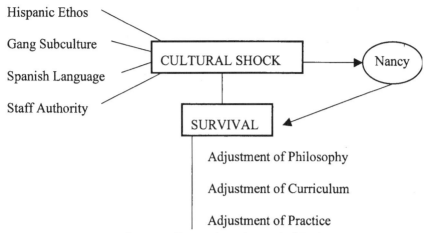

Figure 3.1 A conceptual process diagram from the Survival Study

(p. 147). In the Theatre Response Study, which utilized grounded theory development from seven years of interview data, children's *value* of theatre emerged as the core category. Value of the art form influenced and affected both their formative responses to individual events as they progressed through the study and their summative perceptions of theatre toward the end of the study.

Although developing grounded theory may not be a primary outcome for certain longitudinal studies, Strauss and Corbin's (1998) discussion on the nature of process is essential background knowledge for longitudinal researchers. But this reading must also be accompanied with Dey's (1999) critical analysis of grounded theory. Dey asserts that "[a]ny analysis of process requires some account of the nature of conditions and causes" (p. 180). In *Grounding Grounded Theory: Guidelines for Qualitative Inquiry*, he comments how grounded theory's methodology and methods (as documented by Bernard Glaser, and Strauss and Corbin) do not fully account for the complexities of social interaction, thus limiting the analysis of process. A detailed discussion of such principles as "Process and Causality" (chapter 7) and "Structure and Agency" (chapter 8), and their relation to temporal sequencing, provides additional theoretical underpinnings for analyzing change. The density of these chapters challenges summation in a review, but most notable is Dey's statement to reconceptualize how process is not "a series of slices of time viewed in cross section," but a complex and ever-changing web of "evolution over time" (p. 205).

Epiphanies As Longitudinal Qualitative Data

Denzin (1989) labels significant events in a person's life epiphanies, "inter-actional moments that leave marks on people's lives [that] have the potential for creating transformational experiences for the person." Once these "turning point experiences" occur, "the person is never again quite the same" (p. 15). Such meaningful events or revelations in a participant are moments that alter the direction of future thought and action. They also merit investigation of the participant's contextual and intervening conditions that may help us better understand how or why these epiphanies occur and their consequent impact. The longitudinal researcher should be on the lookout for epiphanies of varying magnitude in data, since they both highlight and locate significant conditions related to change.

An example of an epiphany is a teacher reaching a level of work-related stress so severe that it alters his or her career path within or away from the profession. Troman and Woods (2002) interviewed twenty teachers over a two-year period to study their career adaptation processes through time. The researchers classified these teachers' choices into three broad types of adaptation patterns: retreatism, downshifting, and self-actualization—three detailed processes with more utility and depth than the generic teacher "burnout."

Supplemental quantitative data, proportions, grounded theory, and epiphanies are just four types of general approaches to analyzing change through time. Additional and more specific methods will be reviewed later in this and other chapters. For now, a discussion of qualitative data management, including coding, is necessary before proceeding to the recommended sixteen-question template for guiding longitudinal qualitative data analysis.

Longitudinal Qualitative Data Management

Chronological Assembly of Data

The traditional beginning, middle, and end structure is typical of most stories, and the storytelling model provides one way of organizing or "restorying" (see Ollerenshaw and Creswell, 2002) the master narrative of your data corpus. Aesop wrote short fables with morals. The task for longitudinal qualitative researchers analyzing change through time is somewhat the same: to develop a summary of what happened first, next, and last to the participants in your study, punctuated by a major learning, such as an assertion or theory. A folktale's elements, such as character types, character actions, symbols, and themes, are called *motifs*. Scholars of folklore use standardized and numbered indexing systems for labeling and classifying these motifs. Qualitative researchers do something comparable because the search for motifs in the story of our study is the coding of data.

One basic technique for analyzing change in a participant's data across time is to assemble in chronological order all passages that have been similarly coded. In other words, create a tale with a beginning, middle, and end whose elements are composed of the same motif. For example, the following excerpts from one female participant in the Theatre Response Study illustrate her ability at *story recall*, one particular category of interest to the research team. You won't be able to make sense of her comments because you won't know the plays or characters she's referring to. But notice that her responses from K–2 differ from her responses in grades 4–6 in several ways:

Create a tale with a beginning, middle, and end

Kindergarten: He wanted to go have ice cream with his sister.

Grade 1: Sarah gave the doll to Mrs. Frye.

Grade 2: They were making magic and they were going to show their castle.

Grade 3: [no responses in the story recall category; participant said she was "sleepy" and "tired" and responded minimally during the small-group interview]

Grade 4: The man made a wish, then he goes into the tree. I didn't think he was going to stay trapped in the tree.

Grade 5: She was crying because they sold her daughter as a slave. I thought he looked crazy, that man.

Grade 6: That was sort of sad, in a way, 'cause she told her they could just be friends, but Pip loved the girl.

Obviously, this girl's utterances became longer as she aged and progressed through the study. This was nothing surprising since verbal fluency develops as most children mature. But note that her story recall responses in grades K–2 are basic facts about the action in the play's stories. Story recall in grades 4–6 includes facts as well, but they are now accompanied with *inference making, person perception,* and *emotional response* as new categories that interrelate with story recall. This girl has progressed from a child who simply recounts a story, into someone who connects how the story influences and affects her responses as an audience member. (It is unfortunate that no data were available from grade 3 to assess whether this may have been a transitional year from one pattern of response to another for this participant. But such is the nature of gathering data in the field. Opportunities are sometimes absent or missed.)

Comparing Dynamics through Time

Another strategy for assessing change in field note data is to extract and compare the dynamics of the researcher's observations through time (dynamics will be discussed more fully in the next chapter). Researcher-generated descriptions and interpretations of the social environment and participant action reveal clues as to how, how much, in what ways, and sometimes why something happened during the moments of fieldwork or afterwards in reflection. For example, my field notes of Barry's classroom and public performances throughout the course of one year included the following key words, extracted from narrative passages, to describe the overall qualities or dynamics of his acting (movement, voice, and characterization):

August 24, 1995: sharp, crisp, economic, clear, good volume, articulate, wide variety/range, energetic, believable, "leading man" quality, presence

October 13, 1995: concentrated, focused, precise

October 20, 1995: energetic, focused, detailed, concentrating, honest, clean, active, presence

December 4, 1995: fluid, multileveled, grace, variety

February 22, 1996: low, muddy, slightly inarticulate, intuitive, calm, assured, believable, intimate, detailed

February 23, 1996: detailed, intuitive, spontaneous, low energy, stumbling, strong, parsing well, natural, active, thinking, easy, rushing through, inarticulate, reacts, variety, powerful shifting of moods and emotions, nicely reflective, soft, weak

October 15, 1996: measured, technical, steady, strong, believable

From August through December 1995, no one descriptor appears consistently in all four performance field note entries. The words "energetic," "presence," "variety," variations of "concentrate" (including "focused"), and the synonymous "believable" and "honest" appear in two out of four performances. Like the *Three for All!* game, the task was to find a word, phrase, or assertion that would capture this stage of Barry's acting development, based on the dynamics I recorded. You and I reviewing these same descriptors might generate different interpretations, but I labeled his overall acting quality "elegant stage presence."

February 1996's performances were Barry's experimentation with more spontaneous and intuitive approaches to acting, based on what he had learned in theatre courses, to date. (For the uninitiated, good actors work toward "letting go" of the fundamental yet mechanical approaches they first learn and, with continued experience, begin to trust their artistic impulses during rehearsals and performances.) Unfortunately, Barry was ill during this time period, so my field note dynamics included negative descriptors of his acting quality in addition to positive ones. But even when you're not at optimal performance, the show must go on. So, were the data gathered those evenings "skewed"? No. Did the negative descriptors "count"? Yes. In naturalistic inquiry, what happens, happens; but everything happens in context. Like a show, the analysis must go on. Thus, this stage was labeled, "intuitive, intimate, inarticulate—and ill."

Beginning October 1996, the dynamics used to describe his acting included three words that had not been used up to that time: "measured, technical, steady." He still maintained, though, his ability to create a believable character—an ultimate goal of every performer, and a dynamic Barry maintained throughout this fourteen-month period. This new stage of Barry's artistic development now suggested "disciplined realism." He had become more cognizant of technique's essential jointure with intuitive processes during the creative act.

Dynamics alone do not tell the entire story. Concurrent interviews with Barry, his teachers, and his mother provided additional data to understand the contextual and intervening conditions influencing and affecting his development. These three stages, composed of my own interpretive descriptors, informed me to some degree as to how much, in what ways, and—with supplemental interviews—how and why Barry progressed from one stage through the others.

Analytic Flip Charts

If your longitudinal study is somewhat modest in scope, perhaps the most useful manual tool to analyze longitudinal qualitative data, as it is prescribed here, is a small flip chart similar in format to wall-hanging calendars (see the appendix). But rather than twenty-eight to thirty-one blocks for days of the month on the bottom page, with a large illustration on the top page, each calendar page contains cells for summary answers to the sixteen questions profiled in the next three chapters. Each full-spread page represents a particular time-clustered pond or pool of data from the study. Flipping the pages successively gives you a sense of the study's progression and possible participant change, similar to a cartoon animator flipping plastic cells successively to assess the figures' movement suggested by his or her drawings. If the nuances of change are difficult to decipher from one page's time pool through the next, compare one page of the flip chart to a page from a more distant time pool. I also recommend that you log all entries in pencil for easier revision, since data collected in the future will affect the analysis and interpretation of data collected in the past. Transferring this "analysis-at-a-glance" page onto a word processing template and computer file is another possibility, but I have always found it easier to scan and juxtapose the data by manipulating paper rather than scrolling on a monitor.

Data collected in the future will affect the analysis and interpretation of data collected in the past

Reducing vast amounts of longitudinal qualitative data onto a single page forces you to capture their essence. But by no means is this distillation process intended to replace the necessary detail for a final report. The flip chart is intended as an analytic management tool for the researcher's eyes only, similar to a thumbnail sketch or line drawing before the complete picture is painted in color and exhibited. Customize the content and reformat the layout of the appendix chart to suit your particular study.

Analytic Software and Longitudinal Qualitative Data
My own longitudinal data analyses were conducted before I became acquainted with the various demonstration disks from software developers for qualitative data analysis. I relied on SPSS (Statistical Package for the Social Sciences) PC+, the well-known quantitative data analysis program, for the Theatre Response Study when we experimented with the semantic differential to assess children's attitudes toward theatre (Saldaña and Otero, 1990). For my qualitative data, though, I employed basic word processing programs with boldfaced and underlined key passages from field notes, interview transcripts, and journal entries; handwritten coding in the margins of data hard copies; multiple handcrafted charts, matrices, and diagrams; and index cards for sorting and interrelating salient categories. What I present in this section are the responses of other researchers who have used these data analysis packages, and my own observations and recommendations after sampling one of these programs.

Clandinin and Connelly caution that they "have not found these computerized programs particularly useful in inquiries with massive amounts of field texts of different kinds composed over a span of years" (2000, p. 131). But Manderson, Kelaher, and Woelz-Stirling's massive data management needs for their longitudinal study on women's health requires NUD*IST's (QSR N6) capabilities, particularly for the project's multiple users, "[T]he system must allow ease of use by the research team and must enable the articulation of data with other data sets of different types and from different time periods" (2001, p. 153). Few longitudinal study reports include references to specific programs employed for qualitative data analysis (e.g., Lister et al., 2002), and they generally do not include commentary on the software program's usefulness or their success with it.

Morse and Richards's *Readme First for a User's Guide to Qualitative Methods* (2002) includes a demonstration CD-ROM with a QSR NVivo (version 1.2) tutorial. Demonstration downloads can also be accessed through www.qsrinternational.com. After experimenting with the program, I developed the following major considerations as you work with longitudinal qualitative data and this particular software. The actual program itself will, of course, provide more detailed techniques.

Multiple Research Team Members

Throughout the entering and coding of data, all research team members should ensure that each one is spelling key terms the exact same way during word processing for vital search functions to find all relevant entries (e.g., favor versus favour, Cathy versus Kathy, theatre versus theater, and so on). A glossary, if needed, can provide a reference list of standardized and correct spellings for the project. QSR NVivo's *New Project Wizard: Access* provides log-in and password security measures to protect the confidentiality of participant data. *Properties: Owner* records the name of the particular collector or transcriber of the data should there be several team members working on the project.

Document Files

Data from each case in a small group of participants should be saved in separate files for individual analysis and cross-case comparison through time. It is also recommended that data gathered from separate time pools and ponds (discussed in chapter 4) for each case be saved in separate files (e.g., Nancy.Interview 1.rtf, Nancy.Interview 2.rtf; or Barry Interview.Aug 96.rtf, Barry Interview.Jan 97.rtf, and so on).

Attribute and Sets Functions

The *Attribute* function can specify characteristics of the individual file's data source, such as the gender and ethnicity of the participant, or proportion values in selected categories of data. Most important is the ability to date the particular data documents for chronological review through an attribute's *Values* (e.g., grade level, age, and year). The *Sets* function can organize and classify multiple documents or data sharing similar attributes, or other social characteristics of interest to the researcher.

Document Formatting and Coding

As data are entered onto a document, take a few moments to highlight key words or phrases that seem striking to you by boldfacing, italicizing, coloring, or applying some other rich text feature. These highlighted passages may trigger future in vivo coding or assist with analysis as the documents are reviewed. If you import your qualitative data from a separate word processing program to QSR NVivo, all rich text features will remain intact. Morse and Richards also recommend that different heading styles can be used to represent "different stages or time periods" of data (2002, p. 223).

As you enter and word process data, do some preliminary formatting work by separating lengthy passages of an interview transcript or field notes into short lines or paragraphs, rather than running all the text together. Use (and trust) your instincts to separate passages when you perceive a topic change. For example, the following is an "unchunked" excerpt from an interview with Barry, accompanied with boldfaced text that seemed salient at the time to me:

Do some preliminary formatting

I'm a big—**I'm an idealist, I'm a romantic.** I'm, and I don't just mean in matters of love. I mean, I'm a romantic as far as the way I think, you know? **I'm very feeling oriented.** I think theatre is a very—One thing about it is, it's a very **feeling-oriented institution.** And another thing: it has this **amazing, mysterious stigma** to it. People—You sit out in the audience and you're wondering what's going on here, what's going on backstage. It's like you're backstage and you have this **secret** that the audience doesn't know. And **it's your job to go out there and relay the secret,** and you're telling them the secret, and yet there's still part of it that they don't know, and that they'll never know. And afterwards, when you're done with the show, and the feeling of—**It's an art.** And that's something I used to struggle with, is whether or not it's really an art. Because I'm thinking, I'm using other people's works, there's a director, there's an author, a playwright. Basically, what I'm doing is just relaying somebody else's message. But it really is an art, and **it's an amazing feeling,** and I don't know how to explain it really.

In figure 3.2, the same passage is "chunked" into four smaller units for simultaneous or later coding in NVivo. The coding examples next to the units are, also and appropriately, in vivo and initial, first impression codes for possible future refinement.

An exemplary feature of QSR NVivo is the ability to apply multiple codes to the same passage of text, to subcode a smaller excerpt within a larger coded passage, and to "umbrella" (my term) several coded passages together under one larger code. The *Coding Stripes* feature in the right-hand

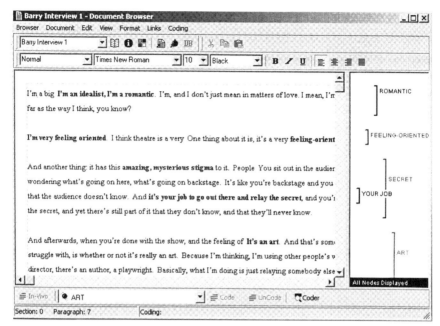

Figure 3.2   A QSR NVivo document screen with Coding Stripes

margin permits you to see your coding labels, which bracket the coded text, at all times. These features allow for initial, open-ended topic coding (Morse and Richards, 2002, pp. 117–19), followed by cyclical readings of the data to add or revise codes related to change (e.g., increases, decreases, and epiphanies).

In NVivo, coding is the act by which references to all text relating to a particular category or code are stored at a container called a *Node*. Since nodes store references to document text, you can browse the references from all documents together in one place through a *Node Browser*. Also, the ability to code is "live," meaning that you can immediately view and code the surrounding context or "code-on" to other categories. This function is of particular interest since you can, if you wish, create general categories during your initial coding that can later be "coded-on" into subtler categories if the data merit it.

It is difficult to code something that is "different" and thus changed in your data unless you first have some basis for comparison. Unless change happens rapidly in your participants, you most likely will not find any evidence of change in your early data sets. Hence, topic coding may be the most suitable approach as you sift through the first few months, if not years, of data. But as you're read-

ing through the interview transcripts, field notes, and documents chronologically, whenever you sense that something—anything—is different than before,
memo, highlight, or code it immediately for
future investigation. I sometimes wrote the

You most likely will not find shorthand code C? for "Change?" in the field
any evidence of change in note margins as a personal alert and reminder
your early data sets to follow up on my intuitive hunch. Sometimes I could find no data to support my C?.
But other times it stimulated a search that
yielded significant results in one form or another. At the very least, it forced me
to review the data once again and gain deeper ownership of the text.

Memos

Use the *Memo* feature as needed for your analytic thoughts while processing data or coding, but especially (if not exclusively) for memos related to
participant change. Since memos are indicated as such through a particular
icon in QSR NVivo, they can be easily batched from a menu. Color-coding
the memos icon can also be applied to separate and identify memos about
change from memos about other topics.

DataBite Links

This feature enables you to establish a link within the transcript or field
note data to separately filed photographs, audio excerpts, video clips, and so
on related to the case and the specific passage in the text. *DataBite Links* become particularly important in longitudinal studies that connect to or build
on previous research studies about natural human development or constructed social processes (discussed in chapter 6). A link to a downloaded article, e-journal article, or bibliographic reference can help you corroborate
whether an observation in your field notes, or an analytic memo about child
development, for example, have been previously noted by other researchers.

Interrelationships

QSR NVivo includes multiple and powerful facilities for exploring possible
interrelationships (discussed in chapter 6) between and among data. *Edit: Find*
conducts a simple word or phrase search in a document to locate where they
occur. *Document Set Editor* "filters" through the data's researcher-established
codes and attributes. By specifying the item, relation, and value of what you're
searching for, the *Editor* links codes and attributes for exploring interrelationships. *Search Tool* finds intersections between coding, attributes, and text to

permit the comparison and contrast of sets of data with particular attributes or codes. Results are stored as coding and can therefore be used as the basis for further searches. *Text Search* codes and counts all instances of a particular word or phrase. *Assay Profile* is an exploratory function, useful when you're uncertain if any interrelationships exist in your data. *Matrix Search* displays its findings in tables and cells, again enabling you to discern possible interrelationships between multiple attributes and nodes (the storage unit for a code).

Modeler

Imagine that a longitudinal qualitative study is exploring how peers, teachers, and family members influence and affect a child's values system from preadolescence to late adolescence. A simple graphic drawn with basic word processing utilities might generate a diagram as shown in figure 3.3.

This modeling serves as a visual tool for theory building. But through QSR NVivo's *Model Explorer*, you can graphically map the major emergent concepts at work with icons, connecting lines, and directional arrows. One possible application of the *Model Explorer* with longitudinal data is to create a separate model for each time period in your study (e.g., Preadolescent Model, Early Adolescent Model, Late Adolescent Model, and so on). The *Model Explorer's Layering* and *Grouping* facilities will then enable you to assess how these models differ and change from one time period through another by overlapping and combining the mapped concepts (see fig. 3.4).

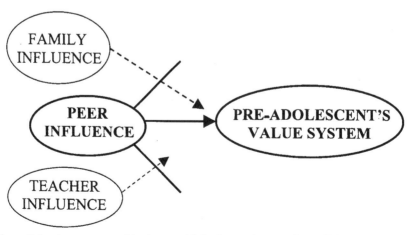

Figure 3.3   A process graphic drawn with basic word processing utilities

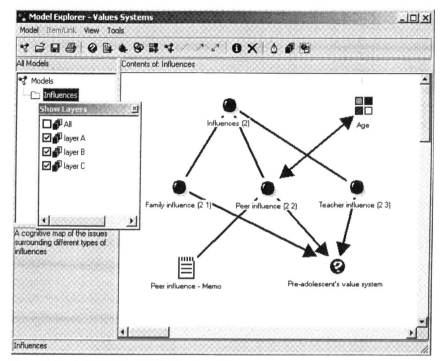

Figure 3.4   A QSR NVivo Model Explorer diagram

Recent computer software and techniques in basic animation hold promise for visually displaying both longitudinal data and results—that is, showing process and change through moving images, rather than through a series of tables, charts, or still graphics on printed pages. As technology advances, this capability may soon be featured in data analytic software.

There is a learning curve with all computer software, including qualitative data analysis programs. None of these, however, "thinks" for you. They are storage and management systems with multiple facilities and functions that enable you to store, chunk, label, organize, and manipulate data for your reflection and analysis. I was satisfied with the basic word processing programs I used for the twenty-month study with Nancy, and the two-and-a-half-year study with Barry. But I wish I had employed something comparable to QSR NVivo or The Ethnograph with the seven-year Theatre Response Study. Though data analysis was concurrent with their collection, manually sorting through 5,000 pages of field notes, interview transcripts, and documents became a massive undertaking. After the study concluded, it took four years of continued data analysis to "get it right." In retrospect, a qualitative data analysis software package would not only have saved me time, but also contributed to a more rigorous and nuanced analysis. The next time I conduct another longitudinal study, I will "shop around" for the most compatible program and use it if I work with one participant in a study three years in length or longer, or with two or more participants in a study one year in length or longer.

Questions to Guide the Analysis of Longitudinal Qualitative Data

There are no prescriptive, systematic, or universal formulas for analyzing longitudinal qualitative data. Each study and its methodology are context-specific and rely on the creative artistry of the analyst to make sense of it all. But regardless of paradigm, regardless of methods, and regardless of topic, what all research studies have in common is the researchers' mantra "I wonder . . . ?" suggesting that there are questions to be answered.

There are questions to be answered

Spradley's "Descriptive Question Matrix" for fieldwork poses relevant questions related to time such as "What spatial changes occur over time?" "How do acts vary over time?" and "When are feeling evoked?" (1980, pp. 82–83) These questions do make time an important facet of ethnographic inquiry, but not its axial focus. I also have difficulty accepting a fundamental premise of social cartography, "Space becomes more important than time in our postmodern mapping discourse" (Paulston and Liebman, 1996, p. 9). Textual answers created for the following questions are one form of "mapping" the ocean of longitudinal qualitative data we collect. However, a body of water's grandeur is not just in the amount of space it occupies on this planet. We can never really understand an ocean's magnitude until we personally experience the time it takes to cross it.

Research is framed and guided by questions, and generating answers for longitudinal studies is assisted through a repertory of analytic methods such as those profiled earlier. But the sheer volume of qualitative data can make the analytic effort burdensome and difficult to track the multiple *types* of change. Ultimately, what might assist the longitudinal researcher is a series of specific questions to consider as the data corpus is collected, reviewed, and coded.

"What changes through time?" *is* the primary question to discern longitudinal trends. But more detailed questions may provide answers that, collectively, form the foundation for in-depth analysis and richer levels of

researcher interpretation. Seasoned researchers may read the following questions and think, "There's nothing new here." Long-term experience does
indeed shape initial, disparate ways of working into a more unified scheme
through time, but these sixteen points of inquiry are intended for novices
who need an accelerated start with a basic, longitudinal analytic framework.
I want my peers front-loaded with this rubric to keep them from experiencing the longitudinal researcher's remorseful statement, "If only I knew then
what I know now."

Wolcott's (1994) three levels of description, analysis, and interpretation
of qualitative data have relevance here and serve as a conceptual framework
for my personal repertory of questions. Chronicling when and what kinds of
changes occur in whom parallel Wolcott's definition of description. Explaining how and why those changes might have occurred, derived after "the iden-
tification of essential features and the systematic interrelationships among
them" (p. 12) is analysis. Explaining the nature and meaning of those
changes, or developing a theory with transferability of the study's findings to
other contexts, is interpretation. Reaching the latter two levels depends on
a solid foundation built from the first.

The following recommended questions are intended to guide the qualitative analysis of longitudinal data—an iterative process but, for organizational
purposes only, divided into three distinct subsets. The five questions in the
first set are ways of framing the data (and must therefore be discussed first).
Framing questions address and manage the particular contexts of the particular study's data by locating them in a processual, analytic ocean, if you will.
The second set of questions is intended to generate descriptive answers. The
third set encourages the researcher to "rise above the data" to richer levels of
analysis and interpretation.

Framing Questions

Five framing questions are posed as data analysis progresses:

1. What is different from one pond or pool of data through the next?
2. When do changes occur through time?
3. What contextual and intervening conditions appear to influence and
   affect participant changes through time?
4. What are the dynamics of participant changes through time?
5. What preliminary assertions (propositions, findings, results, conclusions, interpretations, and theories) about participant changes can be
   made as data analysis progresses?

Descriptive Questions

The second subset of questions generates descriptive information to help answer the five framing questions and the more complex analytic and interpretive questions that follow. Note that these are, in a sense, quantitative in character. Responses to these seven questions could as easily consist of statistics as well as words. But generating meaningful numbers is not the primary goal here. The goal is to generate documented observations of meaningful human actions across time to extract processes (themes, trends, patterns, and so on). This is not necessarily a linear checklist to be answered in the order these questions appear, but an iterative subset of questions to consider on an "as needed" basis as fieldwork progresses and data are reviewed:

1. What increases or emerges through time?
2. What is cumulative through time?
3. What kinds of surges or epiphanies occur through time?
4. What decreases or ceases through time?
5. What remains constant or consistent through time?
6. What is idiosyncratic through time?
7. What is missing through time?

Analytic and Interpretive Questions

The third subset of questions integrates the descriptive information collected earlier to guide the researcher toward richer levels of analysis and interpretation. Like the second subset, these are iterative and their answers may appear during any moment (even during the framing questions review). More than likely, answers will tend to formulate toward the latter rhythms of data analysis. Answers to one particular question may also apply to other questions:

1. Which changes interrelate through time?
2. Which changes through time oppose or harmonize with natural human development or constructed social processes?
3. What are participant or conceptual rhythms (phases, stages, cycles, and so on) through time?
4. What is the through-line of the study?

You'll notice an absence of questions that could identify specific individuals (e.g., Who are the change agents through time? Who resists change through time?). Fullan's (2001) profiles of educational change, for example, are categorized by the particular roles of the teacher, principal, student, parent, and district administrator. This purposeful omission is not intended to diminish the importance of human involvement with change, but to focus more on human perceptions and actions through time—the processes themselves that are more readily identifiable for discerning and thus analyzing change. All the questions assume that human participation and agency are "givens," and it is the researcher's responsibility to keep track of who does what to link or trace changes to their human origins. If the relationship between the researcher and the researched is nurtured through time, the ethnographer becomes part of the participant's life story if change occurs.

Human participation and agency are "givens"

Understandably, there will be an inescapable overlap of data as they are analyzed, since some observations may relate to several questions simultaneously. For example, you might notice that certain data sets interrelate due to certain contextual conditions influencing and affecting participants, yet these simultaneous increases in categories may be due to natural human development. Again, these questions are not a fixed series to be slavishly answered in the order they appear, but a recommended and optional set of tasks the researcher may wish to consider as analysis proceeds. To some, discerning the dynamics of change may possess little or no utility for them. To others, finding rhythms (phases, stages, and cycles) of participant actions may be critical to their particular research questions or agenda. Some studies might stay at the descriptive level deliberately. In other studies, generating theory may or may not be of primary concern. These sixteen questions are tools for longitudinal qualitative inquiry, and not every one of them may be needed to build your particular analytic structure.

Finally, these sixteen questions are certainly not the only ones to consider when analyzing change in longitudinal qualitative data (see the conclusion). In fact, one reader of this book's early draft felt the questions were "not very interesting." I agree. But they are the fundamental and necessary starting points for analysis. Besides, it's not my questions that are supposed to be interesting—it's *your* answers to the questions that are supposed to be interesting.

It's not my questions that are supposed to be interesting— it's your answers to the questions that are supposed to be interesting

A discussion of each question and its analytic principles, accompanied with additional discussion of longitudinal method (e.g., field notes, coding, data management, and so on), plus more examples from various studies, now follows.

CHAPTER FOUR

Framing Questions

Five framing questions are posed throughout long-term research since they weave through all phases, stages, and cycles of data collection and analysis:

1. What is different from one pond or pool of data through the next?
2. When do changes occur through time?
3. What contextual and intervening conditions appear to influence and affect participant changes through time?
4. What are the dynamics of participant changes through time?
5. What preliminary assertions (propositions, findings, results, conclusions, interpretations, and theories) about participant changes can be made as data analysis progresses?

There will be "something borrowed, something new" in terms of the conceptual processes presented here, whose particular combination creates a signature approach to longitudinal qualitative data analysis.

The illustrations for these and other questions are intended as visual supplements to grasp the nature of the inquiry. They can also serve as springboards for any graphic displays you draw to symbolize the flow of data you've collected. Though linear in design for easy recognition, remember that time, change, and the analyses of them are fluid.

What Is Different from One Pond or Pool of Data through the Next?

Beats and Units, Ponds and Pools

Discerning longitudinal change is not a simple matter of tracing a path from start to finish, from point A to point B, or from pretest to posttest, but examining the processual journey along the way (see fig. 4.1). Each month, year, or other time period of a longitudinal study can be seen as a shorter portion of the longer story—like chapters of a novel or scenes from a full-length play. And when all these different periods of data are merged for a full analysis, the data are pooled (Menard, 1991, p. 71), suggesting that smaller subsets of data are ponds (my term).

Studying vast amounts of qualitative data as they accumulate becomes a more manageable effort if the total corpus is chunked into smaller units. But music offers longitudinal researchers a more appropriate metaphor that implies units in time. Glass, a composer, writes, "In Western music we divide time—as if you were to take a length of time and slice it the way you slice a loaf of bread. In Indian music (and all the non-Western music with which I'm familiar), you take small units, or 'beats,' and string them together to make up larger time values" (1996). "Beats of data" imply action, motion, and fluidity—essential conceptual ideas for studying process and change.

First, separate the vast ocean of longitudinal data into smaller, discrete beats—time pools. For example, in the Theatre Response Study, data were gathered from children at each grade level as they progressed through elementary school. Thus, each grade level of interview transcripts (kindergarten, first, second, and so on) became a logical way of dividing the corpus into pools. In my two-and-a-half year study with Barry, the adolescent actor, each public performance (two to three per year) in the school's auditorium became a chronological series of data pools or waves for observing and assessing his artistic

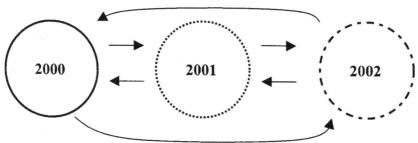

Figure 4.1 **What is different from one pond or pool of data through the next?**

development. In the Survival Study, each year in which data were collected from the teacher (1993, 1994, and 1995) became the three major pools for analysis. Initial separation and deconstruction of the Survival data into categories (e.g., gangs, classroom management, assessment, and so on) rather than time periods could have been an acceptable analytic approach. But dividing longitudinal qualitative data into time pools makes the changes that may have occurred more apparent and the analysis of those changes more efficient to conduct.

Dividing longitudinal qualitative data into time pools makes the changes that may have occurred more apparent

The video documentary *Scared Straight! 20 Years Later* (Shapiro, 1999) profiles the lives of seventeen juveniles (later adults) and "lifers" of Rahway Prison across two decades at specific intervals: 1979, 1989, and 1999. Their initial encounter (an epiphany for the teenagers) was an attempt by the prisoners to scare young lawbreakers out of a potential life of crime. Since 1979, a few of the young people and lifers died from AIDS, drug overdoses, or natural causes. But the majority of the teenagers grew up "straight," and they offer testimony to filmmakers on how the program changed their lives for the better. The longitudinal documentary cuts back and forth between footage from ten-year pools, showing through comparison and stark contrast how an individual's present condition (family-oriented, service-oriented, stable, incarcerated, and so on) differs from his past. The participants' changes are strikingly evident since the follow-up and assessment intervals span one and two decades—a vast amount of time, relatively speaking.

Time pools separated into even smaller beats are ponds. Here is where further subdivision of the data according to a conceptual category rather than time period is more appropriate (although subdivision into shorter time periods is also possible). Within each pool there are dynamic processes at work, and each pond is not a stagnant mass of water but a moving body of fluid data. In the Theatre Response Study, each grade-level pool was separated into two distinct ponds since comparison between groups and genders was intended a priori:

1. Treatment group data from second-site group data
2. Boys' data from girls' data within each major pond above

In the ethnographic Survival Study, ponds were the emergent, researcher-generated categories of the teacher participant's interactions with

1. Students
2. Other fine arts teachers
3. Nonarts teachers
4. School and district administrators
5. School social workers

The student pond was further subdivided into smaller category ponds after their distinctive differences were observed during fieldwork:[3]

- Grades K–6
- Grades 7–8 (arts magnet program students)
- Gang members
- Non-English-speaking students

Data for the life-course study of Barry was organized into various contrasting ponds. The categories emerged during the final stage of analysis when I scripted his life story as an ethnographic performance text. Each pond ultimately became a scene in the final stage production of *Maybe someday, if I'm famous . . .* :

1. Elementary school through secondary school
2. Sports and arts
3. Classroom work and stage production
4. Rehearsal processes and performance dynamics
5. Mother's and teachers' influence
6. Public performances and private thoughts
7. Past accomplishments and future dreams

A longitudinal qualitative study that skillfully merges both time pools and category ponds is Ågren's (1998) study of aging. It included interviews with forty-one men and women at ages eighty-five and ninety-two. After analyzing the transcripts to answer her central question "How does the interviewee experience and adjust to life?" seven category ponds of adjustment emerged that ranged from positive to negative: self-realizing, mature aging, adapting, dependent, resignedly accepting, despairing, and withdrawing. Each of these categories are then illustrated through comparative summaries of life at eighty-five and at ninety-two, with a description of major changes that occur across the seven-year time span. The following is a profile of the dependent category:

Eighty-Five Year Olds (2 men and 16 women)
    The lives of the Dependent were dominated by a deep grief for a deceased spouse or, for the two men, an almost symbiotic dependency upon their wives.

Despite a rather high self-esteem, they felt unable to cope with the present situation on their own. Therefore they turned to, and also received support mainly from their children who now made life worth living.

Ninety-Two Year Olds (2 men and 10 women)
At ninety-two the participants in this category were more physically dependent on others. Dependency could now also be a negative experience. A few were emotionally dependent on caring staff, which was not the case at eighty-five.

Woman: When my daughter visits me all my sorrows disappear. I may be crying but when she comes I become so terribly happy. She says she has so much to do and can not come more often than she does. She has so much to do and . . . . If she knew how much it means to me that she comes (*crying*). I wonder if she understands that? (pp. 110–11)

If general areas for observation or specific categories of change have not been predetermined, each study will have its own particular, emergent, and appropriate categories as determined by the researcher. Ponds are artificial subdivisions of pools, but they become more manageable beats for initial analysis. Even as "ponding" of data progresses, some higher levels of analysis and interpretation are already at work, and the researcher may make some initial observations of change during this procedure. More on this is addressed later in this chapter.

Different, Not "Missing"
Next, begin the systematic comparison of pond to pond, pond to pool, and pool to pool. Notice that "different" rather than "missing" is included in the framing question: What is different from one pond or pool of data through the next? If you look for differences within and between categories, you will be more aware of the many possible contrasts, variability, and dynamics within and between the data. If you look exclusively for what is missing, you limit your search to what is absent rather than present. But compare data carefully. Sometimes a possible answer to "What is different?" may very well be "Nothing at all," yet even this is noteworthy (see the section "What Remains Constant or Consistent through Time?" in chapter 5). Reutter et al.

Look for differences

(1997) observe differences in nursing students' learnings across each year of their four-year preprofessional program by comparing annual pools of interview and survey data. Note how change is described in student "observation" and "needs" by their qualitative differences across time:

As one student said, "the first year I'm learning things, now I'm learning nursing." Students' learning activities are characterized by both observation and practice. Observation in second year, however, becomes more active as students begin to "process" rather than merely "imitate" behaviors of students, faculty, and staff nurses. That is, students begin to critically evaluate their observations and to discriminate between role models. Because of their perceived need to master skills, [second year] students are somewhat more self-centered than in later years in that patients are perceived as "opportunities" to meet students' learning needs. In later years, patients' needs take priority over students' learning needs, as students are now seen as the means to meet patients' needs. (p. 152)

In the Theatre Response Study, second-site participants from seven different schools, comparable to the treatment group in grade level and socio-economic status, were selected each year for cross-site comparison. Analysis of data first began with the treatment group's kindergarten-level interview transcripts and participant observation field notes to discern general categories of child audience response and their proportions within the corpus. This was similar to Strauss and Corbin's (1998) prescriptions for open and axial coding. This part of the process is like filtering muddy water to create a clearer pond. Analysis then proceeded to the second site's transcripts and related field notes for category development and accompanying proportions. This was the second pond.

Next, proportions of both treatment and second-site ponds were compared to note and investigate any differences. For example, three primary categories were the perception processes used by the child in her recall of the event: aural cues, visual cues, and integrated aural/visual cues. At the kindergarten level, treatment and second-site groups relied on aural cues from the play at 16 and 19 percent, respectively, interpreted as a negligible difference. But reliance on visual cues alone totaled 25 percent for the treatment group and 34 percent for the second site. Combined reliance on integrated aural/visual cues also had differing proportions: 14 percent for the treatment group and 4 percent for the second site. Quantitative differences such as these might clue the researcher to state, "This means something." But what? I returned to the transcripts for further comparison of qualitative data pools. One assertion was developed from the observations noted earlier:

In post-performance interviews, children's responses from both sites suggested heavy reliance on visual processing of specific physical actions by the puppets. A second-site child said, "One [of the trees] had a squirrel that dropped that [acorn]." But unlike second-site children, treatment group responses generally integrated both visual *and* aural stimuli from the production in their recall of the story. [A treatment child said,] "The boy, um, he has the pistol. And the snail came up and he started pointing the gun at it, [and the squirrel said,] 'Don't shoot me, I'm a friend.'" (Saldaña, 1996, p. 70)

Other observations emerged as interview transcripts were compared by gender ponds. A simple example is the more frequent references by boys to scenographic elements of the productions (e.g., special effects, lighting, set pieces, and so on). A more subtle difference is the way girls recalled the events using a mixture of replicated dialogue from the play script and descriptions of stage action in extended narratives, a storytelling pattern not as evident among boys.

Difference in Differences
An individual might also be considered a pond within a pool of participants. In the lower grade levels, the thirty children in the Theatre Response Study generally responded in similar ways to theatrical events. "Group" findings as a single pool were the intended analytic and reporting methods. But as participants grew older and developmental complexity emerged, the ocean of response categories expanded, and individual positions within that ocean varied greatly from child to child—that is, from pond to pond. "Small group consensus characterized evaluative response at the early grade levels. Diverse and sometimes opposing interpretations and evaluations of characters, moments, and theatrical elements from the event were most noticeable by the sixth grade level. Not all treatment children by sixth grade demonstrated an accelerated level of critical competence, but the majority did express their personal assessments of what they experienced" (Saldaña, 1996, p. 80).

Analyzing differences from one participant to the next helped me find variations and dynamics within the data pool (discussed later in this chapter). But with greater variability, the more difficult it became to describe "group" findings. Hence, individual cases and their variation within the pool were portrayed through a spectrum of illustrative vignettes in final reports (Saldaña, 1995). And, in findings where a majority or minority of participants exhibited similar responses, terms such as "most," "some," or "a few" were used, preferred substitutes in this case for quantitative proportions such as 76, 42, or 15 percent.

With greater variability, the more difficult it becomes to describe "group" findings

Percentages are indeed useful to portray the distribution of responses within a selected category. Numbers are, in fact, sometimes a better way than words to describe variability—and qualitative purists should be humble enough to admit that. The Gallup Organization's public opinion polls provide us with this type of statistical data in its survey results, and the organization has reached a level of credibility and trustworthiness from my perspective. I am frequently skeptical when social commentary or newspaper editorials attempt to render "national consciousness" or to capture a people's "character" through broad generalizations, for I can often think of at least one exception to the contrary. When I read "Americans are _____ [fill in the blank]" or "As a country we have _____ [fill in the blank]," I question the writer's assumption of authority to represent such a large group and, in the process, negate the diverse opinions diverse individuals may hold. In a qualitative study, differences in participants are frequently the rule, not the exception. Paradoxically, discovering what all those differences have in common is what we're after in an analysis.

Results from pooling multiple case study observations will also be shaped not just by the qualitative lens but by the paradigm filter used for data collection and analysis. In the following two studies, both researchers examined longitudinal outcomes through qualitative lenses, but the analytic filter for one investigator was narrative inquiry, while the other applied grounded theory techniques and assertion development. Each study yielded different outcomes in terms of breadth and transferability.

Barone (2001), in *Touching Eternity: The Enduring Outcomes of Teaching*, interviewed nine student alumni from his original 1983 evaluation study of a high school visual arts program in North Carolina. Twelve years after these students received instruction from Donald Forrister, an outstanding, charismatic, and award-winning teacher, Barone attempted to uncover the influences Forrister may have had on these participants' lives. Barone openly admits that, due to the nature of his arts-based research paradigm, "precise measurements of Forrister's influence in each case is impossible" (p. 143). Nevertheless, Barone renders a portrait of each former student through evocative narrative, followed by interpretive proposals of common bonds. Though few of Forrister's former students later practiced the making of art products, "caring was a recurring theme" (p. 136) in interviews, and Barone posits that "many had achieved Forrister's impressive degree of personal integrity, his tendency to act in accordance with personal proclivities that sometimes ran counter to prevailing orthodoxy. Forrister promoted self-knowledge within his students so that each might act wisely in constructing a unique self-identity, rather than moving to replicate his own" (p. 134).

In contrast, Millar (2002) profiles ten case studies forty years after the initial administration of and experiments with the 1958 Torrance Tests of Creative Thinking. *The Torrance Kids At Mid-Life: Selected Case Studies of Creative Behavior* documents primarily qualitative outcomes from the Tor-

rance Longitudinal Study of Creativity. The goals of the project were to de-
duce the predictive power of the original tests and the life influences and
affects on adult creative achievement. Participants were interviewed in five
areas of interest, such as early influences on creativity, career paths, and accomplishments. Transcripts were analyzed to extract "meaning units"
(Strauss and Corbin, 1990) as data ponds for pooling into themes and trends.
Unlike Barone's artistic narrative profiles, Millar presents each case study interview in an almost verbatim transcript format, accompanied with a descriptive summary of findings at the end of the profiles. The final chapter
"Key Messages for Creative Living" lists forty-seven assertions developed
from the pooled data, such as: "Creativity manifests itself at an early age as
involvement in the 'fine arts' in activities provided by parents; and in schools
that are staffed by teachers with a creative motivation and commitment"
(2002, p. 274); and "Mentors are most helpful in achieving the creative potential of creative persons" (p. 277).

Barone (2001) examines the influence of a particular individual on particular cases. Millar (2002) examines particular cases also, but assesses the
programmatic and naturalistic influences on them with a focus on a phe-
nomenological concept: creativity. The former study's transferability is limited, and intentionally so. The latter study intends a broader applicability of
its assertions to the general population. Both researchers are swimming in an
ocean of longitudinal data, but one seems to be an underwater photographer
capturing the life and beauty that appear mysterious in the depths. The other
seems to be a scuba-diving oceanographer meticulously gathering samples of
that life and beauty for rigorous analysis in a laboratory on dry land. Imagine
what might have resulted if Barone had chosen to interview "the Torrance
kids" and created artistic, narrative renderings of their lives, while Millar interviewed Forrister's former students and systematically analyzed the master
teacher's influences and affects on their creativity. The same participants interviewed by different researchers, using their own preferential paradigms,
would have generated completely different outcomes, even though
both would have worked qualitatively with case studies for the ultimate purpose of pooling results.

Then and Now
I once experimented with analyzing data "backwards"—that is, reading a participant's interview transcript from the final year of a study first, then
reviewing previous transcripts in reverse chronological order, hoping this
comparison technique would reveal new insights. But I learned that I was unable to "keep track of time." Perhaps my future-oriented, chronological

conditioning prevented me from working in this reversionary manner. Whenever some connection or pattern did occur to me using this process, I found myself again going forward in time to later transcripts to make sense of the difference. This "backward" technique, though, might work for other researchers or with particular types of data sets. Working backwards might also assist in tracking previous influences and affects on current conditions. When I reflect on my past to observe how I'm different in the present, I end up thinking forward in time again to map the course of and reasons for change. Moving forward generates analytic insight on development; moving backward generates unforeseen foreshadowing, irony, and regret. I could never remember whether the saying goes, "You don't know where you are or where you're going until you know where you've been," or whether it goes, "You don't know where you've been until you know where you are or where you're going." Perhaps it's both. Søren Kierkegaard's "Life can only be understood backwards, but it must be lived forwards" is both an existential and pragmatic axiom for longitudinal qualitative data analysis.

Photographer Mark Klett replicates historic landscape photographs from the nineteenth and early-twentieth centuries by locating the exact site and best judgment of time of day when the original shot was taken. Zeitlin, an art critic, notes that Klett's work shows how "time erodes the things of the world, and how that pesky creature man accelerates the process. . . . And he shows us that the concept of wilderness is one that is also in constant flux" (2002). The geography and architecture of a historic city's past and present are also compared through the same replication process employed by Campanella and Campanella (1999) in *New Orleans Then and Now*. For example, photographs of the exact same house on a corner of Bourbon Street, taken in circa 1905, 1935, and 1996, are placed next to each other for the viewer to observe and compare the home's differences and similarities through time (pp. 62–63). "Some sequences reflect radical change, others meticulous restoration, others still an interesting inventory of adaptation and evolution" (p. 8). Although photographs are certainly one type of data we can collect and analyze during extended fieldwork, a day's field notes are also "portraits in miniature," as theatre artists like to call stage monologues. Our written documentation through time may hold evidence of pesky human actions in flux, reflecting erosion, restoration, adaptation, evolution, and radical change. But limiting ourselves to analyzing change with a "then and now" rubric is going over time, not through it. Thus, it might be best to think of chronological field note data as a photographic album or diary, with each turn of the page revealing "then, and then, and then, and then, and now." More sequential data ponds and pools permit a more nuanced analysis of change through time.

Glick et al. (1995) provide yet another analogy for analyzing differences across time, "[E]xamining change is analogous to time-lapse photography; change processes can be inferred by researchers who look for differences across a series of snapshots taken at fixed time intervals" (p. 138). Since time is fluid, we do not always have to divide data for analysis into standard units such as weeks, months, or years, or look for change at "fixed time intervals." When appropriate, let the data divide themselves. In other words, when you perceive or interpret that subtle to significant differences appear, regardless of when they happen in the data or time continua, a new beat begins. New pools and ponds are formed.

When appropriate, let the data divide themselves

When Do Changes Occur through Time?

The Researcher As Historian

It is assumed that researchers date and chronicle all field notes, interviews, journal entries, and so on to maintain a documented record of the study as it progresses. Though it may be stating the obvious, knowing or inferring when actions and changes occur is a critical task in longitudinal data analysis (see fig. 4.2). We may label ourselves ethnographers, biographers, or developmental researchers, but another role we assume by default in longitudinal studies is historian. Emerson, Fretz, and Shaw advise, "[E]xperienced ethnographers envision themselves as readers in a more distant future, recognizing that notes should include details and background information sufficient for making sense of them several years hence, when the immediacy of the field experience has faded" (1995, p. 44). All documentation should be sufficiently detailed for future research team members as well if the longitudinal study extends over several years or decades.

Another role we assume by default in longitudinal studies is historian

Not only observed changes but also the contextual and intervening conditions surrounding those changes must be documented. The life-course study of Barry chronicled his artistic development

Jan.   Feb.   Mar.   Apr.   May   June   July   Aug.   Sept.   Oct.   Nov.   Dec.

Figure 4.2   When do changes occur through time?

from kindergarten, as a participant in the seven-year Theatre Response Study, through twelfth grade. The original Theatre Response Study terminated after Barry's sixth-grade school year in 1991, and I did not maintain contact with him until a follow-up study in 1995, his tenth-grade school year, to discern any residual affects on Theatre Response participants. According to his mother, the latter half of Barry's fifth-grade education through the first few months of ninth grade was, as he labeled it, a depressed "dead period." (They reflected on his past during separate interviews conducted in December 1995 with Barry, and February 1996 with his mother.) But this portion of his life was preceded and followed by more successful school periods. After documenting when this "dead period" occurred, I now had to investigate how and why this phase of his life originated and ended. A history of Barry's social worlds before, during, and after this approximately three-year depression revealed how peers, teachers, family members, and Barry interacted to initiate, continue, and eventually suspend this, according to his mother, "horrible, painful, awful time" in his life.

Particular participant changes might also interrelate with social, political, and cultural changes and historic events through time, such as a woman's emergent consciousness of gender roles during the rise of feminism in the 1960s; a young gay man's coming out epiphany to family and friends, motivated by Matthew Shephard's brutal murder in October 1998; or a Phoenix, Arizona, elementary school's increased security measures after the April 20, 1999, shooting massacre at Columbine High School in Littleton, Colorado. Century (2001) notes how applied industrial research in the 1980s influenced the production of new media works by innovative performance artists, changing both the process and representation of exhibition and performance. A state's economic health (or woes) during a particular year eventually influences and affects its public schools' daily operations in myriad ways. What all these examples reinforce is the need to examine participant change through particular periods of time in conjunction with external events and contexts—history.

Chronicling
Longitudinal studies with children and adolescents can chronicle observed changes according to their ages (years and months) or grade levels (with attention paid to the number of weeks or months into the academic year). This allows the researcher to assess whether such changes are part of developmental trends in humans documented in the research literature or changes related to contextual or intervening conditions in the participant's life such as home and school environments, unique classroom learning experiences,

and personal epiphanies. Noting when changes occur also assists in discerning interrelations of events for richer data analysis or for developing conceptual phases, stages, cycles, or other rhythms of human action (discussed in
chapter 6).

Emerson, Fretz, and Shaw also encourage the documentation of action with
transitional markers (e.g., "then," "next," "afterwards," and so on): "Through
actions, characters move through space and time; thus writers aim to capture
the dynamic quality of action and its forward movement—something happens!" (1995, p. 73) Brizuela and García-Sellers (1999) examine first-grade
Spanish-speaking children and their recently immigrated families adapting to
a U.S. school. The researchers profile the adaptation processes of four case
studies through the course of one year using a repertory of general time desig-
nators representing simple beginnings, middles, and endings:

- "At the beginning of the school year . . ."
- "As the school year progressed . . ." and "During the course of the
  school year . . ."
- "During" and "Throughout the follow-up [mediation] . . ."
- "Throughout the study . . ."
- "Toward" and "By the end of the follow-up . . ."
- "By the end of the school year . . ." and "By the time of final assess-
  ment . . ."

These phrases elegantly outline in traditional story formats the adaptation
processes of the children, parents, and teachers involved with the study. The
linearity of narrative's basic "beginning, middle, and end"
sequencing tells tales of transformation.

Tell tales of   A study conducted throughout a traditional aca-
transformation   demic school year could also document observations
                                   with more precision to assess and report when changes
occurred. The precision can be as fine as a specific day,
month, or time period (e.g., from September 8 through October 23; from
the orientation stage in weeks 1–2 through the routine stage in weeks
3–7). Kelly and McGrath go so far as to encourage researchers to specify
the time of day, day of the week, season of the year, and so on data were
gathered, since these particular periods may play a significant role in the
interpretation of data (1988, pp. 72–75). Willett, Singer, and Martin refer to precise event occurrence as "continuous-time data," and events occurring within a finite time interval (e.g., a year or grade level) as
"discrete-time data" (1998, p. 401). Other methodologists prescribe that

data from participant observation could be collected during standardized time frames—for example, during the first week of each month. But life and its accompanying changes, epiphanies in particular, do not always occur at fixed time intervals. Capturing participant change at the moment or during the period it occurs is sometimes due to good fortune—being at the right place at the right time—or interpreted in retrospect once a pool of data has been collected. Change is inferred as data are reviewed and coded, but it is critical that you know what happened when. Our initial training in taking field notes includes diagramming the fieldwork environment, such as a classroom ground plan, with thick descriptions of the artifacts and movement within the space. We should also pay comparable attention to documenting aspects of time in the field site and how it's perceived and valued by participants; how it's realized in such artifacts as watches, clocks, calendars, and posted schedules; and how it's measured, allocated, apportioned, and adhered to hourly, daily, weekly, monthly, and annually.

Later, when I discuss rhythms (phases, stages, and cycles), I'll note that as data from the Theatre Response Study were pooled, my interpretations suggested that general characteristics of children's responses appeared within three separate grade groups: K–2, 3–4, and 5–6. Most elementary educators in the 1980s separated children into two main clusters: K–3 and 4–6. I adopted this traditional but artificial dichotomy in my thinking as I proceeded through the analysis. I sought a discrete turning point in children's responses ending with grade 3 and beginning with grade 4. But as grade 3 data were coded, a host of new response categories emerged that contrasted to the generally positive responses from grades K–2. Also, different response categories emerged in grade 5, while selected categories from grades K–4 data decreased in proportion or disappeared altogether in grades 5–6. Hence, the original plan to pool grades K–3 and 4–6 data was discarded. Noting when these changes occurred helped me develop not two but three distinct stages of children's responses to theatre. An additional lesson here is to permit new codes to emerge as a longitudinal study's data are gathered and analyzed. If we assume that change occurs in participants, then our codes should also change to reflect those differences through time.

Permit new codes to emerge

The precision of chronicling when changes occur also depends on the study's particular research questions and amount of detail needed in final reports. Daily, weekly, monthly, quarterly, annual, and/or decennial reports are generated by various organi-

zations for various reasons, depending on mandated record-keeping procedures, assessment tasks, and timely decision making by self or others. The
amount of detail required for these reports can be as cursory as a paragraph
summary to an exhaustive 300-page document. As a generalization, the
shorter the fieldwork period (e.g., one year), the more detail needed in final
reports. The longer the fieldwork period (e.g., ten years), the less detail
needed in final reports. This advice, though, is superceded by whatever the
researcher or audience may feel is necessary detail for descriptive documentation and a persuasive argument for a study's account.

Recording when changes occur is a ubiquitous task as the researcher
notes such observations as increases, decreases, or idiosyncratic patterns in
the data. Also, the question "When do changes occur through time?" is
closely related to the dynamics of change such as duration, frequency, and
tempo (discussed later). Sophisticated quantitative systems in organization
science, for example, locate and specify change with precision, using such
terms as "inflection points" and "trend lines." Admittedly, I do not possess
expertise in computing these complex quantitative methods. And when I
feebly attempted to find qualitative equivalents to these systems of measurement, it occurred to me that the exercise was both futile and moot
since time and change—including types of change—are contextual to a
study.

What Contextual and Intervening Conditions Appear to Influence and Affect Participant Changes through Time?

Contextualization

Throughout longitudinal data analysis, there is reflection on such time-
oriented questions as when, how often, and for how long certain participant actions occur. But also critical to analysis is investigating how, how
much, in what ways, and/or why these actions occurred—the conditions
involved with change (see fig. 4.3). There is a specific history and course

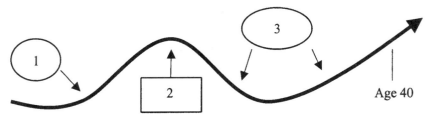

Figure 4.3   What contextual and intervening conditions appear to influence and affect
participant changes through time?

of events to every particular participant, every particular setting, every particular researcher, and every particular study. Contexts are inextricably embedded within each particular research enter-

---
Qualitative data cannot be analyzed in isolation
---

prise. Participant actions are rooted in social and cultural contexts, and what the researcher observes and interprets is also rooted in his or her own social and cultural contexts. Qualitative data cannot be analyzed in isolation. Perhaps this is why so many advise, "Never let the data speak for themselves."

Pettigrew advises that

> the task is to identify the variety and mixture of causes of change and to ex-plore through time some of the conditions and contexts under which these mixtures occur. . . . Context is not just a stimulus environment but a nested arrangement of structures and processes where the subjective interpretations of actors perceiving, comprehending, learning, and remembering help shape process. Thus processes are both constrained by context and shape contexts, in the direction of either preserving or altering them. (1995, pp. 94–95)

Mouat states this interrelationship elegantly, "[T]he individual and society interact complexly so that each affects the development of the other" (1996, p. 84).

A clarification of terms as they are used in this book is necessary here. I borrow principles from Pettigrew (1995) and terminology from grounded theory, but I also advocate my own constructs for this question. Admittedly, these are slippery concepts to grasp because there is no precise algorithm to follow. Like contexts, how you use these concepts depends on how you per-ceive them and how you interpret field data.

Influences and Affects, Interaction and Interplay
"Influences and affects" are constructs I use to replace the traditional, linear "cause and effect." Perhaps it is nothing more than semantics, but I find that the former phrase evokes a more processual way of examining the complexity of change within participants in a qualitative manner, since change forces and consequences are multiple, networked, and collaged, not singular and isolated. I have always perceived "cause and effect" as static nouns. "Influences and af-fects" are not only nouns, they are rich verbs suggesting action and change. Huberman and Miles reinforce that "outcomes" can be discerned from "plots" (chronological events) unfolding through time, "the local processes underlying a temporal series of events and states" (1994, p. 434). These local processes are,

from a dramaturgical perspective, conflicts that participants confront as their contextual and/or intervening conditions, which often stimulate agency, the participants' actions or tactics. Observing participants' tactics as they negotiate conflict (in its broadest sense) helps to structure the plot and provide insight on how individuals act on and possibly change from it—that is, how they are influenced and affected by conflict. Since conflicts are potential sources or stimuli for participant action, and their negotiations with conflicts are suggestive of participant change through time, plotting allows the researcher to reflect on and speculate how and/or why events unfolded as they did. Scudder and Colson's anthropological theory of the Gwembe Tonga in Zambia may hold far more applicability to the human condition than they originally intended as part of their long-term study; "A major finding of our research has been the frequency with which people experiment, assess gains and losses, and decide whether to continue. People weigh their options and make choices, and then justify them if need be" (2002, p. 214).

Change forces and consequences are multiple, networked, and collaged, not singular and isolated

"Interaction," as I use it throughout this book, refers to the reverberative (i.e., continuously back and forth) influences and affects through time between humans, artifacts, physical environments, institutions such as government, structures such as culture, processes such as aging, and/or abstractions such as time. Individuals make sense from their personal interactions with the social and physical worlds. Humans also assign interactions between nonhuman entities, such as time and the physical environment. "Interplay" refers to the associative (i.e., connected, combined, and integrated) influences and affects through time among any of the previously described entities. Individuals in isolation don't just "make sense" of the social and physical worlds; during interplay they construct deeper meaning from their synthesis of those worlds. As an academic, I *interact* on a weekday basis in a university institution's buildings, classrooms, and offices with students, staff, and faculty. The *interplay* comes from heightened awareness of my personal role, responsibilities, and status within that institution, and my necessary social transactions and political negotiations with students and people in power for me to function effectively within that institution. Interaction is reverberative; interplay is associative. Reflecting on how your participants engage in both assists you with determining the web of influences and affects at work.

Interaction is reverberative; interplay is associative

Contextual Conditions

Contextual conditions are the "nested arrangement of structures and processes," the participants' particular givens in their everyday social worlds and their particular interactions with them. For example, a teaching context for an instructor consists partly of interactions with the particular students assigned to or enrolled in the class (e.g., fourth-graders, 75 percent education majors, one deaf student, an obstreperous yet gifted young boy whose parents are currently in the middle of a divorce, and so on), the particular content or curriculum he or she teaches (e.g., advanced placement calculus, mandatory adherence to district or state standards, an elective rather than required course, and so on), and professional interactions with colleagues (e.g., the perceived relationship with the school's principal, whether he or she feels isolated from or bonded to other teachers in the subject area, and so on). Other teaching contexts might consist of such structures and processes as the school's annual budget for classroom materials, the teacher's particular philosophy or pedagogical approach (e.g., whole language versus phonics), and the expertise he or she demonstrates in classroom management.

Social contexts are also critical to longitudinal research and its data analysis. Heinz and Krüger note that in life-course research, "Basic social institutions, mainly the family, education, economy and social policy play a central role in enabling or restricting life-course continuities. The social features of a person, gender, class, ethnicity and citizenship define or frame social differentiations which point to variations of life courses within and across cohorts" (2001, p. 34).

Sometimes, we perceive that day-to-day, consistent environments and routines—contextual conditions—are neither locations of nor stimuli for participant change. But they are. A typical classroom throughout the course of an academic year is a setting where numerous and multiple types of changes occur in both students and teacher. Cumulative television, film, and theatre-viewing experiences change the way children perceive and interpret future viewing experiences. Developmental and incidental changes in their preferences and value systems for entertainment also occur. A consistently boring work environment influences and affects—changes—its employees' social interactions and personal emotional health through time. Structures and processes such as these may not lend themselves to immediately observable changes throughout short-term durations. But in longitudinal contexts and through qualitative data analysis, the

Contextual conditions—the givens—are potential locations of participant change

interpreted changes become more apparent. Hence, contextual conditions—the givens—are potential locations of participant change.

Intervening Conditions

When Pettigrew states that "processes are both constrained by context and shape contexts, in the direction of either preserving or altering them," this suggests to me that even contexts are contextual. Any of the contextual conditions illustrated earlier could also be labeled intervening conditions, depending on how the participant and researcher interpret them. An intervening condition is a contextual condition perceived as a purposeful, unanticipated, or significant structure, process, or human action that influences and affects participant change through time. In other words, some conditions initiate greater change than others. Contextual conditions are background; intervening conditions are foreground.

Contexts are contextual

Action research in education, for example, is in itself an intervening condition since practitioner change is purposeful. Gitlin's two-year project with teachers employed "horizontal evaluation" (2000, pp. 101–103) to examine the contradictions between their intentions and practices. Through this critical and collaborative method, oppressive structures in school culture were challenged and intervention was sought for positive change. This "ethnography of empowerment" (Delgado-Gaitan, 2000) is a research framework that stimulates new and transformative ways of working to break the existent and immobilizing contextual conditions of school culture.

But what of qualitative studies in which action research is not the driving model? For example: To a veteran teacher of twenty years, a deaf student mainstreamed into her classroom—the fifth deaf child she's taught in her career—may be perceived as nothing significant within her teaching context. The deaf student's presence is a given contextual condition. Their interactions are pedagogically appropriate and, for the seasoned educator, routine. But to a first-year teacher who has never instructed hearing students, let alone a deaf student, their interaction processes are perceived by the teacher, the student, and the researcher as problematic.

The novice teacher's inadequate preparation program—a structure and process—which offered no university coursework on exceptional children, is a given contextual condition because the past cannot be altered. Yet, it could also be perceived and labeled as an intervening condition because it plays a significant, albeit antecedent, role in the teacher's forthcoming change process. Her lack of professional knowledge about exceptional children both constrains and shapes her interactions with the deaf student. This inade-quate preparation could preserve their distanced relationship throughout the school year, or it could be one of the factors that influences and affects an alteration—a change—in her teaching practice through personal agency.

Strauss and Corbin (1990) describe how intervening conditions operate on a continuum from positive to negative. The inadequate teacher prepa-ration program could be perceived as a negative intervening condition be-cause it is one of several factors that inhibits effective teacher-student interactions. Structures, processes, or human actions that are positive in-tervening conditions—such as the coincidental offering of district in-service workshops in exceptionality or the principal's mediation by assign-ing a veteran teacher to act as a mentor for the novice—may influence and affect teacher change through time. Edgerton, writing from an anthropo-logical perspective, asserts that traditional practices (contextual condi-tions) as well as change (intervening conditions) can range from adaptive to maladaptive, the latter resulting in "sick societies": "It should be assumed . . . that any belief or practice could fall anywhere along a contin-uum of adaptive value. No belief or practice in question should escape care-ful scrutiny before being deemed beneficial or harmful. It may simply be neutral or tolerable, or it may benefit some members of a society while harming others" (1992, p. 206).

Now, let's examine other implications of and illustrations for the question: What contextual and intervening conditions appear to influence and affect participant changes through time?

Examples of Contextual and Intervening Conditions

Huber and Van de Ven prescribe the search for "antecedents and conse-quences" of change (1995, p. xii). An entry point in the field is not a base-line with which to compare consequent observations, but the start of investigating what antecedent contextual and intervening conditions pre-ceded the researcher's moment of entry to influence and affect the current status. For example, when investigating a first-year teacher's classroom practice, the researcher explores not just the participant's first few days on the job, but her educational background at the specific institutions she at-tended, previous field experience placements, and other influences such as key preservice teacher educators and mentors. Current contextual condi-tions of this teacher exist not only within her classroom but in the entire school: administrators, teaching colleagues, parents, and so on. Additional levels include district personnel, state administrators, and curriculum mandates. But "structures and processes" also exist within individuals; we internalize our experiences and act synchronically. The educational research of Connelly and Clandinin (1988) and Bullough (1989) reminds us that teachers are not just service professionals but people. Their personalities and personal lives influence and affect what they bring to and how they work within the classroom.

Contextual and intervening conditions emerge not only from the broad scope of governments and institutions (Qvortrup, 2000), but even from specific incidences. In the Theatre Response Study, data collected from interviews could only reveal so much about young children's perception and interpretation patterns. Transcript data analyzed without participant observation field notes on the contextual and intervening conditions of the treatment group's school would yield incomplete or skewed results. For example, some fourth-grade children in the treatment group were enrolled in a class whose beloved teacher suffered privately from mental health problems. The teacher was killed by police when he became aggressively violent in public one weekend. The loss of a teacher through this unexpected and tragic manner in the memories of some participants influenced their interpretations of a play-viewing experience that year, *The Arkansaw [sic] Bear*—coincidentally and ironically, a poignant comedy-drama about the death of a beloved dancing bear. Without knowledge of the children's classroom history—the intervening conditions—a researcher analyzing their responses might have been at a loss to explain the difference between their heightened, empathic statements from those children who were not taught by the revered teacher.

But not all conditions were this dramatic. One child's minimal responses to a theatre event in third grade were explained by her admitting to feeling "sleepy and hungry" afterwards. Another child, previously fluent and eloquent in her responses, experienced a sharp drop in response quality during her grade 5 interviews. Later investigation revealed that these introverted actions were also present in the classroom. Her withdrawal was attributed to emotional anxiety because her parents were in the middle of a divorce at that time.

Note how these examples illustrate the way contextual and intervening conditions can influence and affect participant responses. Also note how these conditions can affect the coding and analysis of data. In the first case, there was an interrelationship between the teacher's death (interpreted as an epiphany in several of the children's lives) and the particular play (an intervening condition) viewed that year. In the case of the child whose responses were minimal because she was sleepy and hungry, there was an idiosyncratic proportion that year in her seven years of data. In the third case, response decreased in the child whose parents were in the middle of a divorce. Such descriptive observations as these are inextricably linked to the conditions from which they emerged. Hence, "What contextual and intervening conditions appear to influence and affect participant changes through time?" becomes a ubiquitous question to answer as longitudinal data analysis proceeds.

Contextual and intervening conditions influence and affect participant responses

Finally, keep in mind that, throughout time, change changes. This means that contextual and intervening conditions— the interactive, interplaying, and cyclical nature of structures, processes, and human actions—influence and affect change through time, which influences and affects consequent change through time, which influences and affects consequent change through time, and so on.

Throughout time, change changes

What Are the Dynamics of Participant Changes through Time?

Dynamic Words

In music and stage voice, dynamics refer to expressive performance elements that operate on continua such as tempo (slow to fast), volume (soft to loud), or pitch (low to high). Comparable dynamics in quantitative research are statistical range (e.g., low scores to high scores, or $p < .05$ to $p < .001$, and $r = -1$ to $r = 1$) and changes in rate (acceleration and deceleration). In qualitative research, the dimensions and variability of the data are its dynamics (see fig. 4.4). The applicable continua, however, are not only quantitative in character ("a little" to "a lot" or "negligible" to "extreme"), but also qualitative ("boring" to

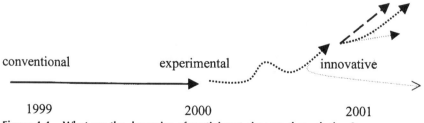

conventional   experimental   innovative

1999   2000   2001

Figure 4.4   **What are the dynamics of participant changes through time?**

"fun," "neophyte" to "expert," or "enthusiastic" to "burned-out"). Dynamics of participant change, most often, can be described using traditional rubrics or Likert-type words—for example, "improved, worsened, remained static" (Rist, 1994, pp. 550–51), or interpreted with words and phrases along a broad, open-ended ocean of antonyms such as "military-like efficiency," "organized to a fault," "neat," "scattered and messy," "so unorganized," and "chaotic."

Verbs, adjectives, and adverbs used in field notes and analytic memos should be selected carefully to note and, to some degree, "chart" the processes observed. A thesaurus becomes an indispensable tool as the researcher observes, constructs, and interprets the dynamics of participant processes. For example, a repertory of answers for the question "What remains constant or consistent through time?" includes a number of possibilities (and their variations): "always," "cohesive," "consistent," "constant," "continuing," "continuity," "endure," "equilibrium," "forever," "habitual," "inertia," "level," "maintain," "ongoing," "ordered," "permanent," "preserved," "routine," "same," "sedentary," "stable," "stationary," "steady," "traditional," and "usual." Answers to the question "What is idiosyncratic through time?" might employ: "aberration," "chaotic," "contradictory," "covary," "displaced," "erratic," "flexible," "fluctuating," "haphazard," "hyperturbulent," "idiosyncratic," "juxtaposed," "messy," "multidirectional," "paradoxical," "serendipitous," "unpredictable," and "varied." The language we use to describe and connote process and change should be chosen carefully, lest we mislead the reader (and ourselves) with what we witnessed in the field. There are both subtle and extreme differences between an environment that is ordered or sedentary, haphazard or unpredictable. Thus, describing the dynamics of change becomes an approximate and highly interpretive act. Hall (1995), for example, tracks the progress of a newly created educational policy from the national through the local school level over the course of three years. The dynamics he uses to describe the consequences that eventually occur within specific schools reacting to state-implemented policy toward the end of the three-year period are "differential, superficial, sporadic, and fragmented transactions" (p. 407).

Describing the dynamics of change becomes an approximate and highly interpretive act

Strauss and Corbin (1998) advocate that a category has properties, its "general or specific characteristics or attributes." The location of that property along a "continuum or range" specifies its dimensions (p. 117). "Dynamics" sounds comparable to "dimensions" or "variability," and the difference may be nothing more than semantic. But to me, "dynamics" suggests more action, a characteristic of time and change. Selected researchers in organization science prescribe the search for such time-oriented dynamics in data as tempo (how fast or slow), frequency (how often), and duration (how long)—quantitative constructs whose precise measurement plays a vital role in findings. But qualitative inquiry's precision does not come from numbers; the precision rests with our word choices.[4]

In Vivo Codes

Using in vivo codes (codes extracted from verbatim participant language rather than the researcher's constructed terms) to chart the dynamics of change through time provides a more participant-centered basis for analysis. Vanover's autoethnographic story "Attunement" (2002) relates his eight-year career with the Chicago public schools. Before he began as a substitute teacher with the system in 1993, he considered himself "a marginal figure," "empty," "scared of things I shouldn't have been scared of," and perceived his life at that time as "a waste." The quality of his family upbringing and early relationships also suggest that "[l]ove wasn't something that came naturally to me. It wasn't something I was good at. It wasn't something that I lived with every day."

Vanover perceives that his initial months of substitute teaching at one particular elementary school in Chicago's West Side were "never easy" and filled with "stupid mistakes" on his part. The African American and Hispanic children the school served were "very poor" and living "hard lives." He continually felt "tired," "always running," and "out of place": "I hadn't grown up in the city, and I didn't know how to act. I didn't understand what was going on around me." After particularly "terrible" days when children treated him "viciously," he felt "shocked," "angry," "worn out," and "sad." He "wept" for the children whom he felt "deserved so much and the world had given them so little, and there wasn't much that I could do to make their lives any better." Yet, when rare "moments of grace" occurred in the classroom, things "worked," "energy rushed," and he felt "alive." Though teaching was "hard work," it gave him a "good feeling." Vanover also attributes part of his personal and professional development to Mr. Johnson, another substitute teacher at the school who served as his "role model" and "exemplar": "He could ride the wave. He could move with the beat. He could take all of his students' love and all their kindness and all of their hopes and all of their fears and give the best part back to them. He could walk into any room in the school and make it his own. Nobody else could."

When Vanover eventually transferred to a Chicago high school a few years later, his daily professional practice and work environment became "easier" and "simpler." In contrast to his initial self-concept before he became a teacher, "I was suddenly the man I wished to be. The Chicago Public Schools taught me how to open up . . . taught me how to love." Participant thoughts, emotions, attitudes, values, and beliefs are all dynamic through time.

Participant thoughts, emotions, attitudes, values, and beliefs are all dynamic through time

Selected longitudinal qualitative studies should pay attention to such dynamics if they are essential elements of a particular research question or if there are emergent in vivo patterns that appear in the data suggesting refined focus and further investigation. But bear in mind that a continuum is merely a straight line with two end points, and "less" and "more" soon become inadequate descriptors of a phenomenon's quality. What we are looking for is what Agar calls the "patterned variation" of phenomena (1996, p. 10). The interpretive nature of qualitative research suggests that an expansive, fluid ocean is a more appropriate metaphor for the ever-shifting location and position of dynamics within the data.

Dynamics of participant change are examined to infer the nuances and subtlety of contextual conditions, to determine the magnitude of intervening conditions' influences and affects, or to place the participant's actions and changes in perspective or contrast to others. In the Theatre Response Study, grounded theory methods were used to analyze final exit interview transcripts to discern the central category at work. And, as Strauss and Corbin (1990, 1998) prescribe, the central category has "dimensions." The children's varying perceptions of theatre's *value* was the resulting central category, yet its dynamics extended beyond "a lot" to "none at all." The key interview question that brought this category to prominence was: Is theatre necessary? Children's initial responses ranged from "yes" to "no"—that is, necessary to unnecessary, a linear continuum. But the analysis went beyond that and located the multilevel dynamics of that value through the children's own words, "After 12 to 16 classroom drama sessions, at least one performance in elementary school presentations, and three to four theatre viewing experiences on an annual basis for seven years, the treatment group, in general, possesses enhanced theatre response skills but a spectrum of values for theatre. These values range from 'boring' (unnecessary) to 'fun' (entertaining), to 'personal' and 'real' (necessary)" (Saldaña, 1995, p. 28).

The analytic narrative further explains how children's value of theatre is based on the personal meaning and payoff they receive from it. Words such as "boring," "fun," "personal," and "real" don't fit neatly on a linear continuum like "unnecessary" to "necessary." But they do cohere in a "value ocean's" multiple locations and depths. It's as if their value of theatre could also be represented according to where they sit in a theatre: in the very front row to get a good view and immerse oneself in the production, in the precise center of the auditorium with no one seated on either side to enjoy the show without distraction, in the last row of the balcony with a best friend so you can talk and play if the production gets boring; or directly on stage as an actor, both nervous and energized while experiencing the performative act.

An individual's attitudes, values, and beliefs change or solidify over time as life experiences from contextual and intervening conditions accumulate. Not all participants may be cognizant of what is held to be true within them, just as the researcher may not always correctly infer or identify what is held to be true within a participant. Both must work collaboratively through time to discover what is "truly" inside one's head at the moments of inquiry. Royce observes that "there is a delicate process of seeing people in action over many years, of seeing similar or different responses to situations or people, that is the only key to recognizing the existence of these values. Once you 'see' these values, you understand them as critical factors that shape behavior in virtually every sphere, from politics to health to making pottery or writing poetry" (2002, p. 27).

What Preliminary Assertions (Propositions, Findings, Results, Conclusions, Interpretations, and Theories) about Participant Changes Can Be Made As Data Analysis Progresses?

Analysis in Progress

Terminology for statements that summarize researcher-constructed analyses of qualitative data vary, and researchers should choose the terms that best suit their ways of working and fit their project goals. The subtle and overt differences between these terms and their natures will not be discussed here, but recognize that each one listed earlier has different meanings and functions in

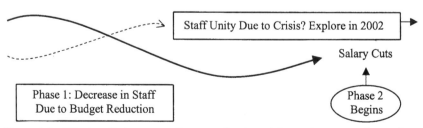

Figure 4.5   What preliminary assertions . . . about participant changes can be made as data analysis progresses?

data analytic methods and reports. For clarity's sake, assertions (Erickson, 1986) will be used later in this chapter to represent the vast array of data summary statements.

Assertions-in-progress are "rough-draft," emergent, conditional statements the researcher formulates during the analytic process. They are observations teased from the data awaiting appropriate revision, refinement, reordering, connection, synthesis, or deletion as analysis progresses. Systematic listing of assertions assists in finding particular themes or trends in the data and should include speculation of how contextual and intervening conditions may have influenced and affected participant change (see fig. 4.5).

This basic process can be found in the discussions of coding, analytic, and theoretical memos of grounded theory. Strauss and Corbin's (1998) miniframework heuristically organizes data into charts or lists that permit comparison of data sets from one time period through another. Miles and Huberman's (1994) time-ordered matrices are another option, as are the intuitive yet systematic procedures of Erickson (1986). Qualitative methods texts advise us to construct these assertions during rather than after data collection, and longitudinal studies add additional considerations. If change is constant, then so is our analysis of it.

> *If change is constant, then so is our analysis of it*

The Future Shapes the Past

As data are examined chronologically (with additional data collection remaining), expect to revise assertions continually, since data located in the future will influence and affect assertions developed in the past. Iterative and cyclical processes are particularly relevant here. Recall the child's game Red Light, Green Light. The caller shouts "green light!" and turns his back to you. You carefully walk or run toward the caller because he can turn around at any moment to shout "red light!" and you must freeze. If you're caught moving, you must return to the starting point and begin again. Imagine now that you get caught moving on "red light!" each time it's called and you have to return to the starting line. But what's frustrating is that at each "red light" you've gotten closer and closer to the caller. You're so close to the goal but must retrace your steps from the beginning each time. You try moving in straight lines and zig-zags, in slow footsteps followed by bursts of speed. But each time you get caught and must return to the beginning.

This process is similar to the analytic pathways through longitudinal data. Imagine that the starting line is your first set of data (year one), and the area you must cross is all the data to be collected after it (years two through seven). As you journey toward the caller (the key assertion), you're developing other assertions along the way. But the "red lights" are new data that don't harmonize with the assertions developed thus far—the discrepant cases or the disconfirming evidence. Hence, you must return to the starting point and begin again. You tried moving in a straight line before (a descriptive assertion), so this time you try moving in a zig-zag pattern (an assertion that incorporates intervening conditions or weaves in interrelated observations). But another "red light" is called (new insights on the emergent theory, a revised conceptual framework, or "present" data that places "past" assertions into a different perspective), so you return to the starting line and begin again. Like the game, this iterative and cyclical process for the analytic player is time consuming, sometimes frustrating, and filled with "red lights." The payoff, however, is cognitive ownership, a deeper understanding of and insight about the data each time the journey across the space-time playing field is made. And when you finally reach the caller and tag him, you replace him and look back at the journey you've just made through the data landscape/timescape. You now have a holistic, panoramic perspective rather than a narrow focus, and are better equipped to formulate a key assertion or through-line that summarizes the journey.

Erickson (1986) recommends that researchers develop a key assertion that represents the salient data corpus and related subassertions to describe the constituent parts of that corpus. These same summary principles can be applied to longitudinal data. The key assertion of a longitudinal qualitative study summarizes how the data, as a whole, reflect general participant changes through time—that is, throughout the course of the study (see the section "What Is the Through-Line of the Study?" in chapter 6). Subassertions can chronicle the more detailed changes at either the "red lights" or designated time markers (e.g., from year through year and from epiphany through epiphany), or your movement through "green lights"—specific periods of time as phases, stages, or cyclical periods (e.g., from grades K–2, 3–4, and 5–6).

An Example of Change in a Case History

Let's examine how preliminary assertions and subassertions can both endure and change throughout an extended period of time. When Barry, a case study participant from the Theatre Response Study, was in third grade, a graduate research assistant wrote the following impressions and assertions about him in 1987 after classroom drama observations and an interview:

> He is very intelligent, learns quickly, and enjoys the process of learning when intellectually challenged. Barry seems to enjoy the drama sessions. He partici-

pates in the drama process, but on an intellectual level, not an internal or emotional level. . . . He can *think* the drama very well. He cannot *show* it. . . . He clearly understands concepts such as pantomime, acting, properties, and plot construction. However, he lacks the ability to appreciate theatre with any emotional commitment. He is not in touch with his emotions, and does not connect with the world with any emotional awareness. His concentration skills and recall ability are excellent. He relates to drama and theatre as an intellectual exercise, not as an experience of himself as a feeling human being.

The research assistant's 1987 assertions that Barry is "very intelligent" yet "lacks the ability to appreciate theatre with any emotional commitment" in third grade endured for the next four years. The principal investigator formulated a similar assertion after a review of Barry's theatre response data from 1984 through 1991, "Data from longitudinal transcripts suggest that Barry doesn't necessarily empathize or sympathize with characters to a large degree, but he does make astute perceptions of them and evaluates the theatre event with critical finesse and insight for his age" (Saldaña, 1995, p. 25).

Barry's intelligence remained strong during his secondary school years, according to his teachers and mother. But the sweeping assertions about his elementary school emotional detachment would be modified as Barry progressed through junior and senior high school. In a revealing and prophetic moment during a final exit interview conducted toward the end of his sixth-grade term in May 1991, Barry confessed, "The psychiatrist, the school psychiatrist said I'm too, uh, I'm more mature than the other kids my age. I'm not looking to please them. I'm looking—and I've set my goals high because I'm more mature than them. That's part of my problem. That's why I'm so depressed usually. It's because I'm more mature than the other kids and I don't fit in."

The emotional turmoil Barry experienced during his upper elementary and junior high school years—a "dead period," as he labeled it—was explained by his mother in a retrospective interview:

Barry went through a really tough time about—probably started the end of fifth grade and went into sixth grade. When he was growing up young in school he was a people pleaser and his teachers loved him to death. Two boys in particular that he chose to try to emulate wouldn't, were not very good for him. They were very critical of him, they put him down all the time, and he kind of just took that and really kind of internalized it, I think, for a long time. . . . At Lakewood Junior High School he had a really tough time, real tough. The first day of school in seventh grade, some—I'll use the term gang-banger, but I don't know—was picking on a little kid, and Barry said, "Hey man, get off his case."

And from that moment on, all of the tension was focused on him. From the time he entered Lakewood to the time he left Lakewood, he was a target by the bad guys. That was a very tough time for him.

Developmental factors, coupled with contextual and intervening conditions such as family and peers, interplayed and interacted throughout this "dead period." The third-grade assertion "He is not in touch with his emotions, and does not connect with the world with any emotional awareness" now required modification. Psychological intervention was necessary to help Barry through his tumultuous early adolescence. When he was a sophomore in high school, he reflected back on his seventh- and eighth-grade years, "There was a period during junior high when I had no theatre in my life, didn't have any exposure to it, and I got really heavy into drugs. I was hanging out with the wrong crowd." His mother added:

> He was never anti-social, but making the statement—the way he dressed, the way he looked. In fact, some of his junior high teachers would call me and say, "I noticed that he's hanging out with some unsavory characters and I think . . . ," you know, that kind of stuff. It was kind of like teaching the dog not to run in the street by getting hit by a car. It was a horrible, painful, awful time. And yet, if it doesn't kill you it'll make you stronger. That's what's happened to Barry.

The assertion that Barry, in sixth grade, didn't "necessarily empathize or sympathize with characters to a large degree" would also change as he progressed through high school and became actively involved with theatre classes and extracurricular play productions. Barry reflected midway through his senior year (December 1996):

> When I came to University High I saw theatre was something that I knew, something that I was interested in. So I came and I got cast in my first show. I got a lead for my first show which made me think, "Whoa—maybe there's something I'm good at here." And I was in the position where there wasn't anything standing in-between me and theatre because there wasn't anything in my life. Drugs had taken up my whole life. And so as soon as I was ready to get out of that, I mean—Theatre helped draw me out of drugs and, in a way, drugs helped draw me into theatre, in that they voided my life of everything else so I was completely empty—completely open towards picking up on theatre. . . . I started cleaning up my act, and that had a lot to do with drama because I had something else, and it was almost intoxicating in and of itself. It gave me the strength to get away from that stuff.

His mother mused, "I'll never forget the day Barry said to me, 'You know, mom, you don't have to buy me all gray and black clothes anymore.'" Through theatre, Barry found a passageway to escape from his emotional limbo, and the art form nurtured within him a new sensibility—a "passion." Barry merged his intellect with his emotions in an integrated, holistic manner during late adolescence, "To me, theatre is intellectual. It's reading, it's analyzing literature—it's *art*. . . . I'm an idealist, I'm a romantic, and I don't just mean in matters of love. I mean, I'm a romantic as far as the way I think, you know? I'm very feeling-oriented. I think theatre is a very . . . feeling-oriented institution. . . . Theatre has instilled me with a very chivalrous attitude towards life."

When Barry was in third grade, the research assistant predicted, "Perhaps as he matures, he will be better able to give better definition to his feelings, and obtain an understanding of drama as an exercise in connecting to inner feelings, and not simply as an intellectual activity." This predictive assertion was supported by the time Barry was in tenth grade—the beginning of his "renaissance": "It was during the longitudinal study that I developed my passion for the arts and began seeing them as something as an idealistic career, an almost—a romantic, bigger than life—you know, *passion*. . . . I don't know how else to put it—the *passion* for the arts."

A human tableaux set in motion is said to be "dynamized" (Boal, 1995), suggesting that once we read and make inferences from its frozen symbols, the tableaux's movement evokes new readings and interpretations as it shifts across time and space. Due to the limitations narrative has on capturing life as it is complexly lived, some methodologists advocate that qualitative research can capture only "snapshots." But extend the metaphor: If we can capture still-image "snapshots" through our writing, can't we also capture brief temporal images such as .avis and video clips through language? (Recall the classic time-lapse films of a flower growing from the ground and blooming in just five seconds. Describe those five seconds of action orally or in writing.) All this depends, of course, on the writer's descriptive flair and the reader's ability to imagine. Since time is a human construction, how we frame it, build it, and live in it is based on our own architectural cognition and imagination.

CHAPTER FIVE

Descriptive Questions

The discussion now turns to seven descriptive questions, whose answers may inform both the framing inquiry outlined in the previous chapter, and the analytic and interpretive inquiries that follow. These descriptive questions are:

1. What increases or emerges through time?
2. What is cumulative through time?
3. What kinds of surges or epiphanies occur through time?
4. What decreases or ceases through time?
5. What remains constant or consistent through time?
6. What is idiosyncratic through time?
7. What is missing through time?

What Increases or Emerges through Time?

Increasing and Emergent Data

A simple emergence or proportionate increase of a variable or category frequency may suggest some type of change (see fig. 5.1). In virtually every quantitative and qualitative longitudinal study I've read, "increased," "grew," and "more" are the words most often used to describe the types of participant changes observed. But when these words are employed as the most frequent descriptors, they provide an oversimplified conception of change processes. When "increased" and "more" are overused, the possibility also exists that only selected phenomena for examination were established early in the study,

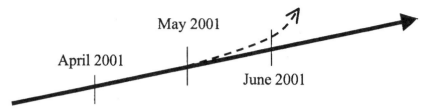

Figure 5.1   What increases or emerges through time?

which narrowed the parameters of future observations and limited the opportunities to discover the complexities surrounding change. For example, in the Theatre Response Study, children's interview transcripts were reviewed to count the number of discipline-specific terms used by child participants throughout the seven-year period. Data suggested that in the upper grade levels

> [b]oth sites grow quantitatively in the number of [theatre] terms used from Grades 3 to 6, but the treatment group tends to incorporate the vocabulary of drama and theatre two to three times more than the second-site group. One overt difference in the treatment group is the more frequent use of terms related to scenography, particularly *lights, props,* and *stage.* The quantity of scenographic terms remains fairly constant throughout the four upper grade levels, but there is apparent growth in the number of performance related terms: *role, voice, accent, dance, sing, belief,* etc. (Saldaña, 1993, p. 322)

The inference made from this observation was an increase in the treatment group's theatre literacy as the study progressed.

In the Survival Study, Spanish-language vocabulary used by the teacher participant during interviews and classroom interactions was nonexistent in 1993 data. But by 1995 such words and slang as "quinciañera," "azul," "rojo," "por favor," "nana," "tata," "mijo," and others were recorded, indicative of her emergent knowledge of Spanish and willingness to incorporate this vocabulary into her speech and classroom interaction patterns with Hispanic youth. But measuring increases through content analysis and category frequencies alone limit the potential of qualitative data analysis for richer levels of meaning.

At the beginning of the Theatre Response Study in 1984, the instrumentation and data analysis were primarily quantitative in character—choices based on available instrumentation to measure the response of the young theatre audience and, in retrospect, choices based on presenting results from this groundbreaking study in "hard statistics" for both advocates and skeptics of the value of arts experiences for children. But as the study progressed, both the research team and outside peer reviewers felt the statistical results from seven years of data gathering revealed nothing more than "numbers of utterances" in predetermined categories, rather than substantive insight about the response of the young theatre audience. One critic encouraged me to reanalyze the transcript contents qualitatively. Hence, qualitative, longitudinal, analytic methods prescribed by Miles and Huberman (1994) and Strauss and Corbin (1990) were employed. Categories and subcategories of perception and response were generated inductively from transcripts. Each response was recoded according to the perception process a child utilized (visual and/or aural), to one of four emergent response modes (cognitive, emotional, evaluative, and behavioral), and to the response's specific content (e.g., character, scenography, and prediction of story outcome). Data from each year's event were examined as case studies for comparison between the treatment and second-site groups, then pooled to discern longitudinal trends.

Throughout time, new and different actions in participants may subtly emerge, but not necessarily with the suddenness of a surge or a 180-degree change after an epiphany (discussed later in this chapter). Wolcott (1994, 2002) did not label his "Brad Trilogy" longitudinal, per se, but the latter two articles (the first published in 1983, the next two in 1987 and 1990) do chronicle a "sneaky kid's" emergent paranoid schizophrenia and its devastating consequences. What began as a profile of a young man's self-imposed exile from mainstream expectations after a tumultuous adolescent period of petty theft and unstable family life, just a few years later turned into a horror story of arson and violence after Brad suffered from depression, severe headaches, and imaginary voices speaking directly to him. The three articles combined are a compelling anthropological life history and textual portrait of emergent mental illness, emergent tragedy, and—from Wolcott's perspective—emergent reflexivity on the meaning of it all.

Quantitative versus Qualitative Increases

Changes in quality throughout time may be accompanied by or synonymous with quantitative increases. One person's quality is another person's quantity, and these differing perspectives influence and affect what is observed in the field. For example, a beginning teacher's inconsistent or mishandled classroom management techniques with children may be interpreted as "ineffective" by two different participant observers. But throughout the course of an academic year, management strategies change for the better—qualitatively to one observer, quantitatively to another.

Qualitatively, this beginning teacher—thrust into his first job without adequate preparation and mentor support, and growing frustrated by the "kiddie chaos" encountered daily in the classroom—*initiates action* to make positive changes in his practice. Quantitatively, there is increased reading of professional literature to learn alternative management strategies, increased dialogue with colleagues for their suggestions, and increased reflection time on ineffective teaching practices.

One person's quality is another person's quantity

To the qualitatively oriented researcher, the teacher's verbal responses to a disruptive child were formerly interpreted as *impulsive* and *reactive* ("Billy, stop talking!"), but are now *rational* and *proactive* ("Billy, you need to listen to these directions so you'll understand what to do."). The quantitatively oriented researcher perceives these same changes across time as an increase in tactful discipline. To the qualitative researcher, a method of dividing the teacher's students into small groups *randomly* is replaced with one who *assigns* small-group membership. The quantitative researcher perceives this action as an increase in small-group organization. The qualitative observer notes that writing topics at the beginning of the school year focused on *mundane* textbook prescriptions, but topics by midyear are changed to *relevant* issues of interest to children, thus enhancing their *engagement*. The quantitative observer notes that writing topics become more authentic. Qualitatively, the teacher used to lecture *slowly* and *bore* the class, but he now lectures *energetically* and *dynamically*. Quantitatively, he now lectures with increased enthusiasm. Qualitatively, the teacher now reports being "happier" and "confident." Quantitatively, he smiles more often.

An increase in teaching effectiveness may be inferred overall, but some of the changes leading to this perceived increase were either quantitative or qualitative in character—*depending on how the teacher's actions were interpreted by the researcher*. Is one orientation better than the other to assess change across time? Or can both work in a complementary or integrated manner? Tashakkori and Teddlie (1998) support the latter, and Miles and Huberman (1994) prescribe it.

Finally, increases across time may suggest certain types of changes, but some of these increases might interrelate with other observed changes or be linked to certain contextual or intervening conditions. If children use more theatre terms as they grow older or if a teacher uses more Spanish language vocabulary the longer she works with Hispanic youth, there are conditions behind these actions and antecedents to their presence. Hence, emergence of, or simple increases in, qualitative categories cannot be examined in isolation. They are only part of the analytic puzzle, particularly if they are interpreted as cumulative (discussed in the next section). Finally, the magnitude or size of change may indicate other factors at work. These surges (also discussed later in this chapter) merit examination separately from otherwise smooth increases in proportions or qualities across time.

Increases might interrelate with other observed changes

What Is Cumulative through Time?

Growth and Development
There are subtle differences between the terms "growth" and "development." The word "growth" implies a quantitative increase across time, such as height, weight, size, number of terms used, length of sentences, grade point average, additions to the workforce, and demographics. Variables or categories affected by growth can be easily counted or somewhat reliably measured, such as those discussed earlier in the section "What Increases or Emerges through Time?" The word "development" implies more qualitative characteristics across time, such as improvement, betterment, and transformation. Developmental variables are more ephemeral, socially constructed, not accessible to precise measurement, and include such concepts as knowledge, empathy, worldview, aesthetic response, and values.

Cumulative Affects
Cumulative affects through time are outcomes of growth and/or development—quantitative and/or qualitative factors interacting or interplaying with each other. A cumulative affect is some type of change discerned by the researcher in participant quality as a result of successive experiences (see fig. 5.2). For lack of a better metaphor, these affects "snowball." The original question for this

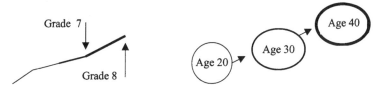

Figure 5.2 **What is cumulative through time?**

section was: What evolves through time? But the implications of the term "evolve" are too broad and confounding. "Cumulative" is a more appropriate, constituent term for describing change of this type.

Growth, primarily quantitative in character, could be readily observed in the increased number of theatre-related terms used by children in the Theatre Response Study. Assessing development in the treatment group, however, could not be left merely to counting and comparing proportions of response categories across time. Some second-site children in grades 5–6 responded hesitantly or superficially when asked about the learning outcomes of the plays' protagonists. For the character of Pip in *Great Expectations*, some children said, "He learned to be a gentleman?" "Not to trust people?" "I think he learned how to judge a person by the inside and not by the outside." In contrast, treatment children commented on the harsh life lessons learned by the characters in the play and interpreted with more depth how the fictional events had parallels to real life, "Any of the things that happened in the play could happen today, like the part where Estella married the wrong guy instead of Pip." The qualitative differences between the two groups' responses, combined with the quantitative differences observed by coding the amount of aural cues used by each group to interpret the play, led me to infer that

> by fifth and sixth grades the treatment group had developed a schema for attending and attending *to* the theatre event. Accustomed to the experience and undistracted by novelty, treatment children may have been more aurally attentive, and thus perhaps better able than second-site novices to focus on and transfer ideas from the fictional, historic worlds of the plays into present-day reality. The cumulative effects of the classroom drama, recreational theatre, and theatre viewing experiences were designated as the most likely causes for these "significant differences" between groups. (Saldaña, 1996, p. 80)

Time Triangulation

Cumulative affects, however, needn't always be accompanied with a quantitative component. For example, in the Survival Study, interviews were conducted with and documents were collected from the teacher participant in late 1993, 1994, and early 1995. I wanted to assess how Nancy's perceptions of the barrio children she instructed had changed throughout the course of twenty months. I searched the interview transcripts, field notes, and written documents for evidence related to her cross-cultural functioning and competency (Banks, 1994, p. 50). The following excerpt from the completed report briefly describes the relevant data record:

During her second month of teaching in 1993, Nancy remarked in an interview, "To me, a person's a person." Thesis documentation of her first year experiences revealed that by 1994 she was willing to adopt the "perspective of the barrios" to learn about the children she taught and to empower herself as an educator. . . . Towards the middle of Nancy's second year in 1995, her insights into Hispanic culture had deepened: "I don't think I saw their version of reality or their world, and now I do. Instead of trying to change it, I understand it." (Saldaña, 1997, p. 41)

These three related ponds of data located across three pools of time served as one of several bases for assertions, embedded in this analysis portion of the report:

Nancy may have entered Martinez School with a Eurocentric conception of drama and personal worldview, but over [the course of a year and a half] she learned to survive by adapting to her classroom environment—the final stage of cultural shock recovery. She did not "go native" or assimilate completely as a Hispanic, but she did demonstrate a willingness to function cross-culturally, thus equipping her with more expertise of the Martinez community, thereby enabling her to reconceptualize drama for her specific teaching context. (pp. 41–42)

Cumulative affects may be discerned from successive ponds of data merging to form larger ponds and pools. In the previous example, three related data sets located across three beats of time served as time triangulation to support the observation of cumulative change. "Before" and "After" summary tables that list the qualities of an environment or participant at the beginning and end of an observation period seem insufficient. At a minimum, one more table labeled "During" should be placed in-between (see fig. 5.3).

Time-triangulation supports observations of cumulative change

Child Development
Studies in child development should be particularly attuned to cumulative affects throughout time, specifically because these profiles can become researcher-constructed phases or stages of childhood and adolescence, such as those formulated by Piaget and Erikson, or the more arts-based conceptions of development by Gilligan. The abundant research literature in the field documents both generalized observations of children at specific ages and the successive patterns of complexity that follow. Cognitive

NANCY'S CLASSROOM PRACTICE

September 1993 ————————————→ April 1995

BEFORE	DURING	AFTER
no conversational applications of Spanish with children	asks children to translate for her and to teach her Spanish words/ phrases	occasional use of "Spanglish" with children and teachers; bilingual posters in room
reluctant to address gang subculture in classes out of personal fear	social worker educates her on gang subculture; learns about her students	incorporates gang characters in original play production; actions: tagging, rapping
feels she's not in "control" of classroom; shouts for attention	experiments with various management techniques; gains self-confidence	feels more in "control" of classroom; uses firm voice, nonverbal strategies
play readings: Eurocentric canon, students not engaged with material	seeks literature resources from school librarian and university theatre	original play production of Mexican American folk tale, La llorona

Figure 5.3   A Before, During, and After process chart from the Survival Study

development, for example, is not just a matter of children learning and knowing more as they grow older, it is learning and knowing in different, more sophisticated ways than before. As various social interactions accumulate, accompanied with the natural, physical growth and development of the brain, the constructions of children's knowledge progress toward enhanced abilities to perceive, remember, differentiate, conceptualize, abstract, and so on. When it comes to researching children, cumulative development is a combination of both biology and social environment.

Maturation is not just quantitative in character (e.g., height, weight, and amount of vocabulary gained), maturation is also qualitatively shaped in such domains as emotional intelligence (Goleman, 1995) and empathy (Lennon and Eisenberg, 1987), depending on the types of social environments and interactions experienced through time. Goleman asserts that "childhood and adolescence are critical windows of opportunity for setting down the essential emotional habits that will govern our lives" (1995, p. xiii). For example, examining how a child develops self-awareness— "observing yourself and recognizing your feelings; building a vocabulary for feelings; knowing the relationship between thoughts, feelings, and reactions"

(p. 303)—is not left merely to counting the increasing number of vocabulary words related to feelings the child learns. The capacity for self-awareness accumulates and evolves as particular life experiences are gained, accompanied with introspective thought and personal reflection on those experiences. Across time, these unique emotion-related encounters with others, and thus with self, accumulate in a qualitative, quasi-exponential manner. It's not that the child becomes "more" self-aware, but rather that he or she becomes better at it, given optimal conditions for development. But always be conscious of idiosyncratic patterns when researching young people (discussed later in this chapter). Dockrell, Lewis, and Lindsay remind us that, from a psychological perspective, "children's behaviour or performance does not necessarily change (develop) in a straightforward and additive manner" (2000, p. 49).

> Always be conscious of idiosyncratic patterns when researching young people

What Kinds of Surges or Epiphanies Occur through Time?

Surges
Escalation of a variable could appear suddenly within qualitative data. Just as we attribute to young children physical growth spurts, so, too, can there be growth and developmental spurts—surges—in qualitative data (see fig. 5.4). An epiphany or critical incident experienced by the participant and documented in the data could also be loosely interpreted as a surge if the event produces relatively sudden changes in or directions of the participant's consequent actions. Royce and Kemper acknowledge that an individual life across decades consists of "uneven terrain . . . the pace of the everyday and the staccato bursts of the extraordinary" (2002, p. xv).

In the Theatre Response Study, proportions of evaluative responses emerged and increased subtly during grades K–4, but a "noticeable evaluation 'growth spurt' occurred in the fifth grade, and an evaluative focus dominated most of the sixth grade responses" (Saldaña, 1996, p. 80). Isaac and

Figure 5.4   What kinds of surges or epiphanies occur through time?

Michael provide a developmental observation in the affective domain as a possible rationale for the "spurt":

> There is likely to be a negative relationship at certain stages of development between age and measured attitudes. Young children . . . respond very positively to most experiences, but begin to differentiate along a broader range of feelings as they grow older and become more discerning, critical, or analytical. The result is a shift from more positive to less positive responses as time passes. Although this observation suggests a negative shift in attitude resulting from the learning experience itself, especially in longitudinal studies, it is probably a developmental shift in the child's maturity level. (1995, p. 234)

However, since this growth spurt did not occur within the second-site group, natural child development was ruled out as the influential contextual condition, and the cumulative treatment of drama and theatre was accepted as a positive intervening condition. Why the surge occurred at the fifth-grade level and not earlier or later in the data record was puzzling. But this was new information, unsubstantiated by previous research. I asserted that the longitudinal study treatment accelerated within the target participants what would happen naturally to the second-site groups at later grade levels.

The rate of a surge can bring negative consequences with it as well, "[S]ocial and cultural change, particularly when it is rapid, leads to decreased physical and mental health as a result of what, for want of a better concept, we can call stress" (Edgerton, 1992, p. 124). The common phrase, "too much, too soon," exemplifies how humans cannot always deal effectively with fast-tempoed change. In the 1990s, the need for educational accountability motivated the implementation of mandatory, high-stakes testing in English and math of Arizona's high school seniors for graduation. The standards-based test was rushed through development and administration by state-level officers, yet they provided virtually no adequate preparation time for local-level teachers and students. A few consequences of this hurried process were: failure by over 75 percent of students in the math portion of the examination, lawsuits over the inequities of testing second-language learners and mentally disabled students, and millions of tax dollars spent to rectify test construction and scoring errors.

Epiphanies

An epiphany is a significant event that takes participant change to a different level, direction, or quality. During this event, the processual wave of participant change becomes unexpected, like a flash flood or sudden rainstorm. The September 11, 2001, terrorist attacks on the U.S. World Trade Center and the Pentagon were epiphanies of tremendous magnitude, particularly for American individuals and thus the sociocultural climate of the country. Depending on the individual's particular background, multiple and accelerated change processes were initiated by this disastrous intervening condition, ranging from a daily reconfiguration of contextual conditions, to a reconceptualization of personal worldview. Media stories during September 2001 and for months afterward focused on such social questions as: How has your life changed? Change dynamics had been exponentially rapid and their trajectories unknown, but I personally felt a sense of normalcy return six months afterward, until terrorist attacks escalated in the Middle East during Easter of 2002, pipe bombs exploded in U.S. mailboxes during the first week of May 2002 ("domestic terrorism," as reported by the media), and more terrorist alerts were announced by the U.S. government that same month. Americans were attempting to and encouraged to bring their lives back to normal, but that quality had now been layered with the idiosyncrasy of terrorism.

To return to a case study focus in epiphanies, in the following passage, both the researcher and teacher participant acknowledge one particular school incident as an epiphany during the first few months of her professional career:

> The origin of the survival theme and its place in the emergent conceptual framework for this study could be found in what Nancy referred to as a turning point in her teaching: One day during her second month at Martinez, gunshots were fired near the campus and students were contained in a designated area for safety. Nancy had never encountered such an emergency and panicked, but she noticed that the Hispanic children showed no fear. Some were bored as if the matter was routine; a few were angered that their recess had been interrupted by gunfire. Nancy reflected in her thesis: "I was no longer in the illusion of the safe environment I had created in my room and my mind. I was in the reality of the inner-city. The illusion that I could take these children into a different world, into my version of reality, had been shattered. . . . This forced me to question why I was really there and the role of drama in the lives of these children." (Saldaña, 1997, pp. 30–31)

From this moment onward, Nancy reconceptualized the purpose of drama with Hispanic youth. "Aftermath" is a term most people use sparingly. But its utterance suggests that a life-changing incident or a tumultuous series of events has occurred, thus altering the present status and people's future actions (see Wolcott, 2002).

My initial interviews with the teacher participant did not include a deliberate search on my part for significant events, turning points, or epiphanies such as the one just profiled. The story appeared in Nancy's personal journal reflections on her first-year teaching experiences without direct prompting from me to document such incidences. I got lucky. The lesson taught me what some biographers and life history researchers have probably known tacitly, summarized in Beverly Donofrio's quote from the film *Riding in Cars with Boys*, "One day can make your life. One day can ruin your life. All life is, is four or five big days that change everything" (Brooks, Ansell, and Sakai, 2001).

When people reflect on their epiphanies, some may speculate on what might have happened if the turning point had not occurred at all. Inquiring about a participant's alternative life-course possibilities may place his or her current conditions in context. I wonder what kind of response I would have gotten had I asked Nancy: How do you think your philosophy and practice would be different today if you had started teaching at a middle-class, suburban school? In the video documentary *Scared Straight! Twenty Years Later* (Shapiro, 1999), one of the former juveniles, Angelo, reflects on the impact Rahway's program made on him and how his life might have been different if "that one day" hadn't happened. His character progresses from a cocky teenager ("Worst thing I ever done is rob a store—and got caught"), to a potential "lifer," then to a humble family man:

> I broke the law three times after I visited Rahway, twice right after, still at the age of seventeen and eighteen. And once about five years ago I had a disorderly conduct, and I did fifteen days in a county jail. It was something that I'm ashamed of, and my wife wanted to tell my kids I was working. I said "No," and I made her come down and visit me at the county jail with my oldest daughter to see me in-between the piece of glass, and told her daddy got in trouble, and this is what happens when you do wrong. If I didn't go to Rahway, I think that I would've done hard time. And if that one day didn't happen, I might not have my family, and my family to me right now is everything. (1999)

Epiphanies do not always have to be this dramatic, however. Significance is in the eye of the participant, not just the researcher-beholder. We should not discount what the participant perceives as an important event in his or her own life. Some attest that reading one particular book, attending one particular film or workshop, or saying one particularly wrong thing at the particularly wrong time, changes something dramatically in oneself. For example, Bullough and Baughman report that serendipitous exposure to a new way of working initiated change in an educator's practice, "Early in her fourth year of teaching, Kerrie attended an International Reading Association conference and obtained a copy of Nancy Atwell's book *In the Middle: Writing, Reading, and Learning with Adolescents* (1987). As she read it, lights went on. She saw within Atwell's program, Reading and Writing Workshop, the possibility of shifting her program toward a writing emphasis and decided to change her entire curriculum" (1997, p. 110).

We should not discount what the participant perceives as an important event in his or her own life

Participant change may be indicated by surges, developmental "growth spurts," or epiphanies—the latter varying in magnitude from life expanding to life altering. But data collected prior to these events should be examined carefully, for it may be that missing or incomplete data records could mislead the interpretation of successive records.

What Decreases or Ceases through Time?

Decrease and Cessation

Certain variables, reflected in a category's proportions, may decrease or disappear all together as a study proceeds (see fig. 5.5). Decreases may be developmentally appropriate, such as most young children's decreasing inattentiveness as they mature. Decreases may be due to decay or memory loss, such as decreased proficiency in a second language if it is not used or reinforced on a regular basis across time. Some decreases may be interrelated with increases in other categories or actions. A decrease in and cessation of smoking might be accompanied with (or replaced by or substituted with) an increase in eating. A counselor working with a male sex offender might observe decreases in the client's profanity and negative references to women throughout the course of treatment, accompanied with changes in the offender's personal grooming habits for the better, and enhanced personal disclosure in self-reports.

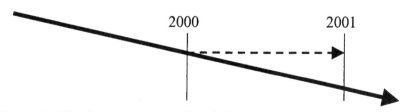

Figure 5.5   What decreases or ceases through time?

Decreases and cessation of actions should be interpreted cautiously because the quality and contents of our field notes themselves change through time. Observations may consist of a broad variety of actions at the beginning of a study, and then on more focused details or categories of emergent importance as fieldwork progresses. Also, the longer we're immersed in the field the more we become familiar with and take for granted what exists in the environment. So, even our field note entries may show evidence of decreased detail and a cessation of logging the contextual conditions. Since later field notes may not include what was initially targeted in early observations, be careful inferring that something in the social setting has "disappeared" when time pools and category ponds are compared. Longitudinal studies that extend for decades are particularly at risk for this problem. New research team members, phased into the study years after it has begun, can refresh the data with additional field notes, which might capture what may be missing from the initial researcher's documentation.

The quality and contents of our field notes themselves change through time

An Example of Decreasing Data

Some decreases may reflect positive changes, others negative. McCammon's (1994) study of four theatre teachers at a secondary school fine arts magnet program examined the dynamics of teamwork and development of collegiality among the group as they progressed through one academic year. Unfortunately, the story profiles a group of teachers whose interpersonal relationships decayed across time.

McCammon's (1994) conceptual framework for this study utilized phases of group development from various studies. She also used proportions as a quantitative tactic to assess the group's change, "Field note data was coded to determine the frequency of teacher talk and levels of collegiality during each phase" of group development: orientation, conflict, resolution, and production (p. 4). Increases in particular categories through these phases, such as "complaints," serve as an indicator of the increased conflict among the group. But decreases in selected categories add to the story.

The group focused primarily on discussions about classes (16.4 percent) at the beginning of the school year in August 1990, an obvious topic for teachers during an orientation phase. But as time progressed, teacher talk about classes decreased to 5.1 percent by the end of the conflict phase in December; rose negligibly to 7.3 percent during the resolution phase; and fell to its lowest level, 3.2 percent, in the final production phase by March 1991. Mc-Cammon observed that

> when the group members had six months' experience working together, the theatre teachers displayed many of the characteristics of teachers from ineffective, low goal consensus schools. They experienced uncertainty about their teaching and consequently spent large portions of their time avoiding talk about school. . . . The teachers talked about their classes only 3.2% of the time. They did not observe each other's classes, seldom collaborated with one another, and spent decreasing amounts of time with one another during lunch because they were avoiding one another. . . . This decrease in teacher talk is both the result of low cohesiveness among the teachers and the cause of continued decreases in cohesiveness. (p. 7)

McCammon notes that teamwork and collegiality within this particular group of teachers did not evolve due to inadequate team training and a school culture that promoted autonomy instead of collegiality.

Decreased proportions in selected categories supported her assertions. But McCammon also notes that "it was hard to watch the teachers' self-confidence and enthusiasm erode slowly over the course of the year" (1994, p. 4). Such categories as "enthusiasm" and "self-confidence" were not part of the proportioned teacher talk. This was a general observation, a holistic overview of the group based on McCammon's long-term fieldwork. This was not a decrease in frequency but a decrease in quality.

Decrease versus Increase

"Is the glass half empty or half full?" is a popular layperson's question to assess one's negative or positive worldview. The same principle can be applied to this discussion, "Is what I'm interpreting a decrease or an increase?" To expand on examples presented at the beginning of this section, as most young children mature, do they become less inattentive or more attentive? Is a smoker trying to quit by smoking less or eating more? Or is the smoker substituting a decrease and cessation of one action for an emergent increase in another? Or are both actions inextricably linked and cannot be examined in isolation? My intuition informs me that if change is due to a decrease in one area (e.g., workplace morale), other types of changes may occur in another area (e.g. decreased efficiency, emergent and increased hostility, cumulative deterioration of a worker's self-esteem, and so on).

If change is due to a decrease in one area, other types of changes may occur in another area

Finally, the researcher's personal worldview may influence and affect how decreases are interpreted. For example, if a particular ethnic group of children's standardized test scores decrease across time, is this due to an increase in the ethnic group's inability to learn or keep up with peers from other ethnic groups? Or is the decrease in test scores due to cumulative increases in discriminatory practices within an educational system that favors one ethnic group over others—increasing the opportunities for some while decreasing opportunities for others? Is the glass half empty due to ethnic deficits, or half full due to social oppression?

What Remains Constant or Consistent through Time?

Some Things Never Change

Postmodernism touts that human beings and societies are always changing, never static, and that constancy or consistency is uncertain. Nevertheless, this question "What remains constant or consistent through time?" does merit a place in the repertory included here. "Some things never change" is a well-known adage, and in some categories of longitudinal data there may indeed be no overt or discernible changes in frequency or quality through time due to the nature of the data collected (see fig. 5.6). But recall another adage, "No news is good news." The good news is that the constant or consistent presence of particular data may reveal something significant at work. The bad news is that the constant or consistent presence of particular data may also reveal nothing out of the ordinary.

Salient and Significant Constancy

In some cases, what appears as a constant, pervasive phrase or pattern in the data corpus may be a regular part of the participant's everyday world. Some phenomena, despite their prominence or reoccurrence in field notes, might be background routine—the given contextual conditions—rather than foreground issues for analysis. For example, in the Survival Study the teacher participant was a theatre director in a grades K–8 fine arts magnet school. The time demands of curriculum and lesson planning, extracurricular play rehearsals, and various production needs of a one-person theatre program

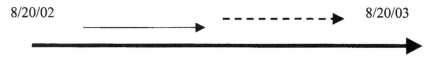

8/20/02   8/20/03

Figure 5.6   What remains constant or consistent through time?

made "lack of time" a consistent phrase in field notes and interview transcripts. But "lack of time" is a phrase echoed by other school theatre directors, even veterans to the profession. (These days, in fact, lack of time seems a permanent construct of most people's lifestyles.) Focusing on Nancy's lack of time would have been relevant if the study's goals focused on such issues as time management or teacher burnout. Lack of time also would have played a role if grounded theory's constant comparison of data had been employed. But the goals and methodology of the Survival Study, coupled with my ethnicity, made lack of time an irrelevant, albeit constant, category for examination, "I develop this report with my cultural worldview—my knowledge, attitude, value and belief systems—as an Hispanic raised in an environment not as impoverished but somewhat similar to the Martinez School youth. The ethnic lens I used throughout this process brought selected issues to the foreground into sharper focus for analysis" (Saldaña, 1997, p. 27). Hence, what emerged from the study was Nancy's occasional use of the terms "survive" and "survival" in the data corpus across time:

October 1993: "The way I look at drama . . . is a tool and discipline that's going to help these kids be productive citizens who will survive until the age of 18."

December 1994: "Something more important [than learning] may be occurring due to the fact that a particular child entered the building and classroom—survival."

February 1995: "For a lot of junior high schoolers, I think [drama's] going to be, um, a means of expression . . . and a tool to help them survive."

March 1995 (researcher's field notes): Nancy has a blue file rack labeled "Daily and Substitute Survival Kit" with a folder for each class.

"Survival" is a common perspective for beginning teachers in inner-city school settings (Lancy, 1993, pp. 168–87). And since the study's inner-city educational contexts were relevant, the teacher participant's perspectives and conception of teaching drama with Hispanic youth were key areas for analysis. From October 1993 through March 1995, the term appeared not necessarily with numeric frequency but with salient and significant constancy in the data. In other words, survival as a theme held summative power for all major and minor categories. To use another common adage that may apply, "Less is more."

Terms can appear not necessarily with numeric frequency but with salient and significant constancy

Latency

There is no guarantee that what you may observe as constant patterns will remain after you leave the field. With children in particular, consistent presence yet "nongrowth" in particular categories might suggest latency, and developmental change may occur at a later time. For example, one child in the Theatre Response Study, when asked who the best actor was in the plays she had viewed (and prompted with "Why?"), gave similar responses across three grade levels with little elaboration across time:

Grade 2: The Meateaters. . . . They act good.
Grade 3: Lucy. . . . She was funny.
Grade 4: The Bear, because he acted real good. I like the way he act.

Other children throughout the same grade levels were able to articulate various rationale for their choices, which progressed from a basic *memory of lines* or *enjoyment of the character*, to a more complex *awareness of acting challenges*. Unlike the aforementioned child whose responses remained constant across three years, other children's responses suggested a cumulative awareness of the art of acting. Here are another child's responses to the best actor question across the same three grade levels:

Grade 2: All the actors, um, they got all their lines right.
Grade 3: Probably, hm, probably Snoopy, because he had, um, a good reaction to what's going on in the play.
Grade 4: Well, I'd say I liked, see, uh, the two bears, because it took a lot of hard training to get to know all those dances.

Immersion in the field for an extended period will reveal not only changes but possible "nonchanges," for lack of a better term. Nonchanges can be indicative of positive stability, but in negative contexts they can indicate inefficiency, stagnancy, bad habits, or dysfunction. Interviewing the participant about her life and social world before you entered the field and reviewing past archival documents will give you a sense of history to compare with what is actually observed during fieldwork. In the following passage, Nancy describes how her actions toward teacher colleagues changed in response to a two-year-long, nonchanging "battle":

During her first year Nancy acculturated to the non-arts teachers' requests to please them, even though she felt their expectations of the drama program, particularly with primary age children, were unrealistic: "During the whole first

year, I continually had to fight the battle of 'When are we going to have a performance?' Teachers tended to believe that if their class could not produce a
play or performance for an audience from what we were doing in the classroom,
I wasn't doing my job as a drama teacher." . . . The "battle," as Nancy put it,
was still being waged during her second year at Martinez [School]: "Last year I
did whatever they wanted. And this year, I do have to fight for it, but I can also
say, 'I don't think so.'" (Saldaña, 1997, p. 39)

"Nothing Is Happening"

Finally, be cautious of automatically assuming that constancy is evident because "nothing is happening" in the field. Extensive fieldwork can become
monotonous after awhile, particularly if the day-to-day routines of ordinary
social life are examined. What might be interpreted as consistency in participant actions through time might be attributed to the researcher's boredom
and an inability to "make the familiar strange," as the ethnographic saying
goes. What may be interpreted by the researcher as nothing more than daily
routines might be significant and essential daily rituals for the participant's
sense of continuity, stability, or ways of working. However, what is constant
or consistent through time might also suggest that something is missing
through time (discussed later in this chapter).

Daily routines might be significant and essential daily rituals

Cultures are not fixed social systems; they
are constantly evolving as they maintain
essential—and sometimes self-destructive—
traditions. Some people label themselves "crea-
tures of habit," and they may adhere to
constant and consistent patterns of action
across long periods of time whether they are aware of them or not (Tuchman, 1994, p. 311). Edgerton asserts that "most populations are reluctant
to change their traditional beliefs and practices . . . and often they fail to
understand the implications of changing conditions, believing the lessons
of the past will continue to serve them well in the future" (1992, pp.
58–59). Though we say that "times change and people change," the latter
do not always.

Constancy and consistency are indicators of patterns, cues for extracting
themes, and baseline data for possible future change. The challenge for
ethnographers then is to determine whether stable and ubiquitous data are
background noise or foreground issues—"familiar" or "strange" phenomena
to dismiss or analyze. Paradoxically, change itself can be constant and consistent through time, but not necessarily at moderate tempos or regular
rhythms. The patterns may appear to be idiosyncratic. Yet idiosyncrasy itself

can be constant and consistent through time. (A feedback loop is evident here, but don't let yourself get caught in it.)

What Is Idiosyncratic through Time?

Idiosyncratic Data

Idiosyncrasy is a phenomenon that complicates both quantitative measurement and qualitative assessment of change in longitudinal research. In qualitative analysis, idiosyncrasy refers to data patterns that are inconsistent, ever-shifting, multidirectional, and, during fieldwork, unpredictable (see fig. 5.7). Recall that the Theatre Response Study transformed qualitative categorical data into proportions. In the following table, notice how the proportions of "aural processing" varied as treatment children progressed through the study:

Category of Response: Replication of Characters' Dialogue during Interviews

Grade	Proportion
K	8%
1	12%
2	22%
3	19%
4	16%
5	25%
6	17%

The fluctuating proportions from grades 3–6 negated the smooth pattern of quantitative increase that appeared in grades K–2.

An observed trend in grades K–2 data was constant growth in aural processing, interrelated with a decline in visual processing of the theatre event. Preliminary assertions suggested that the treatment productions themselves may have played a role in this phenomenon (i.e., their content became less visual and more verbal), but I also attributed the influence to factors of child

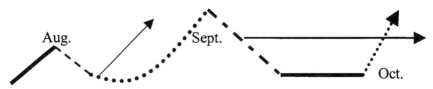

Figure 5.7   What is idiosyncratic through time?

development. As children mature, there is more active selection and inter-pretation of information received, particularly through listening skills (Mussen et al., 1990, pp. 303, 318).

Grades 3–6 proportions, however, revealed that both visual and aural pro-cessing of the theatrical event were actually idiosyncratic, due to varying amounts of visual and aural stimuli present in several different theatre pro-ductions and based on what children themselves chose to focus on in free-response interviews. In addition, aural processing was proportionately higher among the treatment group in the upper grade levels than second-site par-ticipants, suggesting that the drama/theatre treatment was yet another posi-tive intervening condition at work.

One plausible reason may have been an unreliable coding system that skewed resulting proportions. Another and more likely reason may have been highly contextual conditions interacting and interplaying with each other through time. Children's responses in the study were gathered after seven specific theatre events accompanied with a multitude of intervening conditions. "What ifs" entered the analytic picture as I speculated on what might have happened, could have happened, or should have happened. In other words, it was an attempt to analyze and thus justify why the data were idiosyncratic:

> [The] assertions profiled in this report would have been completely different had *Step On a Crack* been selected for presentation instead of *The Arkansaw [sic] Bear* in fourth grade; or if *Great Expectations* had been performed in fifth grade instead of sixth. Likewise, more substantial response might have been given by Barbara, a Holdeman [School] participant, if she hadn't been sleepy and hungry the day she attended *Snoopy!!!*; or if Sharon's parents had not been going through a divorce the same year she saw *Big River*. These profiles may have been completely different if *Most Powerful Jujus* would have had a stronger company of performers; if *Home Away from Home* had not included a pre-performance workshop in puppetry; if Hispanic actors had been cast to portray selected leading roles; or if the playwright of *Snowbirds* had chosen a male protagonist instead of a female. Even the accompanying classroom drama component of the study might have affected children's responses had the instructors chosen different learning objectives or content. (Saldaña, 1996, pp. 68–69)

Idiosyncrasy As a Pattern
Strauss and Corbin caution that some phenomena and behaviors do not lend themselves to orderly, consistent development (1990, p. 156). "Messy" and "slippery" are terms sometimes used to describe the complex, oscillating,

and erratic nature of human life documented in field notes and interview transcripts. But as Agar posits, "Randomness is not necessarily bad news" (1996, p. 178). Idiosyncrasy is sometimes a legitimate way to explain random and unpredictable human actions and observations—the "miscellaneous" bin for data that do not fit into an analytic framework—if it can be supported and justified. To adopt a concept from chaos theory, idiosyncrasy can be a pattern (oxymoron intended) and not to be dismissed, especially with data gathered from the perspectives of young children (Knapp, 1997) and adolescents (Fine and Sandstrom, 1988). Individual differences will occur within a group of participants, especially among young people. As Eisner so astutely reminds us, children and adolescents "have their own ideas, motives, needs, and feelings about what they want to do and be. When a group of twenty-five or thirty get together, our ability to predict and control outcomes or processes becomes even more questionable" (1991, p. 102).

Idiosyncrasy can be a pattern

If children and adolescents are groups with inherent idiosyncrasy then, by default, these patterns appear in one of their most prominent environments: school. But young people are not the only participants who experience erratic change. Idiosyncratic patterns also appear in ethnographic studies of classroom teaching practice. Murray (1998) examines the two-year journey of three elementary school teachers incorporating drama into their curricula. Though she summarizes the individual journeys of these teachers "at the end of the first year" and "over the second year," she also details the idiosyncratic shifts (along with the contextual and intervening conditions) that occurred in her participants' perceptions and applications of the art form throughout the study, "[In] appropriately dramatic form, the views and voices once raised are now too rich, varied, numerous, and complicated to be simplified into a final, neat, narrative plot line. This is the story of people who come together, people who stay apart, people who try, people who change, people who refuse, people who care, people who fear, people who risk, people who hide, people who start, people who quit, people who finish" (p. 188). Thus, school and education are two highly idiosyncratic constructs, despite current attempts to "standardize" student outcomes and teaching curricula.

Reconceptualizing Patterns

Too often, when we think of patterns we associate them with symmetrical or consistent repetition such as carefully arranged floor tiles, heartbeats, or rush-hour traffic on selected days of the week and year and during specific hours of the morning and evening. I am amazed at the infinite number of ways humans construct repetitive patterns in their material products. In my office alone I detect patterns in my bookshelves, my air conditioning vents, the rows of florescent light tubes, the squares created by the wire mesh of my "in" and "out" baskets, and even in the graphic symbols contained in a replica of an Aztec calendar hanging on my wall. But patterns can also consist of multirhythmic, asymmetrical, and seemingly fluctuating strings of action, such as an improvisational jazz session, the ebb and flow of customers shopping in a mall throughout the course of a weekday, or a period from a preschooler's free play: role-playing a parent in a game of House, riding her tricycle, chasing a dog, spinning around, then refocusing her attention suddenly when she discovers a caterpillar climbing a tree. In other words, a pattern is constructed by a researcher, and whether it's interpreted as repetitive or idiosyncratic is, like contexts, contextual.

Florida labels a particular yet large cluster of people who work in selected professions as "the creative class," a unique social group "whose function is to create new ideas, new technology, and/or new creative content" (2002, p. 8). Awareness of this emergent class and its ethos, however, was not immediately apparent. Some social critics may have viewed the 1990s as a decade of tumultuous uncertainty, but Florida explains how the seemingly idiosyncratic was a pattern in process, "Society . . . is changing neither in random chaotic ways, nor in some mysterious collective-unconscious way, but in ways that are perfectly sensible and rational. The logic behind the transformation is still in progress. But lately a number of diverse and seemingly unconnected threads are starting to come together The deeper pattern, the force behind the shift, can now be discerned" (p. 4).

Florida's observations cemented during reviews of occupational data and interviews with members from the "creative class" itself. The transferable lesson from this constructed concept is that idiosyncratic phenomena, as perceived by the researcher, are not like a miscellaneous assembly of jigsaw pieces from multiple puzzles that do not and cannot fit together. Rather, idiosyncratic data are like miscellaneous craft items—beads, feathers, glitter, paint, fabric scraps, and so on—awaiting assembly to create a new and unique artistic product.

A category or construct that appears erratic or fluctuates in the data may indicate contextual and intervening conditions interacting and interplaying with each other through time. This unique pattern, though, may set limits on the transferability of findings to other contexts. Idiosyncratic patterns may also arise when the dynamics of participant actions reach extreme ends of a continuum or extend across multiple locations in the ocean of data. When idiosyncrasy appears in the data, the possibility of a flawed coding system should not be ruled out, nor should the possibility that an insufficient amount of data exist for analysis. Finally, idiosyncrasy can be approached as a challenge for the researcher to assemble or creatively construct a new pattern or a pattern in process.

What Is Missing through Time?

"Notably Absent" Data

The universe of the data corpus is what exists for analysis. Certainly, we work with what we have and, when needed, return to the fieldwork site for more data to fill the missing gaps. During the analytic cycle, however, there may be data that the researcher somehow intuits should be there but aren't—"notably absent," as Strauss and Corbin (1990) write (see fig. 5.8). For example, in a simple content analysis of theatre-related terms used by children in postperformance interviews, a variety of theatre personnel appear such as actors, directors, and designers. But missing from seven years of transcripts is the term "playwright," one of the central creators and key collaborators of theatre production. The inferences made from this missing term was that either children did not see this as an essential role when responding to the play, or the teaching/research team did not effectively instruct children on the playwright's function in theatrical production. (Of course, idiosyncrasy could be at work here. Some children may have known but simply not have chosen to use the term during interviews.)

As data collection progresses simultaneously with data analysis, the researcher may become aware of critical areas not initially addressed in a preestablished interview or observation protocol. Way, in her engaging three-year longitudinal qualitative study of urban adolescents, writes how one problem surfaced and was resolved across time in interviews with her predominantly ethnic minority participants:

> After the first year of interviews, I sat down to . . . think about what was and what was not being asked. Immediately I was struck by the absence of questions

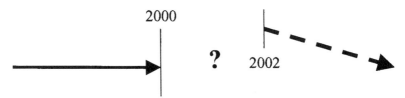

Figure 5.8   What is missing through time?

concerning discrimination and oppression. . . . In the second year of interviews, we attempted to address this situation by asking the students whether they felt that their "race, ethnicity, or gender would make it more difficult for them to do what they wanted to do in the future." Reviewing their responses after these interviews . . . we realized that we were not asking the right questions. . . . In the third-year interviews, we headed straight to the heart of the matter. We asked the adolescents whether they experienced racism or sexism. (1998, p. 205)

This fine-tuning of Way's interview protocol generated provocative answers from her young participants as the study progressed. It was a wise choice to rectify what was missing from the first year's database, which led to deeper insights on a salient theme.

Present and Missing Data
In chapter 4, I noted when comparing ponds and pools, "If you look for differences within and between categories, you will be more aware of the many possible contrasts, variability, and dynamics within and between the data. If you look exclusively for what is missing, you limit your search to what is absent rather than present." I do not intend to contradict myself here, but that advice applied to that process. When you examine "What is missing through time?" you refocus your search for what is both present *and* missing.

Just because something is missing doesn't mean that nothing is being influenced and affected. Consider how we sometimes take for granted or do not appreciate what is present until it is suddenly or unexpectedly missing from our lives. Recall the earlier discussion on whether the glass was half empty or half full. The metaphor applies here as well. In my introspective moods, I contemplate what's missing from my own life—the half empty part. Sometimes I can pinpoint those voids with accuracy. At other times, I'm at a loss to clarify what I really want, "Life's good, but something's missing and I don't know what it is—my glass is only half full."

Just because something is missing doesn't mean that nothing is being influenced and affected

What is missing or absent from my life affects my perceptions of what is present—and vice versa. This suggests that if something is missing, then there might be something else in its place—something present.

In the Survival Study, Nancy's in-service teacher workshops offered by the school and district were irrelevant for her immediate needs as a beginning teacher or drama specialist. Math manipulatives, computers, and other topics were presented, but nothing in these professional development seminars covered her most critical needs: communicating with children who knew little English, interacting with students who may be gang members, and understanding the ethos of Hispanic youth and the culture of poverty. Missing from her experiences were such structures and processes as preservice preparation in multicultural education and in-service education for site-specific conditions. Thus, present in her initial teaching experiences were *trial and error, hit and miss,* and *learning by doing.*

During Barry's "dead period," missing from his junior high school years were classes and extracurricular programs in theatre production. But what was really missing could be interpreted and combined in different ways: acceptance by peers, self-esteem, direction, fulfillment, purpose, and so on. It was not until he became involved with theatre in high school that the things missing from his life were now present.

Final exit interviews with participants, conducted during the latter portion of a longitudinal study, are not only opportunities for closure or assessment, they are also researcher opportunities to confirm whether the absence or presence of particular phenomena or data have shaped their course of actions (or nonactions) across time. For example, the Theatre Response Study presented a treatment of productions from a traditional canon of plays for young audiences. One of the final exit interview questions asked children to share what they both liked and disliked about theatre. Cumulative experiences may have played a role in affecting their personal preferences for theatre content and their attitudes toward the art form (Saldaña, 1995, p. 20):

> Out of 26 theatre viewing experiences, only two were non-traditional in genre: *This Is Not a Pipe Dream* (surrealism) in Grade 4, and *The Nose* (absurdism) in Grade 6. *After seven years of conventional, mainstream experiences the treatment group, in general, possesses conventional, mainstream preferences for theatre:* comedies and adventures with an exciting, comprehensible story and variety in its staging. We can speculate that the treatment did not provide a diversity of genres for their experiential base. But we can also speculate that this diversity may have had no effect on influencing their consequent likes and dislikes toward the end of the study. (p. 28, emphasis in the original)

Noticeably absent categories may suggest that the constancy or consistency of contextual conditions, or the as yet undetected intervening condition, might inhibit the presence of something to emerge. What is missing could also be the consequence of a decrease that occurred earlier in the chronological data record. Contemplating "What is missing through time?" is a worthwhile exercise to both reflect on how the absence of something may influence and affect participants, and to exhaust the possibilities of what might have been, could have been, or should have been present during the study.

CHAPTER SIX

Analytic and Interpretive Questions

The discussion now turns to an examination and integration of descriptive data, and observations culled from framing questions, in more complex ways to hopefully yield analytic and interpretive insights from your longitudinal study. The four questions addressed in this chapter are:

1. Which changes interrelate through time?
2. Which changes through time oppose or harmonize with natural human development or constructed social processes?
3. What are participant or conceptual rhythms (phases, stages, cycles, and so on) through time?
4. What is the through-line of the study?

Which Changes Interrelate through Time?

Interrelationship

In qualitative studies, the researcher looks for overlapping ponds or pools of data within and across beats of time suggesting interrelationship—a tight and more complex connection between and among the multiple processes involved with change (see fig. 6.1). Whether perceived by a participant or inferred by a researcher, interrelationships are human constructions, reflections on the interactions and interplay of social action or phenomena. We attune ourselves to these connections to better understand the intricacies and interconnectedness of change forces. Gently breaking the surface of a body of water sends ripples

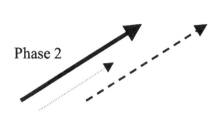

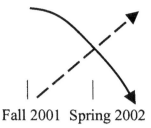

Fall 2001 Spring 2002

Figure 6.1   Which changes interrelate through time?

outward, merging with other ripples, splashes create waves that disturb and sub-sume the ripples, and the tide swells to overtake and gather everything in its path. The ocean is ever moving and ever changing, just like our social worlds.

Longitudinal qualitative data are examined chronologically, categorically, and thematically in a longitudinal study. Linear data displays and matrices allow the researcher to scan observations repeatedly to assess the general processual flow of changes through time. This iterative process of data scanning across rows and columns may reveal links or interrelations between sets of observations, leading the researcher to infer possible contextual or intervening conditions influencing and affecting particular ponds and pools of data. Interrelationship may also be suggested when similar or related answers appear in response to several of the sixteen questions simultaneously. As stated earlier, sometimes an increase in certain actions may be accompanied by a decrease in others. Taken together, these composite actions constitute an adaptation or evolution of sorts (Emerson, Fretz, and Shaw, 1995, p. 111).

Throughout this book, I stress that there will be an inescapable overlap of data as they are analyzed since some observations may relate to several of the sixteen questions simultaneously. My own experiences in longitudinal qualitative data analysis also taught me that certain actions in data may suggest other actions—for example, an increase interrelates with a decrease, contextual conditions influence and affect participant development, and constancy in data might suggest that something is missing. If you wish to be highly systematic and thorough, you can construct a sixteen-by-sixteen-cell matrix to examine not just the interrelationships, but how one question intersects with the other fifteen, if relevant (e.g., when does an increase, decrease, surge, cessation, and so on occur through time? What are the dynamics of the contextual and intervening conditions, constancy, idiosyncrasy, stages, and so on through time?). A three-dimensional matrix will expand the analytic possibilities even further (e.g., what contextual conditions influence and affect increases in certain participant actions that suggest a new pattern of development?). To a certain point, these analytic matrices can generate new combinations of data clusters and possibly reveal how one answer plus another answer (plus another answer) intersect to form an entirely new answer. Depending on the magnitude of your data, the capabilities of qualitative data analysis software, such as QSR NVivo, can make these searches easier to conduct.

The linear intersections of rectangular cells, however, seem incompatible with the fluid and *Certain actions in data* blended nature of qualitative data. Imagine a *may suggest other actions* clear glass tank of water with various colors of liquid dye poured into it, each color representing an answer or pool of qualitative data to one of the sixteen questions profiled in chapter 3. Rather than stirring the water to mix all the colors together, you allow the natural currents and flows of dye to blend with each other in the tank. These combinations of two or more dyes create new colors—new ponds, new pools, and new answers. This is the conceptual process for analyzing both interrelationships and change in longitudinal qualitative data. It is systematically elusive, but I can think of no other analogy to describe the way your answers to these questions eventually blend together.

Examples of Interrelationship

In the Theatre Response Study, treatment children's responses in the category of *evaluation* were proportionately higher in grades 5–6 than in grades K–4. Most children's comments transcended mere descriptive recall of the event and focused on evaluation of such elements as scenography, acting performance, and, from a few children, the structure of the play script. An interesting interrelationship was observed between the children's ability to critique the acting and their developmental ability to separate the real actor from the fictional character he or she portrayed. Before grade 5, most children evaluated the effectiveness of a performance based on the character's appealing qualities, such as humorous actions and dialogue. But by grade 5, treatment children generally referred not to the character in their evaluative commentary, but to the actor *portraying* the character. The heightened developmental ability to separate performer from character emerged during the same grade levels *evaluation* as a category increased. Child development was attributed as the contextual condition for children's ability to separate fictive characters from real actors, and the cumulative drama/theatre treatment was seen as a positive intervening condition that enabled children to critique acting performances with more depth than second-site youth.

But identifying a simple influence and affect is not this neat. Additional contextual and intervening conditions at work added layers of complexity to the previous analysis. I learned how context is a complex "nested arrange-ment of structures and processes" when I attempted to explain how a child's gender possibly influenced and affected his or her responses to theatre:

> Studies in perception and response to theatre, in which gender is a variable for examination, are minimal. Ingersol and Kase noted that "the enjoyment of plays is defined as an aspect of the feminine role" (p. 42). In the small group interview condition, boys may have withheld sincere response to the theatre event due to self-consciousness among peers (Davis and Evans p. 65; Eisenberg). But the Grades 1–2 productions featured female protagonists, possibly lending more per-ceived similarities and interest for girls. If gender differences in child develop-ment are examined, the heightened perceptions and responses from girls may be attributed to their higher IQs in the early years and their increased performance in verbal fluency and verbal comprehension (Mussen et al. p. 356). At the same time, the socialization that boys and girls receive from peers, family, school, and mass media contribute to patterns of intellectual development: The patterns of achievement for males and females are consistent with cultural stereotypes about appropriate behaviors for men and women. American children learn early that reading, art, and verbal skills are stereotyped as feminine. (Saldaña, 1993, p. 356)

Evaluative response and attention to dialogue before grade 5 had been proportionately higher from girls than from boys. But in grades 5–6, boys' proportions of evaluative response and attentiveness to dialogue increased and the girls' decreased. Child development literature offered no plausible explanation for this observation. Yet, a scan of categories across time re-vealed that this interrelationship was indicative of an interaction between the genders of child audience members and the gender of the central protag-onists in the theatre productions.

When children in grades 2–3 were asked to identify their favorite and "best" actor, boys generally chose male performers while girls chose female performers as their preferences, even though the ensemble casts featured fe-male protagonists and an equal balance of men and women (Saldaña, 1989). In grades 5–6 however, the plays' central protagonists were Huckleberry Finn from the musical Big River, and Pip from an adaptation of Charles Dickens's Great Expectations. These predominantly male stories with boy characters in active roles and female characters in passive, traditional roles suggested that gender of the central protagonists, interacting with genders of child audience members, emerged as intervening and contextual conditions, respectively, that possibly influenced the observed increase in attention to dialogue and evaluative commentary from boys and the decrease from girls.

"Gender" and "school" are more than constructs; they are cultures. Chil-dren develop not only as individuals, but also as individuals within and between multiple cultures and subcultures. Corsaro and Molinari reinforce how longitudinal ethnography is essential for developing theory in the sociology of childhood (2000, p. 180) and, along with Scott (2000), assert that the collective processes to which children belong change concurrently with their members. "What unites different life course studies is that they view human development over individual, social and historical time. . . . First, we need to understand how early events and influences persist and fade across the life course in a changing world. Second, we need to understand how an individual's actions and societal change are reciprocally linked" (Scott, 2000, p. 116).

The charges may be difficult to meet, for "[t]here are ubiquitous individual differences in adolescent development, and they involve connections among biological, cognitive, psychological, and social factors—and not any one of these influences acting either alone or as the 'prime mover' of change" (Lerner et al., 2001, p. 12). The challenge, then, is to wear multi- and interdisciplinary lenses and filters as you examine qualitative data, and to collage or network, rather than rank, the interrelated factors influencing and affecting change.

Collage or network, rather than rank, the interrelated factors influencing and affecting change

Integrated Methodologies

Finally, just as proportions of categories function as a quantitative tactic for discerning change across time, statistical correlation can lead to or support observations of qualitative interrelationships across time. Braver and O'Connell (1998), in *Divorced Dads: Shattering the Myths*, combine primarily quantitative methods (e.g., surveys and demographic data) with qualitative methods (interviews) across a three-year period to track patterns that developed among divorced parents. Most noteworthy was the methodological decision to survey and interview each parent separately, *"Asking any two divorced parents the same question about nearly anything will almost certainly garner far different responses. There are two sides to every story, and up until now, it appears only one side has been recorded"* (p. 33, emphasis in the original). Bar graphs throughout the text illustrate multiple disparities and disagreements between "what mothers say" and "what fathers say" in response to various questions. The statistical evidence profiled in the book brings several positive and negative correlations to the surface, such as, "[I]f a mother had *previously* restricted visitation, the father was significantly more likely to *later* withhold some child support" (p. 172, emphasis in the original). Causal analysis, not interviews ("It's inappropriate to attempt to answer this question by simply asking people"), led to the assertion that "[f]athers both pay child support and maintain emotional involvement *because* they feel parentally enfranchised, not vice versa" (p. 170).

Braver and O'Connell downplay the qualitative component of their study and even the paradigm itself, "Unlike the comparatively objective quantitative method, the more 'interpretive' . . . qualitative method leaves more room for researchers' judgements, biases, and ideologies to color their interpretations" (1998, p. 167). Yet, despite the rhetoric of statistical rigor advocated throughout the book to support the validity of their conclusions, Braver and O'Connell also rely on excerpts from newspaper articles and interviews with divorced parents to inform their general public and policy-making readerships. The emotion-laden quotes, vignettes, and stories not only illustrate or exemplify the statistical findings, but the narratives also support and give human meaning to the numbers. *Divorced Dads*, perhaps unintentionally, is an example of quantitative and qualitative data corroboration and correlation.

If category proportions have been calculated for qualitative data, standard statistical operations can be employed as a tactic to bring any possible correlations to the surface for closer scrutiny (see Cairns, Bergman, and Kagan, 1998). The preceding descriptive questions that log such phenomena as increases, decreases, and idiosyncrasy in data certainly help. But from my own experience, the eventual observation of interrelationships between ponds and pools of data is one that emerges after multiple readings of data and its reduction into visual displays, plus extended reflection on their possible connections and overlap.

Figure 6.2, an excerpt from Ludwig Beethoven's Symphony No. 5, Movement 1, illustrates the notes to be played simultaneously from five different string instruments. The conductor's score includes each individual instrument's sheet music formatted in rows (indicated through staffs) and columns

Figure 6.2   An excerpt from a conductor's musical score

(indicated through measures) on single pages. The orchestra conductor controls the tempos, holds, and rests of the piece with his baton as musicians create different yet interrelated sounds through time. Each instrument, literally as well as figuratively, has a specific part to play in the overall symphonic scheme.

Consider how this musical notation system could be applied to longitudinal qualitative data display and thus analysis, with each row representing either a single case from a group of participants or a particular variable about a case, and each column representing a pond or pool of time. Not only will this method permit cross-case comparison as participants progress through a study, it may also provide insights on possible interrelationships. One could

	EIGHTH GRADE *adagio* *piano* "It's kind of a dead period"	NINTH GRADE *allegretto* *mezzo forte* "Whoa—maybe there's something I'm good at here"	TENTH GRADE *andante* *mezzo forte* "I'm very feeling-oriented"
FROM DRUGS	- "I got really heavy into drugs" - "Drugs had taken up my whole life"	- "Theatre helped draw me out of drugs" - "[I] quit everything I was doing, all the drug use" - "Drugs helped draw me into theatre in that they voided my life of everything else, so I was completely empty, completely open towards picking up on theatre"	
FROM CHURCH	- "I've been going to church my whole life, but I have a hard time subscribing to certain beliefs"	- "I've been doing a lot of soul searching since [my drug use]"	- "I don't wanna go to Sunday school any more"
FROM THEATRE	- "I had no theatre in my life, didn't have any exposure to it"	- "[Theatre] was almost intoxicating in and of itself. It gave me the strength to get away from [drugs]" - "I got cast in my first show . . . a lead"	- "I think theatre is very spiritual for me . . . it's my version of church"

Figure 6.3   Barry's spiritual fulfillment as a "muscial score"

even take the display and analysis so far as to include the dynamics of change's tempos through such musical terms as *allegro, presto, moderato,* and so on, and change's magnitude through such volume terms as *forte* and *pianissimo* (see fig. 6.3).

Various changes throughout time can be multiple and can interrelate positively or negatively in complex ways through reciprocity—that is, interaction or interplay. Miles and Huberman's (1994) time-oriented matrices may help display the variables' relationships with each other, as can Strauss and Corbin's (1998) integrative diagrams for "best fit" conditional paths (see fig. 6.4).

It's as if the researcher is looking for "side affects" of sorts, from a root factor, variable, or category. Think of those complex layouts of thousands of dominoes standing in intertwined and multileveled patterns. When the first domino is tipped over and the successive tiles fall, sometimes the initiating pattern can break into multiple tracks of dominoes falling simultaneously, which then crisscross and overlap like DNA strands. This is the metaphor for complex "causality": multiple paths of action in various patterns and directions that sometimes weave into and then away from each other.

Finally, just as with statistical correlation, qualitative interrelationship does not necessarily imply causality, and not everything that links in a matrix suggests an authentic interrelationship. Likewise, when interrelationship cannot be supported by the available evidence, but you sense that there should be some type of connection, return to the field if possible for additional observation or interview data to confirm or disconfirm your hunch. Logic, common sense, life experience, intuition, and—first and foremost—good data are needed to weave the possible interrelationships at work.

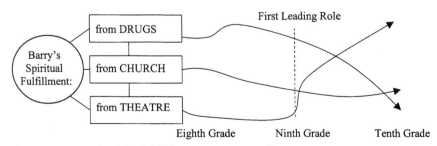

Figure 6.4   Barry's spiritual fulfillment as a process diagram

Which Changes through Time Oppose or Harmonize with Natural Human Development or Constructed Social Processes?

Development and Process

An awareness of and sensitivity to the way most children and adults of both genders and of different ethnicities develop naturally and/or socially through time, or the way human actions tend to progress and change in particular social contexts, are essentials when reviewing and analyzing longitudinal data. Knowledge of cognitive, physical, emotional, and other domains of human development is useful to determine if change in the participants is due primarily to natural or social processes rather than the result of intervening conditions (see fig. 6.5). As children grow, their oral language fluency should naturally increase, as should the complexity of their vocabulary. Inference-making skills, however, may differ from child to child within the same grade level and may develop in varying qualities of sophistication through time. Complicating the matter further is how gender, ethnicity, and other variables may also affect their inference-making ability and the communication of that ability to an interviewer, or the interpretation by a participant observer.

Patton notes that a change theory "bears the burden of specifying and explaining assumed, hypothesized, or tested causal linkages" (2002, p. 163). Previous research that examines phases, stages, cycles, or other social processes in particular contextual conditions may provide conceptual frameworks, clarifications, support, guidance, or even challenges for any observed changes in the data. For example, Winkelman's (1994) stages of cultural shock—tourist, crisis, adjustment, and adaptation—can be applied readily to such contexts as studies of foreign students attending U.S. universities, North American anthropologists conducting fieldwork in Third World countries, or white, middle-class teachers instructing in inner-city schools. The stages of cultural shock, according to Winkelman, are both sequential and cyclical. Knowledge of these stages provides a template, if appropriate to the particular longitudinal research study, to discern whether the data record of change harmonizes

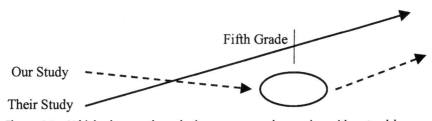

Figure 6.5   Which changes through time oppose or harmonize with natural human development or constructed social processes?

with or disconfirms previous findings. Other examples of social and contextual human processes are Kübler-Ross's well-known stages of death and dying (1969), Huberman's professional life cycle of teachers (1989), theoretical models of the coming out process for gays and lesbians (Blumenfeld, 1998), stages of ethnic identity development (Benjamin, 1998), processes leading to enhanced social consciousness (Adams, 1997), stages in modifying addictive behaviors (Prochaska, DiClemente, and Norcross, 1992), progressive adaptation of infertile couples to biological childlessness (Daniluk, 2001), and factors leading to teacher burnout (reviewed in McCammon, 1992). Models such as these are our observations of social patterns. In a positivist sense, these constructions/theories are also our attempts to explain, predict, and control human actions in particular contexts.

Previous research may provide conceptual frameworks, clarifications, guidance, support, or challenges

Previous research on development and social process can (and should) be challenged as well. New paradigms and new knowledge contribute to the reconstruction of scholarship. Yates and McLeod (1996), researching adolescent gender development over a period of seven years, survey and compare the contested body of feminist work on psychology, epistemology, and moral development. They hope to rectify the shortcomings of earlier longitudinal quantitative studies through their qualitative approaches. Based on their preliminary fieldwork with young people, "The issue of what has been striking to us raises questions not only about what we noticed because it seemed to be news in relation to the existing literature, but also about how we can maintain some openness to areas which are for us already saturated with theory via the literature" (p. 92). Yates and McLeod do not "build" on previous work; they deconstruct it critically in order to maintain an open mind for what may emerge over seven years, and to prioritize their young participants' individual biographies over definitive accounts of adolescent development.

An Example of Developmental Change

A simple example of how a child development stage may have influenced and affected responses to theatre viewing emerged in third- and fourth-grade transcripts of the Theatre Response Study. Mussen et al. refer to a phenomenon that occurs in middle childhood: "emotional ambivalence" (1990, pp. 412–13). This is a period when new emotions, such as guilt, are experienced but seem confusing to the child because there are no labels for them. Children described poignant, bittersweet, or ironic moments from play productions by combining the only emotional vocabulary they knew, "Sorta happy and sorta sad." Children also used descriptive metaphors and similes, "A different kind of happy—a floating happy." Without knowledge of the childhood stage of emotional ambivalence, their responses might have been perceived as an inability to infer and interpret character actions and emotions as portrayed by the actors.

In grades K–6, proportions in the categories of *story* and *character* generally decreased and increased, respectively, across seven years. These two literary elements are closely intertwined, for a story is about characters and characters move the story forward. Coding was cautious: a *character* code was applied when the child spoke *about* the character, but an entry was coded as *story* when the child described the *character in action*. The resulting proportions were surface indicators of some type of qualitative change, but of what? The intervening condition of the play script content becoming more complex in later grade levels was ruled out, as was the seven-year drama/theatre treatment, since second-site participants also exhibited the same changes through time. Instead, natural child development presented a plausible reason why this change may have occurred:

> As treatment and second-site children progressed from kindergarten through sixth grade, there was a self-initiated and preferential shift from story to character in post-performance discussions of theatre events. In later childhood, young people become more sensitive to the complexities of human behavior through such developmental skills as person perception and inference. This factor, rather than the treatment, was designated as the primary cause for the shift. (Saldaña, 1996, p. 80)

An Example of Processual Change

The Survival Study illustrates how Nancy, as an inner-city school teacher, experienced a previously constructed social process: the sequential and cyclical cultural shock and adaptation stages profiled by Winkelman (1994). His stages became part of the conceptual framework for approaching the study and analyzing its data in a longitudinal overview. Nancy entered the teaching profession as what Winkelman calls a tourist in a culturally unique site, yet she faced crises when her Eurocentric approach to drama did not engage the Hispanic students, "After seven years of university education, Nancy prepared herself thoroughly for her first day of public school instruction. She reflected in a confident tone: 'I knew my craft. I thought: I was trained, I was ready for this, I can handle this situation.' Then she spoke with weariness: 'I did my lesson plans—and nothing turned out the way I thought it would. Absolutely nothing'" (Saldaña, 1997, p. 25).

Nancy then adjusted her teaching philosophy, curriculum, and classroom practice to meet the needs of her inner-city students and to make learning more relevant to their ethos. There was no particular evidence in the data that allowed me to state with confidence that Nancy finally adapted to the school culture on a specific day or even within a specific time period. Nancy herself could not identify when this turning point occurred. But actions observed toward the latter five months of the twenty-month longitudinal period—such as her more frequent use of Spanish language vocabulary, increased knowledge of barrio culture, more meaningful content choices for dramatic exploration (e.g., Mexican American folklore and gang issues), and her professional insights shared with preservice teachers—suggested she had, to a comfortable degree from the researcher's holistic perspective, adapted her practice for a more compatible fit with the culture of the children she taught.

An Example of Developmental and Processual Change

A final example illustrates the complex interaction and interplay among adolescent development, gender, class, and ethnicity, and how previous research both supports and contradicts new findings. Way, in *Everyday Courage: The Lives and Stories of Urban Teenagers*, questions why the lower-class girls (predominantly of color) in her study "have the courage and strength to speak out in relationships when many white, adolescent girls and women from middle- or upper-income families appear to have great difficulty" doing so (1998, p. 105). Note how Way addresses this question by weaving the observed changes across time with developmental research in her field:

> [Since] many of the girls in the study seemed more willing to speak openly in their junior and senior years than in their freshman and sophomore years, it is possible that girls from different socioeconomic, racial, and ethnic backgrounds find it particularly difficult to speak out in early adolescence. Hormonal changes, school transitions, and other shifts in their lives, including their growing cognitive capacity to understand cultural expectations, may silence most girls during this period. The capacity for open expression may increase as girls' lives stabilize when they reach late adolescence. Previous studies focusing on the silences among primarily white middle- and upper-class adolescent girls have focused on those who are in early to midadolescence. Had we interviewed the girls only in their first two years of high school, outspokenness would have been a barely detectable trend rather than a pervasive theme. Researchers have, however, detected such silences among adult middle-class women as well, which suggests that there may be differ-

ences across social class, race, and ethnicity in the willingness and ability to speak one's mind. (p. 107)

Way's findings did not harmonize with previous research. Her attunement to the integrated social constructs of age, gender, class, and ethnicity added new layers of knowledge for developmental research with young people, a quality desired in contemporary studies (Lerner et al., 2001).

Transferability of Developmental and Processual Observations

What if the researcher chooses to transcend the particular longitudinal observations of an individual or small group's development in order to generalize to a larger or broader population? Schofield (2002) presents several methodological strategies, such as multi- or representative site selection, for increasing the "generalizability" of qualitative research; while Spradley (1980) illustrates six levels of ethnographic writing ranging from specific incidences to universals as a means of progressing from the particular to the general. Prediction of how other populations will act is inferred when we attempt to generalize through theory, but Patton cautions, "[I]ndividual outcomes, impacts, and changes that result from participation in some set of activities are seldom predictable with any certainty. Moreover, the meaning and meaningfulness of such changes as do occur are likely to be highly specific to particular people in particular circumstances" (2002, p. 525).

For example, Lister et al.'s (2002) panel of sixty-four young adults for a three-year study of their developing political attitudes includes a representation of the young general population in terms of gender, ethnicity, education, employment, and age (from sixteen to twenty-two). This sample spectrum enhances and lends support to any transferable findings the researchers may develop when the study concludes, but the situated time period of the study (1999–2002, which includes a general election year) and its geographic location (Leicester) will limit the extent of those findings to other countries and possibly other time periods in the near future, depending on the social and political climates at that time.

Development, as noted earlier, is an elusive phenomenon to abstract into precise predictive theory. Teacher development can be so particular and personal that a single story may defy and negate the generalized patterns observed and constructed by researchers. Diamond and Mullen assert that "[a] teacher's self-movement is not relentlessly unilinear; it includes pauses and cyclic returns. Development proceeds in a manner other than as in a projectable curve like a cannon shot. Development cannot be 'measured' by using linear, rational tools" (1999, p. 68). Heinz and Krüger, discussing contemporary challenges for social research, note that "life-course arrangements are becoming more dynamic, less standardized and more self-directed" in Western nations (2001, p. 29). Hence, these solo rhythms of change, influenced and affected by one's contextual and intervening conditions, merit reexamination of their unique patterns for comparison against previously held assumptions of universal change.

Development is an elusive phenomenon to abstract into precise predictive theory

The Theatre Response Study research team began the project in 1984 with an idealistic vision that seven years of continuous drama and theatre-viewing experiences for a group of sixty-four children would mold and create sixty-four gifted directors, playwrights, and actors for the art form's future. This prediction was maintained but appeared less likely once we approached the end of the study in 1991 and analyzed the less-than-hoped-for magnitude of change in the thirty remaining participants, which included Barry, our "rising star." But what if one, two, or more of those original participants start directing Broadway plays, receive the Pulitzer Prize for playwriting, or win an Academy Award for Best Actor twenty years from now? The interim period between what I wishfully think will happen and what actually does happen is hope, not prediction. To our knowledge, none of the original participants are actively pursuing full-time careers in theatre or film as of 2002. This is hardly surprising, for no evidence exists in the qualitative data we collected that something like this was bound to happen with any certainty. Predictions about the participants' futures after a study is completed are always a risk. But predictions developed *before* and *during* a study for possible outcomes toward the *end* of the study are more realistic opportunities to develop and test assertions-in-progress, and to refine them as confirming and disconfirming evidence emerges.

Selected longitudinal quantitative procedures (eerily labeled "survivor probability" and "hazard modeling") attempt to examine the multiple and possible predictors that vary through people's lives, such as income, education, marital/family status, and how these interacting variables might determine "whether and when individuals are likely to experience a target event" (Willet, Singer, and Martin, 1998, p. 403) or how the variables might predict "how *different life contexts* may lead to *similar outcomes* . . . and how *similar life contexts* may lead to a variety of *different developmental outcomes*" (p. 407, emphasis in the original). Longitudinal quantitative data analysis acknowledges both the linearity and nonlinearity of developmental pathways and human life trajectories, as does longitudinal qualitative research.

But the power of the qualitative paradigm rests with its ability to examine with more descriptive depth the multiple dimensions of social contexts and individual human agency in concert with other individuals' human agency, and thus the multiple variables and predictors interacting and interplaying through time. But elegance should not be ruled out automatically. Depending on what the data suggest, sometimes the answers to whether and when something might occur can be quite direct. A common rejoinder by someone who discounts an easy answer is, "Well, it's not that simple," to which I reply (if the solution seems possible or plausible), "It doesn't have to be that complicated, either."

Elegance should not be ruled out automatically

What Are Participant or Conceptual Rhythms (Phases, Stages, Cycles, and So On) through Time?

Life Rhythms

The natural cycles of our world, such as sunrise and sunset and seasonal change, combined with the human need to sequence and construct patterns in life, and social traditions to acknowledge such markers as birthdays and anniversaries, motivate us as researchers to seek "the implicit rhythm of particular social systems" (Pettigrew, 1995, p. 100). Researchers may find serial, cumulative, or repetitive actions embedded within and woven throughout the vast tapestry of longitudinal data. These rhythmic action clusters—the pattern of patterns—can take many forms according to how the researcher

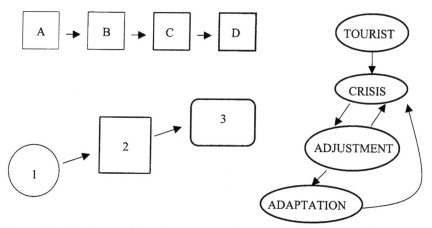

Figure 6.6   What are participant or conceptual rhythms (phases, stages, cycles, and so on) through time?

observes them in data: linear, sequential, cyclical, multitempoed, improvised, choreographed, and so on (see fig. 6.6). Observations and analyses of social life throughout an extended period of time may generate insight into the rituals humans have created—consciously or unconsciously—in their particular settings. Reflection on these rituals may ultimately reveal that there are implicit short- or long-term rhythms to par-

ticular contexts and sequential or developmental patterns that transfer to other contexts. In other words, what we are trying to analyze and apportion are the theoretical periodicities of human action, such as the transition sequences of the life course. But any theoretical pattern constructed by the researcher will most likely be general—rarely will it apply perfectly to every case.

Analyze and apportion the theoretical periodicities of human action

---

Phases

First, there are differences between a phase, a stage, and a cycle. The popular saying "It's just a phase he's going through" suggests a short-term anomaly or deviation from average, expected, or appropriate developmental behavior. A somewhat stereotypical example is the angst-ridden teenager who wears black clothing during a portion of his adolescent years—such as Barry did when he began high school. The phase may end when this period of depression ceases and a more colorful wardrobe is selected. *Entertainment Weekly* subjectively apprises the public of the latest fashion and cultural trends by informing us what's "in," what's "so five minutes ago," and what's "out."

A phase can also be a more typical rather than an atypical portion of a particular process or system. Most new ventures, such as the first day on the job, the first days of school, or the first week of fieldwork, include what might be labeled an initiation or orientation phase in which all participants become acquainted with and accustomed to new ways of working. Other phases follow, depending on the particular process or system and its contexts. According to Fullan, even the change process itself in educational reform has three broad phases:

> Phase I—variously labeled initiation, mobilization, or adoption—consists of the process that leads up to and includes a decision to adopt or proceed with a change. Phase II—implementation or initial use (usually the first two or three years of use)—involves the first experiences of attempting to put an idea or reform into practice. Phase III—called continuation, incorporation, routinization, or institutionalization—refers to whether the change gets built in as an

ongoing part of the system or disappears by way of a decision to discard or through attrition. . . . [E]vents at one phase can feed back to alter decisions made at previous stages, which then proceed to work their way through in a continuous interactive way. (2001, p. 50)

Characteristic of a phase is a beginning and end, though these may not necessarily exist as specific moments in time or be defined and contained by specific initiating and concluding actions. An epiphany, however, may set a new course of participant actions in motion, suggesting the beginning of a new phase and/or the conclusion of the previous one. Glick et al., addressing longitudinal studies in organization science, prescribe the search for "absolute beginning and end points of the change process" (1995, p. 144). Granted, some events may have discrete beginnings and endings. When a not-for-profit organization receives news that its annual funding will be severely decreased, the initiating action begins a new phase of change as budgets are readjusted and survival strategies are implemented for the next fiscal year. But many participant changes in social science investigation are gradual and subtle, sometimes not immediately apparent until months or years of data are summarized and reduced to a single page or matrix. Think of viewing a two-hour videotape on fast-forward for ten minutes. By compressing that video, we can look deductively for both gradual and sudden changes in its contents and interpret the transformations. Unfortunately, by sacrificing the experience of viewing the video in real time or slow motion, we lose opportunities to observe the nuances of change and their distinct separation into discrete phases. A metaphor: Think of longitudinal data as a run-on sentence. Our task is to find the appropriate places to insert commas (phases), periods (stages), and new paragraphs (cycles). Or, consider a dramatic metaphor: A phase is a scene; a stage is an act; and a cycle is a trilogy of plays.

Stages
The saying "a stage of life" suggests a longer period in a person's lifetime, during which the actions are composed of particular qualities—typical or atypical—in human development. Adolescence, a period of roughly five to seven years and characterized by particular biological, cognitive, psychological, and social changes is one example. "Midlife crises" or "major life transitions" for many adults in their late thirties through early fifties are other examples. Each academic year of a four-year baccalaureate program can be perceived as a stage of student development. Reutter et al. interviewed and surveyed a panel of nursing students from their freshman through their senior year to study their socialization processes, "Data were analyzed by comparing data from students within

the same year for similarities and differences in their perspectives. Comparisons were also made between years, that is, comparisons between all the students in first year and all the students in second year, and so on. Finally . . . the data were examined to see what changes could be observed in students as they progressed from year to year" (1997, p. 151).

The researchers observed that the preprofessionals' learning and socialization progressed from a functionalist through an interactionist approach. Each academic year or stage was assigned a descriptive phrase based on the primary theme in the data: First Year: "Learning the Ideal"; Second Year: "Confronting Reality"; Third Year: "Becoming Comfortable with Reality"; and Fourth Year: "Extending beyond the Reality of Student Practice."

One major difference between a phase and a stage is that the latter suggests cumulative progression of some sort. The development and experiences during infancy, early childhood, and later childhood accumulate to shape to a large degree a young person's adolescence. These stages, in turn, create a foundation for the next stage: young adulthood. Some researchers may call these stages "passages," suggesting not only time-bound periods, but also movement between one and the other. Like phases, a stage has a beginning and end, though they may not exist as specific moments in time or be defined and contained by specific initiating and concluding actions. And in both, duration becomes a critical dynamic to examine change processes.

A stage suggests cumulative progression of some sort

Adams stresses that "human beings are never 'in' a stage. Stage is a metaphor for growth or change," and sequential stages exhibit greater "complexity" and "differentiation" (1997, p. 40). Hence, stages could also include descriptions of transitional processes—the threshold between periods. We're taught that in graphic conceptual mapping of qualitative data, what's important is not only the category boxes or bins, but also the lines and arrows connecting them. The same can be said of stages. What's important is not only how a stage is defined and characterized, but how or why participants make their transition from one stage through the next (see fig. 6.7).

Petrocelli (2002) describes four transition processes between five stages in the Transtheoretical Model (TTM) of counseling. One example includes:

From Preparation to Action
    Clients at the preparation stage have taken small behavioral and mental actions necessary for change. These actions indicate their potential commitment and may be enhanced through exploration of reasons for and against changing

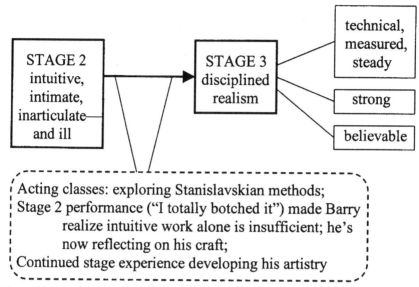

Figure 6.7   A transition-through-stages process diagram from the Barry Study

and an inventory of strengths and weaknesses that may serve to promote or in-hibit particular strategies. . . . [The] process of self-liberation tends to be most prevalent for individuals when attempting to change with or without therapy interventions. Gestalt therapy is the leading approach that has been identified as fitting most appropriately with the respective process of TTM at the prepa-ration stage. (p. 26)

Stages may be perceived not as stationary levels of a staircase, but as a moving escalator. A stage is not a still-life portrait, but an action-filled video clip. Surges or epiphanies can set a new stage in motion, but the cumulative nature of stages makes the distinct separation of them within the data more difficult for the researcher to discern. Also, some stages can be cyclical (ex-plained in the next section), such as Winkelman's cultural shock and adap-tation, which he calls "both sequential and cyclical. The shift from crises to adjustment and adaptation can repeat as one encounters new crises, requir-ing additional adjustments" (1994, p. 122).

Cycles

Cycles are repetitive waves of clustered participant actions. For example, do-mestic violence can be cyclical when the actions carry across generations: Children who are abused grow up to be parents who sometimes abuse their children who grow up to be parents who sometimes abuse their children, and so on. Some of us may be acquainted with people we label "burnout personalities" who go through self-destructive cycles: They work hard, they get overwhelmed, they crash, they recover, they go back to work, they work hard, they get overwhelmed, they crash, they recover, they go back to work, and so on. An intervening condition such as counseling, a reorganization of workplace conditions, or an epiphanic episode of self-realization after personal or material loss might break these self-destructive cycles. Frequency, tempo, and duration of actions become critical dynamics to examine in patterns such as these. For example, Wolcott (1984) observes that the annual cycle of the elementary school principalship in the 1960s was neither the nine-month academic year, nor the twelve-month calendar year. The principal's annual cycle was "instead comprised of an endless array of overlapping cycles of about 19 months' duration" (p. 181), which included preparatory planning for the next school year during the current one, plus the current year's administrative closure after classes ended. Year-round school schedules in some districts and the administrative demands of today may influence and affect a new cycle duration for its leadership.

A small but important distinction to make here is the difference between *cyclical, routine,* and *ritualistic.* For example, an obsessive compulsive's need to complete a number of specific and particular tasks before going to bed might be ritualistic. But the unswerving, mandatory consistency of those tasks each night makes them routine. These routine actions repeated through time become cyclical. My morning workday ritual consists of making coffee, listening to messages on my voice mail, turning on the computer to read e-mail, checking my office mailbox, then prioritizing the day's tasks. The specific daily actions are my rituals; the consistency of them is my routine; and the repetitive, daily occurrence of them throughout a week, a month, or a year, is my morning work cycle.

Multiple Rhythms

When reviewing longitudinal qualitative data, examine clusters of patterns or routines and rituals that could be constructed into phases, stages, and/or cycles, or new multirhythmic patterns all together. As noted earlier, some stages may be cyclical, and one or more phases may be embedded within a stage whose related parts may or may not be the sum of a stage's whole. For example, in the Theatre Response Study grades K–1 children recalled particular, small visual details from larger scenic elements on stage, but this response pattern dissipated in grade 2. Among the many other patterns consistent during the first three years of the study, their two-year attention to visual detail was just one phase within the longer three-year stage of response:

Stage One, Kindergarten through Second Grade—Me and the World of the Play:
   The child attends to what the play "is." Interpretations center on the immediate worlds created by the production. The story and the enjoyment received from the event are of primary importance to the child: "How can I be part of this event?" (Saldaña, 1996, p. 81)

Later, most grades 3–4 treatment children, in their natural developmental period of emotional ambivalence, described poignant, ironic, or bittersweet moments in plays by combining the only emotion vocabulary they knew, "Sorta happy and sorta sad," or "A different kind of happy—a floating happy." This response pattern, observed in two ponds of data collected a year apart from each other, is a typical phase within the middle childhood stage. In my interpretation of results, the children's emotionally ambivalent responses were but one pattern among several in grades 3–4 data that characterized an introspective and reflexive stage of child audience response:

Stage Two, Third through Fourth Grade—The Play and My World:
   The child still attends to the world of the play, but now examines how that world affects his or her own personal world. There is introspection and the beginning of critical examination: "What does this event have to offer me?" (Saldaña, 1996, p. 81)

As data from the Theatre Response Study were pooled, my interpretations suggested that general characteristics of children's responses appeared within three separate grade groups: K–2, 3–4, and 5–6. Several drama education handbooks for teachers separate elementary activities into two levels: K–3 and 4–6. This traditional but artificial dichotomy was my mode of thinking as I proceeded through the analysis and sought a discrete turning point in children's responses ending with grade 3 and beginning with grade 4. But as I coded grade 3 data, a host of new response categories emerged that contrasted to the generally positive responses from grades K–2. Hence, the original plan to pool grades K–3 data was discarded. Again, different response categories emerged in grade 5 as children interpreted stage characters with greater accelerated depth than previous levels. At the upper elementary grades, their ability to separate actor from character interrelated with higher evaluative responses. Also, selected categories from grades K–4 data would decrease in proportion or cease all together in grades 5–6. Hence, the third stage of children's responses to theatre emerged:

Stage Three, Fifth through Sixth Grade—The Play and the World around Me:
   Evaluation of the event is based on the child's own world of experiences and values. Some children extend beyond the immediate world created by the

play to find similarities between its fictional action and reality. Interpretations of characters transform into personal perceptions of the human condition: "How successful is this event and how is it relevant to my life?" (Saldaña, 1996, p. 81)

I suspect that three general ponds of data may appear in other longitudinal qualitative studies with grades K–6 children, due primarily to an interrelationship with the researcher's particular data and general developmental trends of youth. Just as Bogdan and Biklen (1998) recommend that each day's field notes be given a summarizing title to capture the major theme of the observations, so should ponds and pools of data be appropriately titled with a brief synthesis and summary to capture their essence.

Specific lengths of time cannot be used to differentiate a phase from a stage (e.g., a phase is one year, but a stage is two through five years). Time—including the property of duration—is contextual to each particular research project. For example, Berliner (1997) examines "the development of expertise" in classroom teachers and observes cumulative qualities particular to this profession depending on the number of years of experience. Berliner labels these teachers "novices" (1–2 years), "advanced beginners" (2–3 years), "competent" (3–4 years), "proficient" (5 or more years), and "expert" (beyond 5–6 years). Note that there is no specific cut-off point in terms of years for his conceptual stages, rather, there is overlap. Individual teacher personalities and contexts prevent a rigid time frame from being established. Simply put, some teachers develop expertise faster (or slower) than others.

Specific lengths of time cannot be used to differentiate a phase from a stage

Just as an orchestra conductor establishes and controls the tempo of a musical performance, contextual and intervening conditions can decelerate, accelerate, or maintain the "implicit rhythms" of participant actions, attitudes, values, and belief systems within phases, stages, cycles, and long-term evolutionary patterns. Benjamin (1998, pp. 242–43) cites and pools other researchers' work to profile five stages of ethnic identity development: preencounter or conformity, encounter or dissonance, resistance or immersion, introspection, and integrative or internalization. The first two stages progress from an initial denial or ignorance of racist environments (preencounter or conformity), through "personal experiences with prejudice that leads the individual to question the beliefs and assumptions she/he held during the previous stage" (242). In the encounter or dissonance stage, the individual's development from the first toward the next stage will depend on the types or amount of prejudicial encounters and the ability to reflect critically on their impact with regards to personal ethnic identity. In the resistance or immersion stage, some may angrily reject the dominant culture, elect a separatist and tightly defined cultural lifestyle, and remain in this stage. Others, depending on contextual and intervening conditions, may negotiate and resolve personal identity issues to progress toward the latter stages of introspection and integrative or internalization. The point is that a specific number of months or years, or even general types of epiphanies, cannot function as rigid borders or markers for these five stages. Progression and/or regression from one through the other depend on participant agency, social interactions, and contextual and intervening conditions.

Phases, stages, and cycles are traditional patterns for constructing time-based flows to human actions. But Dey reminds us that "there can be a multiplicity of temporal perspectives" (1999, p. 218), and phases, stages, and cycles are just three options available to us. Hargreaves et al. describe the motion of change in a five-year education study as a "distinctive spiral pattern of urgency, energy, agency, then more energy in schools where teachers made significant changes in their practices. . . . When the conditions were right and the necessary supports were provided, these bursts of energy led in an upward spiral to an increased sense of agency and productivity, which in time released even more energy as the spiral continued" (2001, pp. 119–20).

The vertical spiral pattern is also employed in counseling's stages of change in the Transtheoretical Model for problem behaviors, which progress through client precontemplation, contemplation, preparation, action, and maintenance (Petrocelli, 2002, p. 24). James Pinkerton ("Anything Goes," 2002) interrelates two time models when he observes how the cyclical nature of cultural permissiveness now interplays with the linearity of technology. The latter, he comments, has generated "new styles of confession and revelation" (p. V2) in media and cyberspace. Modern American culture will most likely not cycle or pendulum swing back as far to a conservative ethos.

Chapman, reviewing the feminist literature on constructions of adolescence, cites the work of psychoanalyst Louise Kaplan, who argues that the teenage years are a period of embattlement between past and future selves, "Adolescence is a time of active deconstruction, construction, reconstruction—a period in which past, present, and future are rewoven and strung together on the threads of fantasies and wishes that do not necessarily follow the laws of linear chronology. The adolescent phase of life is not a mere space of time that stands between the past of infancy and the future of adulthood" (1999, p. 5).

This reconception of a period in human development is just one way recent scholarship explores the "fuzzy" and "blurred" nature of traditional time-based boundaries and meanings. Bill Maxwell confirms that "[y]outh is Janus-faced. It looks into the past and into the future simultaneously. It looks into the past when it takes from history and tradition only what it needs to ground itself in the present. Once grounded, youth creates and invents, dragging older generations into the stream of change and new experience" ("Who Are . . . ," 1999, p. E24).

Recent interpretive research also explores artistic metaphors from such fields as dance, music, and theatre to shape ethnographic observations into more complex, performative, and improvisational patterns (Janesick, 1994; Saldaña, 1999). Rhythm is an element common to all art forms but most readily applied to music, and its varieties are infinite. The rhythmic patterns you detect in your data may be as progressively steady and symmetrical as Johann Pachelbel's "Canon in D" or as varied, unpredictable, and complex as Philip Glass's *Einstein on the Beach*. How we each live our lives through time, and thus how we interpret and reconstruct it as researchers, depends on the qualitative compositions we hear in our minds.

What Is the Through-Line of the Study?

The Through-Line As Change

Actors and directors working on a play production collaborate to define each character's through-line—that is, the prominent, consistent flow throughout the course of the script that drives his or her action. In Henrik Ibsen's *A Doll's House*, Nora's through-line is her growing awareness of how traditional turn-of-the-century gender roles in marriage have oppressed her development as a woman—indeed, as a human being. In Luis Valdez's *I Don't Have to Show You No Stinking Badges*, Ronnie, a Harvard law student, returns home to his parents in flux about his future. The character's through-line in this tragicomedy is a tormented trial-and-error search for his life purpose embedded within the social context of his ethnic identity. In most realistic theatrical events, the audience watches characters in action and interaction as they *change* during the course of the play. These changes

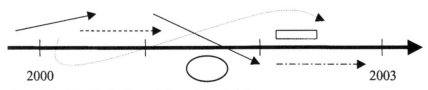

2000   2003

Figure 6.8 What is the through-line of the study?

are the results of how (and if) they achieve their wants, needs, and desires through personal agency—tactics—against the agency of opposing forces—obstacles.

A longitudinal qualitative study also benefits from a through-line that describes, connects, and summarizes the researcher's primary observations of participant change (see fig. 6.8). Methodologists have used various terms or processes to identify what I label as a through-line: Strauss and Corbin's (1998) central category, Erickson's (1986) key assertion, Miles and Huberman's (1994) central phenomenon, Fetterman's (1998) crystallization, Smith's (2001) dominant variables, and Holloway et al.'s (1995) leitmotiv. A graduate student (Brown, 1997) once labeled what I was seeking from her dissertation's final chapter—a passage that summarized the essence of her case study's longevity in the teaching profession—as the "killer paragraph." Artists will call this phenomenon the essence of a work, or an "Ah-ha!" moment—an aesthetic experience of emotional, meaning-making impact. Call it what you will, the through-line can be a single word, a phrase, a sentence, or a paragraph with an accompanying narrative that describes, analyzes, and/or interprets the participant's changes throughout time by analyzing its thematic flow—its qualitative trajectory. Depending on the interpretations the researcher conceptualizes from the data corpus, the through-line may also suggest the *meaning* of changes observed.

> A through-line describes, connects, and summarizes the researcher's primary observations of participant change

Elements of the Through-Line

The through-line may be strikingly evident within a descriptive database, or it may be a researcher's interpretive construction of the longitudinal phenomena. A through-line can emerge from systematic datum-by-datum analysis or from imaginative, holistic conceptualization of the corpus. There is no magic algorithm for answering this question, but there is one stipulation: The through-line focuses on changes through time.

From the Theatre Response Study, grounded theory analysis of final exit interviews with child participants yielded a flow conceptualized as a single word—*value*—when they were asked: Is theatre necessary? Note how the following through-line is described with an explanatory narrative that includes (a) references to time ("seven years" and "throughout this period"), (b) processual terms ("shaped," "developed," and "affected"), and (c) markers or descriptions of beginnings, middles, and/or endings of the participants' journey at various locations through time ("sixth grade"):

A core category in these final exit interviews is *value*. Children's personal experiences with and thus memories of theatre events have provided a background for reflection at the sixth grade level. Their current preferences for content may have been shaped by seven years of particular treatment experiences. Throughout this period, participants have developed and exhibited a spectrum of theatre perception and response skills. Also throughout this period, family members may have directly (or indirectly) affected their children's personal experiences with and attitudes toward theatre, while peers may currently be influencing their publicly displayed attitudes toward the art. These factors are just some of the contributors to a sixth grade child's personal perceptions of theatre's necessity—i.e., its value—now and in one's future. (Saldaña, 1995, pp. 25–26)

The through-line can be a simple, descriptive key assertion. Also from the Theatre Response Study, "A seven year treatment of classroom drama, recreational theatre, and theatre viewing experiences generated developmental, cumulative, and sometimes idiosyncratic 'significant differences' in audience response between the [treatment] participants and second-site children . . . in this study" (Saldaña, 1996, p. 70).

A through-line can consist of an extended, interpretive narrative that includes references to time, processual terms, and markers. From the Survival Study:

Over the course of a year and a half, Nancy did not make any sweeping generalizations about Hispanics; she was attentive to social complexity and perceptive of cross-ethnic differences. Nancy may have entered Martinez School with a Eurocentric conception of drama and personal worldview, but over time she learned to survive by adapting to her classroom environment—the final stage of cultural shock recovery. She did not "go native" or assimilate completely as a Hispanic, but she did demonstrate a willingness to function cross-culturally, thus equipping her with more expertise of the Martinez community, thereby enabling her to reconceptualize drama for her specific teaching context. (Saldaña, 1997, pp 41–42)

An In Vivo Through-Line

The participants' own language may often reveal a through-line operant in their lives. Search the interview transcripts and field notes for recurring in vivo words or topics that appear to hold meaning for the respondent across time. Remember, too, that it is not just numeric frequency that suggests importance. Importance can also rest with infrequent yet salient words that hold summative power for other categories that have emerged. Just as "survival" was a through-line for Nancy's work as a beginning teacher, "spiritual" was the in vivo axis for Barry's conception of theatre and his artistic development as an actor.

Barry was raised in a moderately religious family environment. Spirituality, in its traditional Christian sense, was practiced by his parents during his childhood and early teenage years. His mother shared in an interview during Barry's junior year in high school:

> He's highly valued at our church. He's been a leader in the youth group for years. But just in the last month he's said, "You know, I don't wanna go to Sunday school anymore, I don't wanna go to youth group. I think that the kids there are hypocrites because they'll say, 'I'm a Christian,' and then they'll turn around and make fun of each other." That really bugs him. . . . He said, "I think I can share my spirituality better by being happy around people, and not being afraid to talk about what God's done in my life." OK, I can't argue with that. He's in a much higher plane in that respect than a lot of adults I know.

Throughout the course of the longitudinal study, Barry's spiritual beliefs were evident, but the church's contributions were gradually supplemented (if not replaced) by the spiritual fulfillment he also received from theatre. Barry reflected, "the theatre is someplace that I feel so comfortable in. When those lights go down, and I'm sitting in the audience, it's like I lose all self and I become one with the show. It becomes almost a spiritual thing. I think theatre is very spiritual for me."

Just as Barry detested the hypocrisy of his peers in his church's youth group, he detested the amateurishness his fellow thespians exhibited during rehearsals and performances, "I try to relay to people that just because it's high school theatre, that doesn't mean that we can go out and just goof around. Sometimes I have a real problem with turning people off because I take it so seriously." Barry's psychological intervention in sixth grade was intended to help him resolve his feelings of being misunderstood by others. Five years later, he was still experiencing that dilemma, "I think a lot of people don't understand the spiritual connection that I feel. I kind of assumed that other actors feel that way because I see it in some people's eyes—you know, some people have the passion. But some people just don't understand."

When you search for through-lines, take note of the contexts in which the in vivo word or phrase is embedded. As Barry's interview transcripts were reviewed during analysis, "spiritual" appeared whenever the church and performance were addressed, suggesting an interrelationship:

> What I learned in acting classes will stick with me and I will use it subconsciously when that moment of character takes place, when that moment of concentration and focus takes place. People talk about learning how to act, and I think my feeling towards it is: it's just a spiritual thing, it just happens. . . . When I'm backstage and I'm ready to perform, there's a bond with the people around you and with you in the theatre. There's all this nervous energy there. . . . It's making a spiritual connection with your audience and drawing them into the show, saying, "Look, this is my character, this isn't me up here."

Philosophers and theorists dating as far back as Aristotle have long recognized the connections between religion and theatre, so one may propose that the formulation of this through-line is nothing new or significant in terms of general knowledge. But what *is* unique to this life history is Barry's artistic maturity and his integration of the aesthetic and spiritual domains, qualities often missing in other adolescents who tend to focus solely on the "fun" and glamour of theatrical activity. Barry articulated not just personal meaning but a higher purpose when I asked him, "What do you get out of Theatre? What's the payoff?":

> I've been going to church my whole life, but I have a hard time subscribing to certain beliefs. When I found theatre, it was—I keep saying it's a spiritual experience. I really believe it is. That's when everything is *right*. When people come to the theatre, it's my job to draw them out of trying to figure out how to pay the bills, or trying to figure out how to pass their midterms. It's my job to draw them into my world, and to show them what a spiritual connection it is, what a real world theatre is. It's my job show them the little things in life that are truly beautiful. So, theatre's a very spiritual thing. It's my version of church.

Hence, the assertion I composed describing Barry's through-line was: From his sophomore through senior years in high school, Barry gradually interchanged the insufficient spiritual fulfillment he received at church with the more personal and purposeful spiritual fulfillment he experienced through theatre.

Other Types of Through-Lines
Through-lines needn't always derive from in vivo codes or a repertory of standard psychological or sociological constructs. Arts-based research offers simile and metaphor as ways of conceptualizing a through-line. Diamond and

Mullen even use the devices to describe the process, "Until sorted like beads onto a chain, events have no inevitable order. They remain separate, haphazard, episodic, and broken until, like a newspaper or film editor, we impose on them a sense of unfolding or collapsed purpose. . . . We project meaning onto our development to see it as some combination of flowing-blocked, smooth-abrupt, lush-arid, intense-deadened, causal-random, isolated-patterned" (1999, pp. 79–80).

As a theatre artist, I call on my knowledge of plays and playwrights to describe my mental states and totality of life thus far. Perhaps only theatre practitioners would truly understand me at first instinct when I say, "My life has been a Chekhovian play." To nonartists who may have no knowledge of what this reference means, my similes and metaphors can emerge from more everyday understandings, "My life's been one long rush hour with the radiator overheating." Similes and metaphors capture the aesthetic totality of a phenomenon, experience, or a life and, like data, they should never speak for themselves. Any accompanying narrative should explain the specific connotations made and parallel life associations drawn from "rush hour" (e.g., the frustration, the sense of going nowhere, or feeling locked in), and why "the radiator overheating" is an essential addendum to the image (e.g., feeling pressured or holding in one's boiling rage).

Some might perceive that collapsing vast amounts of longitudinal qualitative data into a single through-line is a reductionistic, structuralist task that negates the inherent complexity of a study or a human being. Constructing the through-line is not the ultimate analytic or interpretive goal of a longitudinal study, nor is it intended as a "grand theory" for a participant's life course. It is just one of several data summary strategies for springboarding into more extended and complex storytelling. To me, a through-line is simply a way of allowing my mind and perhaps others' to grasp the conceptual essence of the overwhelming magnitude of longitudinal data. Think of yourself going to your high school reunion where you run into a friend you haven't seen for ten years. When you ask "So, how's life been treating you?" most often we hear a summary statement first, "Oh, okay, I guess," "Not so good," or "Well, it's been an adventure." Then you might hear some of the details of those past ten years. But had it not been for that opening summary—that essence—you would have been inadequately prepared for the consequent narrative, and possibly would have gotten lost in the vast litany of year-by-year details. Hence, a through-line of a longitudinal study is not just an analytic or interpretive summary of findings, it can also function as a reader's through-line for a sense of continuity.[5]

Boal, a theatre artist-activist who developed a series of intricate session designs for therapeutic intervention through drama, prefaces the necessity of his lengthy directions to workshop participants with, "Things can be complex without being complicated." I feel the same insight holds for a longitudinal qualitative study and its accompanying presentation. The final report should "be complex without being complicated," and the through-line, albeit one of the latter outcomes of data analysis, serves as a way of holistically introducing or summarizing the complexity of that epic journey to the audience.[6]

> "Things can be complex without being complicated"

Conclusion: Looking Back at the Journey

Additional Questions

New and different research questions will emerge, particular to the study at hand. In fact, the initial stages of a longitudinal study may generate unexpected areas of inquiry worth pursuing if the researchers "allow the participants' responses to modify our concerns [and] to prompt other questions" (Yates and McLeod, 1996, p. 91).

Since each research study is contextual and particular, so are its questions. Smith, examining "significant school change" for an awards process, asked the following questions for an evaluation of each site:

- How meaningful is the change? Is it substantial rather than superficial?
- How deep and broad is the change? Is it systemic, rather than isolated?
- How is the change focused? Is it student centered, looking at teaching and learning?
- How is it measured? Is it solution or outcome oriented? (2001)

These questions appear to examine the dynamics and contextual and intervening conditions involving change through time. Since change is contextual, it makes sense that this particular awards process developed specific sets of questions and accompanying criteria for evaluation purposes.

Some answers raise new questions, and the learnings you acquire through longitudinal qualitative data analysis may generate inquiries beyond how, how much, in what ways, and why. These higher-order questions may relate to matters of policy, practice, and meaning. As I observed Nancy teach lower-income, Spanish-speaking children in her inner-city school setting, my long-term residency at the school reawakened both pleasant and painful memories of my own upbringing in a barrio. Her emergent educational philosophy and teaching practices conflicted with my personal assumptions of effective pedagogy. I found myself questioning my own attitudes, values, and beliefs as a university professor, questioning the presumptive authority of national standards in the arts, and questioning my methods of preservice teacher education. Critical reflection on why things are as they are leads to contemplation on how things could or should be—another worthwhile exercise in developing your sensitivity to change processes.

Questions are tools. It takes an expert craftsperson to work well with them, and a creative artist to use them in inspiring ways. A local television promotion for the film *Contact* stated, "In time, every question finds its answer." I cannot anticipate or predict the specific types of questions that may emerge from the analytic processes of your own particular longitudinal study, but I do encourage you to go beyond the sixteen questions profiled in this book. They are not comprehensive; they are starting points for discovering something more, something new, something deeper.

Go beyond the sixteen questions

I also encourage you not to pose a question directly related to your study into your final report unless you're willing to attempt an answer—or at the very least, a guess or a hunch. There has been a recent trend in qualitative inquiry to reflect deeply on elusive meanings generated from a project and then develop "tough questions." What personally annoys me is that sometimes these tough questions are rarely accompanied by tough answers, an inaction that puts us in parentheses, paralysis, and stalemate. This limbo of inquiry can, to some degree, be a healthy gestation period because the formulation of questions brings initial order to our confusion (Saldaña, 2001b). But I invest my limited and precious time reading research reports for answers, insight, and—if the writer's really good—profound revelation (Saldaña, 2001a), not for unanswered questions. There is no guarantee that a richly worded question will generate an equally rich answer. Sometimes, the "toughest" and most provocative questions are elegant: What is art? Does God exist? How do you *really* know?

The Journey's End

As I stated at the beginning, "What changes through time?" *is* the primary question for longitudinal qualitative studies. Theatre artists know that to maintain audience engagement with a play production, the script and its performance must continually arouse curiosity so that spectators will ask themselves: What happens next? As I reflect on my seven-year journey with kindergarteners through twelfth graders, my twenty months with Nancy, and my two and a half years with Barry, I realize I was asking myself all along: What happens next?

The questions presented in this book for assessing change should produce constructive answers along the way for novice researchers analyzing longitudinal qualitative data. Again, let me emphasize that these questions are not intended as a linear checklist to be answered in the order they were discussed. They are intended as iterative subsets of questions to consider on an "as needed" basis as fieldwork progresses and data are reviewed through time. To summarize and conclude:

Framing Questions
What is different from one pond or pool of data through the next? Studying vast amounts of qualitative data as they accumulate becomes a more manageable effort if the total corpus is divided into smaller units: beats of data, which imply action, motion, and fluidity—essential conceptual ideas for studying process and change. First, separate the vast ocean of longitudinal data into smaller, discrete time pools such as months or years. This will make the changes that may have occurred through time easier to identify and the analysis of those changes more efficient to conduct. Second, separate the time pools into even smaller beats: ponds. Here is where further subdivision of the data according to category, rather than time period, is more appropriate—although subdivision into shorter time periods is also possible. If general areas for observation or specific categories of change have not been predetermined, each study will have its own particular, emergent, and appropriate categories as determined by the researcher. Results from pooling multiple case study observations will be shaped not just by the qualitative lens but by the paradigm filter used for data collection and analysis.

Next, begin the systematic comparison of pond to pond, pond to pool, and pool to pool. Look for differences within and between categories to become more aware of the many possible contrasts, variability, and dynamics within and between the data. If you look exclusively for what is missing, you limit your search to what is absent rather than present. The "then and now" comparison limits the observations of adaptation and evolution. More sequential data ponds and pools permit a more nuanced analysis of change through time. Also, compare data carefully. Sometimes a possible answer to "What is different?" may very well be "Nothing at all," yet even this is noteworthy.

Since time is fluid, we do not always have to divide data for analysis into standard units such as weeks, months, or years, or look for change at fixed time intervals. When appropriate, let the data divide themselves. In other words, when you perceive or interpret that subtle-to-significant differences appear, regardless of when they happen in the data or time continua, a new beat begins. New pools and ponds are formed.

When do changes occur through time? Though it may be stating the obvious, knowing or inferring when actions and changes occur is a critical task in longitudinal data analysis. Date and chronicle all field notes, interviews, journal entries, and so on to maintain a documented record of the study as it progresses. Particular participant changes might interrelate with such contextual and intervening conditions as social, political, and cultural changes and historic events through time. Knowing when actions occurred will assist with charting such observations as increases, decreases, or idiosyncratic patterns. This ubiquitous task also enables you to examine the dynamics of change such as duration, frequency, and tempo, which then supports the development of conceptual phases, stages, cycles, or other rhythms of human action. Thus, permit new codes to emerge as a longitudinal study's data are gathered and analyzed. If change occurs in participants, then codes should also change to reflect those differences through time.

Longitudinal studies with children and adolescents, in particular, should chronicle observed changes according to their ages (years and months) or grade levels (with attention paid to the number of weeks or months into the academic year). This allows the researcher to assess whether any changes are part of developmental trends in humans documented in the research literature or related to contextual or intervening conditions in the participant's life such as home and school environments, unique classroom learning experiences, and personal epiphanies. Comparable attention should be given to documenting aspects of time in the field site as much as space.

Some methodologists prescribe that data from participant observation or interviews could be collected during standardized time frames (e.g., once a year over three years). But life and its accompanying changes, epiphanies in particular, do not always occur at fixed time intervals. Capturing participant change at the moment or during the period it occurs is sometimes due to good fortune—being at the right place at the right time—or interpreted in retrospect once a pool of data has been collected and change is inferred as data are reviewed and coded. The linearity of narrative's basic "beginning, middle, and end" sequencing tells tales of transformation. The use of transitional markers (e.g., "first," "then," "at the beginning of the fifth month," "towards the end of the study," and so on) provides the reader with a sense of process as participant change is described through time.

What contextual and intervening conditions appear to influence and affect participant changes through time? Critical to longitudinal qualitative data analysis is investigating how, how much, in what ways, and why certain actions occurred—the conditions involved with change. There is a specific history and course of events to every particular participant, setting, researcher, and study. Contexts are inextricably embedded within each particular research enterprise. Participant actions are rooted in social and cultural contexts, and what an individual researcher observes and interprets is rooted in his or her social and cultural contexts. Qualitative data cannot be analyzed in isolation, and in most cases we should not ask data to speak for themselves.

Influences and affects are constructs to replace the traditional, linear cause and effect. The former word choices are not just nouns, but rich verbs suggesting action and change, and evoke a more processual way of examining the complexity of change within participants. Change forces and consequences are multiple, networked, and collaged, not singular and isolated. Observing participants' tactics as they negotiate conflict (in its broadest sense) provides insight on how individuals act on and possibly change from it—that is, how they are influenced and affected by conflict. Since conflicts are potential sources or stimuli for participant action, and their negotiations with conflicts are suggestive of participant change through time, plotting allows the researcher to reflect on and speculate how and/or why events unfolded as they did. Interaction refers to the reverberative (i.e., continuously back and forth) influences and affects through time between humans, artifacts, physical environments, institutions, structures, processes, and/or abstractions. Individuals make sense from their personal interactions with the social and physical worlds, and assign interactions between nonhuman entities. Interplay refers to the associative (i.e., connected, combined, or integrated) influences and affects through time among any of the entities described. Individuals don't just "make sense" of the social and physical worlds; during interplay they construct deeper meaning from their synthesis of those worlds.

Contextual conditions are the participants' particular givens in their everyday social worlds and their particular interactions with them. These givens consist of personal actions, agency, structures, processes, and such social constructions as gender, class, and ethnicity. Contextual conditions are locations of and stimuli for numerous and multiple types of participant change. Structures and processes may not lend themselves immediately to observable changes through short-term durations, but through longitudinal study and the analysis of its qualitative data, the interpreted changes become more apparent. Since contexts are contextual, some conditions initiate greater change than others. Any contextual condition could be labeled an intervening condition, depending on how the participant and researcher interpret them. An intervening condition is a contextual condition perceived as a purposeful, unanticipated, or significant action, structure, or process that influences and affects participant change through time. Contextual conditions are background; intervening conditions are foreground, and can range from positive to negative impact.

One's entry point in the field is not a baseline with which to compare consequent observations, but the start of investigating what antecedent contextual and intervening conditions preceded the researcher's moment of entry to influence and affect the current status. Also, throughout time, change changes. This means that contextual and intervening conditions—the interactive, interplaying, and cyclical nature of structures, processes, and human actions—influence and affect change through time, which influences and affects consequent change through time, which influences and affects consequent change through time, and so on.

What are the dynamics of participant changes through time? In qualitative research, the dimensions and variability of the data are its dynamics. Applicable continua are not only quantitative in character (e.g., "a little" to "a lot"), but also qualitative (e.g., "boring" to "fun," "enthusiastic" to "burned out"). Dynamics of participant change can be described using traditional rubrics or Likert-type words, or interpreted with words and phrases along a broad, open-ended ocean of antonyms. But bear in mind that a continuum is merely a straight line with two end points, and "less" and "more" soon become inadequate descriptors of change in a phenomenon's quality. Using in vivo codes to chart the dynamics of change through time provides a richer and more participant-centered basis for analysis.

Identifying and describing the dynamics of change are approximate and highly interpretive acts. Verbs, adjectives, and adverbs used in field notes and analytic memos should properly note and, to some degree, chart the processes observed, particularly with such time-oriented dynamics as tempo, frequency, and duration. The language we use to describe process and change should be chosen carefully, lest we mislead the reader (and ourselves) with what we witnessed in the field. Dynamics of participant change are examined to infer the nuances and subtlety of contextual conditions, to determine the magnitude of intervening conditions' influences and affects, or to place the participant's actions and changes in perspective or contrast to others. Se-lected longitudinal qualitative studies should pay particular attention to dy-namics if they are essential elements of a particular research question or if there are emergent patterns that appear in the data suggesting refined focus and further investigation.

What preliminary assertions (propositions, findings, results, conclusions, in-terpretations, and theories) about participant changes can be made as data analy-sis progresses? Qualitative methods texts advise us to analyze data during as well as after data collection, and longitudinal studies add additional consid-erations. If change is constant, then so is our analysis of it. As data are ex-amined chronologically (with additional data collection remaining), expect to revise assertions continually, since data located in the future will influ-ence and affect assertions developed in the past. These iterative and cycli-cal tasks may become time consuming and sometimes frustrating. The payoff, however, is cognitive ownership and deeper understanding of the data and a holistic perspective rather than a narrow focus, equipping you to formulate a key assertion or through-line that summarizes the journey.

Erickson (1986) recommends that researchers develop a key assertion that represents the salient data corpus and related subassertions to describe the constituent parts of that corpus. These same summary principles can be ap-plied to longitudinal data. The key assertion of a longitudinal qualitative study summarizes how the data, as a whole, reflect general participant change throughout the course of the study. Subassertions can chronicle the more de-tailed changes at designated time markers or the movement through specific periods of time such as phases, stages, and cycles.

Descriptive Questions

What increases or emerges through time? In longitudinal studies, a simple emer-gence or proportionate increase of a variable or category frequency may sug-gest some type of change. Some of these increases might interrelate with other observed changes or be linked to certain contextual or intervening conditions. Changes in quality throughout time may be accompanied by or synonymous with proportionate increases. One person's quality is another person's quantity, and these differing perspectives influence and affect what is observed in the field. Nevertheless, both approaches can work in a com-plementary or integrated manner. Measuring increases through content analysis and category frequencies alone, however, limits the potential of qualitative data analysis for richer levels of meaning. In many longitudinal studies, "increased," "grew," and "more" are words often used to describe the types of participant changes observed. When these words are employed as typical descriptors, this suggests an oversimplified conception of change processes. The possibility also exists that only selected phenomena for examination were established early in the study, which narrowed the parameters of future observations and limited the opportunities to discover the complexities surrounding change.

Throughout time, new and different actions in participants may subtly emerge, but not necessarily with the suddenness of a surge or a 180-degree change after an epiphany. Emergence of or simple increases in qualitative categories cannot be examined in isolation, for they are only part of the analytic puzzle, particularly if they are interpreted as cumulative. Also, the magnitude or size of change may indicate other factors at work. These surges merit examination separately from generally smooth increases in proportions or qualities across time.

What is cumulative through time? A cumulative affect is some type of change in participant quality as a result of successive experiences. Cumulative affects may be discerned from successive ponds of data merging to form larger ponds and pools. For example, three related data sets located across three beats of time serve as time triangulation to support an observation of cumulative change.

There are subtle differences between the terms "growth" and "development." "Growth" implies a quantitative increase across time such as height and weight. "Development" implies more complex qualitative characteristics across time, such as improvement, betterment, and transformation. Developmental variables are more ephemeral, socially constructed, not accessible to precise measurement, and include such concepts as empathy and values. Cumulative affects through time are outcomes of growth and/or development—quantitative and/or qualitative factors interplaying or interacting with each other. Studies in child development should be particularly attuned to cumulative affects because these profiles can become researcher-constructed phases or stages of childhood and adolescence. But always be conscious of idiosyncratic patterns in research involving young people, since developmental change does not always occur in a neatly linear or additive manner.

What kinds of surges or epiphanies occur through time? Just as we attribute to young children physical growth spurts, so, too, can there be growth and developmental spurts—surges—in qualitative data. If the longitudinal study is a field experiment, certain treatments may accelerate what would happen naturally to second-site participants at a later time. Social and cultural changes may produce negative consequences if the rate of change is too fast. An epiphany or critical incident experienced by the participant and documented in the data could also be loosely interpreted as a surge if the event produces relatively sudden changes in, or directions of, the participant's consequent actions. Participants might not think to disclose significant events or turning points from their lives, so researchers should include such inquiry during longitudinal data collection. What the participant him- or herself perceives as an important event should not be discounted. The magnitude of an epiphany and its consequent affects vary. Finally, data collected prior to these surges and epiphanies should be examined carefully, for it may be that missing or incomplete records could mislead the interpretation of successive records.

What decreases or ceases through time? Some decreases in certain actions may be developmentally appropriate for young participants, and some decreases may be interrelated with increases in other categories or actions. But the researcher's personal worldview may influence and affect how decreases are interpreted. A decrease of action to one observer may be perceived as an increase of a different action to another. All decreases and cessations should be interpreted cautiously when time pools and category ponds are compared, because the quality and contents of our field notes themselves change through time. Initial observations may consist of a broad variety of actions, and then consist of more focused details or categories of emergent importance as fieldwork progresses. Also, the longer we're immersed in the field the more we become familiar with and take for granted what exists in the environment. Thus, field note entries may show evidence of decreased detail and a cessation of logging the contextual conditions.

What remains constant or consistent through time? Constancy and consistency are indicators of patterns, cues for extracting themes, and baseline data for possible future change. What is constant or consistent through time might also suggest that something is missing through time. Nonchanges can be indicative of positive stability, but in negative contexts they can indicate inefficiency, stagnancy, bad habits, or dysfunction. In some categories of longitudinal data, there may be no overt or discernible changes in frequency or quality due to the nature of the data collected. The constant or consistent presence of particular data may reveal either something significant at work or nothing out of the ordinary. In some cases, what appears as a constant, pervasive phrase or pattern in the data corpus might be background routine—the given contextual conditions—rather than foreground issues for analysis. Likewise, some codes may not appear with numeric frequency but may still hold salient and significant constancy if they possess summative power for major and minor categories. In some cases of coding, less is more.

Interviewing the participant about his or her life and social world before you entered the field, and reviewing past archival documents, will give you a sense of history to compare with what is actually observed during fieldwork. With children in particular, consistent presence yet "nongrowth" in particular categories might suggest latency, and developmental change may occur at a later time. Be cautious of automatically assuming that constancy is evident because "nothing is happening" in the field. Cultures are not fixed social systems—they are constantly evolving as they maintain essential and sometimes self-destructive traditions. Paradoxically, change itself can be constant and consistent.

What is idiosyncratic through time? In qualitative analysis, idiosyncrasy refers to data patterns that are inconsistent, ever-shifting, multidirectional, and, during fieldwork, unpredictable. Idiosyncratic patterns may arise when the dynamics of cumulative actions reach extreme ends of a continuum or extend onto multiple locations of a data landscape/timescape. A category that fluctuates in the data may indicate contextual and intervening conditions interacting and interplaying with each other through time. Also, some phenomena and behaviors do not lend themselves to orderly, consistent development. Idiosyncrasy is sometimes a legitimate way to explain random and unpredictable human actions and observations if it can be supported and justified. But when idiosyncrasy appears in the data, the possibility of a flawed coding system should not be ruled out, nor should the possibility that an insufficient amount of data exist for analysis.

Too often, we associate pattern with symmetrical or consistent repetition. But patterns can consist of multirhythmic, asymmetrical, and seemingly fluctuating strings of action. Idiosyncratic phenomena, as perceived by the researcher, are not like a miscellaneous assembly of jigsaw pieces from multiple puzzles that do not and cannot fit together. Rather, idiosyncratic data are like miscellaneous craft items awaiting assembly to create a new and unique artistic product. Idiosyncrasy is a pattern and not to be dismissed from analysis, especially with data gathered from the perspectives of young people. Frequent idiosyncrasy, however, may set limits on the transferability of findings to other contexts.

What is missing through time? Just because something is missing doesn't mean that nothing is being influenced and affected. Examining what is missing also entails a search for what is present. During the analytic cycle, there may be data that the researcher somehow intuits should be there but aren't. Noticeably absent categories may suggest that the constancy or consistency of contextual conditions, or the as-yet-undetected intervening condition, might inhibit the presence of something to emerge. What is missing could be the consequence of a decrease that occurred earlier in the chronological data record.

The researcher may become aware of critical areas not initially addressed in a preestablished interview or observation protocol. Final exit interviews with participants, conducted during the latter portion of a longitudinal study, are not only opportunities for closure or assessment, but are also researcher opportunities to confirm whether the absence (or presence) of particular phenomena or data have shaped their course of actions (or nonactions) across time. Throughout data collection and analysis, contemplating what is missing is a worthwhile exercise to both reflect on how the absence of something may influence and affect participants, and to exhaust the possibilities of what might have been, could have been, or should have been present during the study.

Analytic and Interpretive Questions

Which changes interrelate through time? Interrelationship is the researcher's observation of overlapping ponds or pools of data within and across beats of time—reflections on the interactions and interplay of social actions or phenomena. Graphic data displays and matrices permit the researcher to scan summarized observations repeatedly to assess the general processual flow of changes through time. This process may also reveal links or interrelationships between sets of observations, leading the researcher to infer possible contextual or intervening conditions influencing and affecting particular ponds and pools of data. Interrelationship may also be suggested when similar or related answers appear in response to several of the sixteen questions simultaneously. Certain actions in data may suggest other actions—for example, an increase interrelates with a decrease or constancy in data might suggest that something is missing. Various changes through time can interrelate positively or negatively in complex ways, similar to multiple paths of action that sometime weave into and then away from each other. But qualitative interrelationship does not necessarily imply causality, and not everything that links suggests an authentic interrelationship.

Just as proportions of categories function as a quantitative tactic for discerning charge across time, supplemental statistical correlation can lead to or support observations of qualitative interrelationships across time. When interrelationship cannot be supported by available evidence, return to the field if possible for additional observation or interview data to confirm or disconfirm your hunch. Logic, common sense, life experience, intuition, and good data are needed to weave the possible interrelation-ships at work.

The conceptual process for analyzing both interrelationships and change in longitudinal qualitative data is like observing various colored dyes mixing together in the natural currents of water or wearing multi- and interdiscipli-nary lenses and filters to collage or network, rather than rank, the interre-lated factors influencing and affecting change, particularly in developmental studies. The eventual discovery of interrelationships between ponds and pools of data is one that emerges after multiple readings of the corpus, data reduction into visual displays, and extended reflection on all possible con-nections and overlap.

Which changes through time oppose or harmonize with natural human develop-ment or constructed social processes? Knowledge of cognitive, physical, emo-tional, and other domains of human development for children and adults of both genders and various ethnicities is useful to determine if change in the longitudinal study's participants is due primarily to natural or social processes, or is the result of intervening conditions. Previous developmental or social research may provide conceptual frameworks, clarifications, guid-ance, support, or even challenges for any observed changes in the researcher's longitudinal data. Constructed social processes that may be outlined in phases, stages, and cycles provide templates, if appropriate to the particular study, to discern whether the data record of change harmonizes with or disconfirms previous findings. In a positivist sense, these constructions and theories are also attempts to explain, predict, and control human actions in particular contexts.

If the researcher chooses to transcend the particular longitudinal qualita-tive observations of an individual's or small group's development in order to generalize to a larger or broader population, strategic writing that progresses from the particular to the general, and multi- or representative site selection, might be employed. The transferability of these theoretical models for pre-diction, however, is risky. A relatively large spectrum of participants may en-hance and lend support to any transferable findings the researcher may assert, but the situated time period, geographic location of the study, and the study's own particular contexts may limit the extent of that transfer. It may be best to limit and test predictions through assertions-in-progress within the time parameters of the longitudinal study itself.

Longitudinal qualitative data analysis acknowledges both the linearity and nonlinearity of developmental pathways and human life trajectories and can examine in depth the multiple dimensions of human agency in concert with social institutions and thus the multiple variables and predictors inter-acting through time. But personal development is an elusive phenomenon to abstract into transferable theory. Solo rhythms of change, influenced and af-fected by individual human agency and one's contextual and intervening conditions, merit reexamination of their unique patterns for comparison against previously held assumptions of universal change.

What are participant or conceptual rhythms (phases, stages, cycles, and so on) through time? If ample longitudinal qualitative data exist, participant changes could be apportioned into theoretical periodicities of human ac-tion. Researchers may find serial, cumulative, or repetitive actions embed-ded within and woven throughout the vast tapestry of the data corpus. These rhythmic action clusters—the pattern of patterns—can take many forms according to how the researcher observes them in the data: linear, se-quential, cyclical, multitempoed, improvised, choreographed, and so on. Phases, stages, and cycles are traditional patterns for constructing time-based flows to human actions, but they are just three available options. One major difference between a phase and a stage is that the latter suggests cumulative progression. Cycles are repetitive waves of participant actions. Multirhythmic pattern combinations are also possible; for example, one or more phases may be embedded within a stage, and some stages may be cyclical.

Phases, stages, and cycles can consist of typical or atypical portions of a particular longitudinal process or system. Characteristic of these time-based constructions are beginnings and endings, though these may not necessarily exist as specific moments in time, or be defined and contained by specific initiating and concluding actions. Descriptions of phases, stages, and cycles should include notation of their theoretical frequency, tempo, and duration, plus explanations of transitional processes—the threshold between periods that determines how or why participants make their transition from one period through the next. But a specific number of months or years, or even general types of epiphanies, cannot function as rigid borders or markers for these theoretical periodicities. Contextual and intervening conditions can decelerate, accelerate, or maintain the rhythms of participant actions, attitudes, values, and belief systems within phases, stages, cycles, and long-term evolutionary patterns. Progression and/or regression from one through the other depend on participant agency and social interactions.

What is the through-line of the study? The through-line is a holistic summary of the data corpus that captures a thematic flow or qualitative trajectory. It consists of a single word, phrase, sentence, or paragraph with an accompanying narrative that describes, analyzes, and/or interprets the researcher's primary observations of participant change through time. A through-line's explanatory narrative includes references to time, processual terms, and markers (beginnings, middles, and/or endings of the journey at various locations through time). The through-line might employ an in vivo code with summative power for other major categories or incorporate such representational literary devices as simile or metaphor to capture the essence or meaning of participant change. A through-line is not the ultimate analytic or interpretive goal of longitudinal qualitative data analysis. It is only one of several data summary strategies to springboard into more complex storytelling.

Finally, don't be intimidated by the months, years, or even decades of commitment required to collect and analyze longitudinal qualitative data. The longest journey begins with a single step. And every journey changes us in some way for the better.

Appendix: Longitudinal Qualitative Data Summary

Data Time Pool/Pond: From ___/___/_____ Through ___/___/_____

Study: _____Researcher(s):_____

(when possible or if relevant, note specific days, dates, times, periods, etc. below; use appropriate DYNAMIC descriptors)

DATA TIME POOL/POND: FROM ___/___/_____ THROUGH ___/___/_____

STUDY:_____RESEARCHER(S):_____

(when possible or if relevant, note specific days, dates, times, periods, etc. below; use appropriate DYNAMIC descriptors)

INCREASE EMERGE	CUMULATIVE	SURGE EPIPHANY	DECREASE CEASE	CONSTANT CONSISTENT	IDIOSYNCRATIC	MISSING

CONTEXTUAL/INTERVENING CONDITIONS INFLUENCING AND AFFECTING CHANGES ABOVE

DIFFERENCES ABOVE FROM PREVIOUS DATA SUMMARIES

(circle and connect above, then analyze) INTERRELATIONSHIPS

CHANGES THAT OPPOSE/HARMONIZE WITH HUMAN DEVELOPMENT/SOCIAL PROCESSES	PARTICIPANT/CONCEPTUAL RHYTHMS (phases, stages, cycles, etc. in progress)

PRELIMINARY ASSERTIONS AS DATA ANALYSIS PROGRESSES (refer to previous data summaries)	THROUGH-LINE (in progress)

Notes

1. "Affects" (instead of "effects") is a deliberate term choice, and its use will be explained later in the text. I developed the construct "influences and affects" years before Goodall's work, which states that "good scholarly new ethnographic writing *affects* and *influences* us" (2000, p. 195). It was frustrating to review both previously and newly published works in qualitative research as I wrote this manuscript, only to discover that what I thought was an original idea on my part had already been developed by someone else. On the other hand, those discoveries reassured me that my thinking was "on the same page" with reputable scholars in the field. I do give credit where credit is due through references, but any similarities you may notice between my ideas and others' not credited are purely coincidental.

2. Thanks are extended to my research colleague Laura A. McCammon for her contributions to this section, extracted from an earlier coauthored paper (Saldaña and McCammon, 2000).

3. Smaller ponds could be called "puddles" if you wish to extend the metaphor. See Fink (2000), who documents the life cycle of an innovative school across time through various separate ponds or "frames": leadership, structure, teachers' work and lives, and so on.

4. Ironically, the field of psychology, with its predominant quantitative measures from questionnaires and scales, also relies on dynamics to describe findings. Winefield et al., in *Growing Up with Unemployment: A Longitudinal Study of Its Psychological Impact*, interpret their participants' attitudes (collected primarily from quantitative instruments) through such terms as "very positive," "more optimistic," and "a heightened level of aspiration" (1993, pp. 146–47).

5. I read Agar months after I came up with this idea, only to discover he had already written a comparable analogy (1996, pp. 57–58). We differ, though, on the function of the initial summary response.

6. For elegant examples of how longitudinal qualitative studies can be complex without being complicated, read Ågren's "Life at 85 and 92: A Qualitative Longitudinal Study of How the Oldest Old Experience and Adjust to the Increasing Uncertainty of Existence" (1998), McCammon's "The Story of Marty: A Case Study of Teacher Burnout" (1992), and Reutter et al.'s "Socialization into Nursing: Nursing Students As Learners" (1997). For a mesodomain analysis of educational policy, read Hall's "The Consequences of Qualitative Analysis for Sociological Theory: Beyond the Microlevel" (1995). And for an insightful overview of longitudinal method in anthropology with examples of participant change in a fieldwork study, read Epstein's "Mysore Villages Revisited" (2002). There are doubtless many more excellent longitudinal qualitative studies in print that I have not had the good fortune to read, and I welcome your recommendations to continue my personal learning. E-mail your references to: Johnny.Saldana@asu.edu. It is not difficult to access the available literature; it is just difficult for me to survey everything relevant from multiple disciplines.

References

Adams, M. 1997. Pedagogical frameworks for social justice education. In M. Adams, L. A. Bell, and P. Griffin (eds.), *Teaching for diversity and social justice: A sourcebook* (pp. 30–43). New York: Routledge.

After the terror. 2002. *Arizona Republic*, 10 March, p. A15.

Agar, M. 1994. *Language shock: Understanding the culture of conversation*. New York: William Morrow.

———. 1996. *The professional stranger: An informal introduction to ethnography* (2nd ed). San Diego: Academic.

Ågren, M. 1998. Life at 85 and 92: A qualitative longitudinal study of how the oldest old experience and adjust to the increasing uncertainty of existence. *International Journal of Aging and Human Development* 47, no. 2: 105–17.

"Anything goes" attitude looks like it's here to stay. 2002. *Arizona Republic*, 14 July, p. V2.

Areen, J. 1992. Legal constraints on social research with children. In B. Stanley and J. E. Sieber (eds.), *Social research on children and adolescents: Ethical issues* (pp. 7–28). Newbury Park, CA: Sage.

Banks, J. A. 1994. *Multiethnic education: Theory and practice* (3rd ed.). Boston: Allyn and Bacon.

Barone, T. 2001. *Touching eternity: The enduring outcomes of teaching*. New York: Teachers College Press.

Benjamin, R. 1998. Middle schools for latinos: A framework for success. In M. L. González, A. Huerta-Macías, and J. V. Tinajero (eds.), *Educating latino students: A guide to successful practice* (pp. 239–267). Lancaster, PA: Technomic.

Berliner, D. 1997. The development of expertise. Paper presented at the Arizona State University Superintendent Lecture Series, December, Tempe, AZ.

Blumenfeld, W. J. 1998. Adolescence, sexual orientation and identity: An overview. In L. Mitchell (ed.), *Tackling gay issues in school* (pp. 28–39). Watertown, CT: GLSEN Connecticut and Planned Parenthood Connecticut.

Boal, A. 1995. *Games for actors and non-actors*. (A. Jackson, trans.). New York: Routledge.

Bogdan, R. C., and Biklen, S. K. 1998. *Qualitative research in education: An introduction to theory and methods* (3rd ed.). Boston: Allyn and Bacon.

Braver, S. L., and O'Connell, D. 1998. *Divorced dads: Shattering the myths*. New York: Tarcher/Putnam.

Brizuela, B. M., and García-Sellers, M. J. 1999. School adaptation: A triangular process. *American Educational Research Journal* 36, no. 2: 345–70.

Brooks, J., Ansell, J., and Sakai, R. (Producers). 2001. *Riding in cars with boys*. [Film]. (Available from Columbia Pictures)

Brown, C. L. 1997. Longevity and the secondary theatre arts teacher: A case study. Ph.D. diss., Arizona State University.

Bullough, R. V., Jr. 1989. *First-year teacher: A case study*. New York: Teachers College Press.

Bullough, R. V., Jr., and Baughman, K. 1997. *"First-year teacher" eight years later: An inquiry into teacher development*. New York: Teachers College Press.

Bury, A., Popple, K., and Barker, J. 1998. You've got to think really hard: Children making sense of the aims and content of theatre in health education. *Research in Drama Education* 3, no. 1: 13–27.

Cairns, R. B., Bergman, L. R., and Kagan, J. (eds.). 1998. *Methods and models for studying the individual*. Thousand Oaks, CA: Sage.

Cairns, R. B., and Rodkin, P. C. 1998. Phenomena regained: From configurations to pathways. In R. B. Cairns, L. R. Bergman, and J. Kagan (eds.), *Methods and models for studying the individual* (pp. 245–64). Thousand Oaks, CA: Sage.

Campanella, R. and Campanella, M. 1999. *New Orleans then and now*. Gretna, LA: Pelican.

Century, M. 2001. Cultural laboratories. Paper presented at the Arizona State University Institute for Studies in the Arts, Tempe, AZ.

Chapman, J. 1999. *Female impersonations: Young performers and the crisis of adolescence*. Unpublished manuscript.

Christensen, P., and James, A. 2000. *Research with children: Perspectives and practices*. London: Falmer.

Clandinin, D. J., and Connelly, F. M. 2000. *Narrative inquiry: Experience and story in qualitative research*. San Francisco: Jossey-Bass.

Coleman, L. M. 2001. Young people's intentions and use of condoms: Qualitative findings from a longitudinal study. *Health Education Journal* 60, no. 3: 205–20.

Connelly, F. M., and Clandinin, D. J. 1988. *Teachers as curriculum planners: Narratives of experience*. New York: Teachers College Press.

Cooper, A. 1998. Mind the gap! An ethnographic approach to cross-cultural workplace communication research. In M. Byram and M. Fleming (eds.), *Language learning in intercultural perspective: Approaches through drama and ethnography* (pp. 119–46). Cambridge: Cambridge University Press.

Corsaro, W. A., and Molinari, L. 2000. Entering and observing in children's worlds: A reflection on a longitudinal ethnography of early education in Italy. In P. Christensen and A. James (eds.), *Research with children: Perspectives and practices* (pp. 179–200). London: Falmer.

Creswell, J. W. 1998. *Qualitative inquiry and research design: Choosing among five traditions*. Thousand Oaks, CA: Sage.

Daniluk, J. C. 2001. Reconstructing their lives: A longitudinal, qualitative analysis of the transition to biological childlessness for infertile couples. *Journal of Counseling and Development* 79, no. 4: 439–49.

Davies, K. 1989. Women and time: Weaving the strands of everyday life. Ph.D. diss., Lund University.

Deldime, R., and Pigeon, J. 1989. The memory of the young audience. *Youth Theatre Journal* 4, no. 2: 3–8.

Delgado-Gaitan, C. 2000. Researching change and changing the researcher. In B. M. Brizuela, J. P. Stewart, R. G. Carillio, and J. G. Berger (eds.), *Acts of inquiry in qualitative research* (pp. 389–409). Cambridge, MA: Harvard Educational Review.

Denzin, N. K. 1989. *Interpretive interactionism*. Newbury Park, CA: Sage.

———. 1994. The art and politics of interpretation. In N. K. Denzin and Y. S. Lincoln (Eds.), *Handbook of qualitative research* (pp. 500–15). Thousand Oaks, CA: Sage.

———. 1997. *Interpretive ethnography: Ethnographic practices for the twenty-first century.* Thousand Oaks, CA: Sage.

———. 2001. The reflexive interview and a performative social science. *Qualitative Research* 1, no. 1: 23–46.

Dey, I. 1999. *Grounding grounded theory: Guidelines for qualitative inquiry*. San Diego: Academic.

Diamond, C. T. P., and Mullen, C. A. 1999. Mirrors, rivers, and snakes: Arts-based teacher development. In C. T. P. Diamond and C. A. Mullen (eds.), *The postmodern educator: Arts-based inquiries and teacher development*. New York: Peter Lang.

Dockrell, J., Lewis, A., and Lindsay, G. 2000. Researching children's perspectives: A psychological dimension. In A. Lewis and G. Lindsay (eds.), *Researching children's perspectives* (pp. 46–58). Buckingham: Open University Press.

Edgerton, R. B. 1992. *Sick societies: Challenging the myth of primitive harmony*. New York: Free Press.

Eisner, E. W. 1991. *The enlightened eye*. New York: Macmillan.

Emerson, R. M., Fretz, R. I., and Shaw, L. L. 1995. *Writing ethnographic fieldnotes*. Chicago: University of Chicago Press.

Epstein, T. S. 2002. Mysore villages revisited. In R. V. Kemper and A. P. Royce (eds.), *Chronicling cultures: Long-term field research in anthropology* (pp. 59–80). Walnut Creek, CA: AltaMira.

Erickson, F. 1986. Qualitative methods in research on teaching. In M. C. Wittrock (ed.), *Handbook of research on teaching* (3rd ed.) (pp. 119–61). New York: Macmillan.

Fabun, D. 1967. *The dynamics of change*. Englewood Cliffs, NJ: Prentice-Hall.

Fetterman, D. 1998. *Ethnography* (2nd ed.). Thousand Oaks, CA: Sage.

Fine, G. A., and Sandstrom, K. L. 1988. *Knowing children: Participant observation with minors*. Newbury Park, CA: Sage.

Fink, D. 2000. *Good schools/real schools: Why school reform doesn't last*. New York: Teachers College Press.

Flaherty, M. G. 1996. Some methodological principles from research in practice: Validity, truth, and method in the study of lived time. *Qualitative Inquiry* 2, no. 3: 285–99.

———. 1999. *A watched pot: How we experience time*. New York: New York University Press.

Flick, U. 2002. *An introduction to qualitative research* (2nd ed.). London: Sage.

Florence, N. 1998. *bell hooks' engaged pedagogy: A transgressive education for critical consciousness*. Westport, CT: Bergin and Garvey.

Florida, R. 2002. *The rise of the creative class*. New York: Basic.

Foster, G. M. 2002. A half century of field research in Tzintzuntzan, Mexico: A personal view. In R. V. Kemper and A. P. Royce (eds.), *Chronicling cultures: Long-term field research in anthropology* (pp. 252–83). Walnut Creek, CA: AltaMira.

France, A., Bendelow, G., and Williams, S. 2000. A "risky" business: Researching the health beliefs of children and young people. In A. Lewis and G. Lindsay (eds.), *Researching children's perspectives* (pp. 151–62). Buckingham: Open University Press.

Fullan, M. 1999. *Change forces: The sequel*. London: Falmer.

———. 2001. *The new meaning of educational change* (3rd ed.). New York: Teachers College Press.

Gitlin, A. D. 2000. Educative research, voice, and school change. In B. M. Brizuela, J. P. Stewart, R. G. Carillio, and J. G. Berger (eds.), *Acts of inquiry in qualitative research* (pp. 95–118). Cambridge, MA: Harvard Educational Review.

Glass, P. 1996. *Music in twelve parts*. [Brochure]. New York: Nonesuch Records.

Glesne, C. 1999. *Becoming qualitative researchers: An introduction* (2nd ed.). New York: Longman.

Glick, W. H., Huber, G. P., Miller, C. C., Doty, H. D., and Sutcliffe, K. M. 1995. Studying changes in organizational design and effectiveness: Retrospective event histories and periodic assessments. In G. P. Huber and A. H. Van de Ven (eds.), *Longitudinal field research methods* (pp. 126–54). Thousand Oaks, CA: Sage.

Goldberg, P. D. 1977. Development of a category system for the analysis and response of the young theatre audience. Ph.D. diss., Florida State University.

Goleman, D. 1995. *Emotional intelligence*. New York: Bantam.

Goodall, H. J. 2000. *Writing the new ethnography*. Walnut Creek, CA: AltaMira.

Graue, M. E., and Walsh, D. J. 1998. *Studying children in context: Theories, methods, and ethics*. Thousand Oaks, CA: Sage.

Graveline, F. J. 1998. *Circle works: Transforming eurocentric consciousness.* Halifax: Fernwood.

Grieg, A., and Taylor, J. 1999. *Doing research with children.* London: Sage.

Hager, L., Maier, B., O'Hara, E., Ott, D., and Saldaña, J. 2000. Theatre teachers' perceptions of Arizona state standards. *Youth Theatre Journal* 14: 64–77.

Hall, P. M. 1995. The consequences of qualitative analysis for sociological theory: Beyond the microlevel. *The Sociological Quarterly* 36, no. 2: 397–423.

Hallebone, E. L. 1992. Use of typologies for "measuring" self-identity change: Methodological issues in longitudinal qualitative research. *Quality and Quantity* 26, no. 1: 1–17.

Hargreaves, A. 2000. Model schools in mortal contexts: The fate of sustainability. Paper presented at the annual conference of the American Educational Research Association, April, New Orleans, LA.

Hargreaves, A., Earl, L., Moore, S., and Manning, S. 2001. *Learning to change: Teaching beyond subjects and standards.* San Francisco: Josey-Bass.

Hawking, S. 1988. *A brief history of time.* New York: Bantam.

Heinz, W. R., and Krüger, H. 2001. Life course: Innovations and challenges for social research. *Current Sociology* 49, no. 2: 29–45.

Holloway, S. D., Rambaud, M. F., Fuller, B., and Eggers-Piérola, C. 1995. What is "appropriate practice" at home and in child care? Low-income mothers' views on preparing their children for school. *Early Childhood Research Quarterly* 10: 451–73.

Holmes, R. M. 1998. *Fieldwork with children.* Thousand Oaks, CA: Sage.

hooks, b. 1994. *Teaching to transgress: Education as the practice of freedom.* New York: Routledge.

Huber, G. P., and Van de Ven, A. H. (eds.). 1995. *Longitudinal field research methods.* Thousand Oaks, CA: Sage.

Huberman, A. M. 1989. The professional life cycle of teachers. *Teachers College Record* 91, no. 1: 31–57.

Huberman, A. M., and Miles, M. B. 1994. Data management and analysis methods. In N. K. Denzin and Y. S. Lincoln (eds.), *Handbook of qualitative research* (pp. 428–44). Thousand Oaks, CA: Sage.

Isaac, S., and Michael, W. B. 1995. *Handbook in research and evaluation* (3rd ed.). San Diego: Edits.

Janesick, V. J. 1994. The dance of qualitative research design: Metaphor, methodolatry, and meaning. In N. K. Denzin and Y. S. Lincoln (eds.), *Handbook of qualitative research* (pp. 209–19). Thousand Oaks, CA: Sage.

Johnson, S. 1998. *Who moved my cheese? An amazing way to deal with change in your work and in your life.* New York: Putnam's.

Kelly, J. R., and McGrath, J. E. 1988. *On time and method.* Newbury Park, CA: Sage.

Kemper, R. V., and Royce, A. P. (Eds.). 2002. *Chronicling cultures: Long-term field research in anthropology.* Walnut Creek, CA: AltaMira.

Kidder, T. 1989. *Among schoolchildren.* New York: Avon.

Knapp, N. F. 1997. Interviewing Joshua: On the importance of leaving room for serendipity. *Qualitative Inquiry* 3, no. 3: 326–42.

Kübler-Ross, E. 1969. *On death and dying*. New York: Macmillan.

Kvale, S. 1996. *InterViews: An introduction to qualitative research interviewing*. Thousand Oaks, CA: Sage.

Lancy, D. F. 1993. *Qualitative research in education: An introduction to the major traditions*. New York: Longman.

LeCompte, M. D., and Preissle, J. 1993. *Ethnography and qualitative design in educational research* (2nd ed.). San Diego: Academic.

Lee, O., and Yarger, S. J. 1996. Modes of inquiry in research on teacher education. In J. Sikula (ed.), *Handbook of research on teacher education* (2nd ed.) (pp. 14–37). New York: Macmillan.

Lennon, R., and Eisenberg, N. 1987. Gender and age differences in empathy and sympathy. In N. Eisenberg and J. Strayer (eds.), *Empathy and its development* (pp. 195–217). New York: Cambridge University Press.

Lerner, R. M., Lerner, J. V., De Stefanis, I., and Apfel, A. 2001. Understanding developmental systems in adolescence: Implications for methodological strategies, data analytic approaches, and training. *Journal of Adolescent Research* 16, no. 1: 9–27.

Levine, R. 1997. *A geography of time*. New York: Basic.

Lewis, A., and Lindsay, G. (eds.). 2000. *Researching children's perspectives*. Buckingham: Open University Press.

Lincoln, Y. S., and Guba, E. G. 1985. *Naturalistic inquiry*. Newbury Park, CA: Sage.

Lindsay, G. 2000. Researching children's perspectives: Ethical issues. In A. Lewis and G. Lindsay (Eds.), *Researching children's perspectives* (pp. 3–20). Buckingham: Open University Press.

Lippincott, K. (Ed.). 1999. *The story of time*. London: Merrell Holberton.

Lister, R., Smith, N., Middleton, S., and Cox, L. 2002. Negotiating transitions to citizenship: Summary of key findings. Unpublished report.

Manderson, L., Kelaher, M., and Woelz-Stirling, N. 2001. Developing qualitative databases for multiple users. *Qualitative Health Research* 11, no. 2: 149–60.

Marshall, C., and Rossman, G. B. 1999. *Designing qualitative research* (3rd ed.). Thousand Oaks, CA: Sage.

Masson, J. 2000. Researching children's perspectives: Legal issues. In A. Lewis and G. Lindsay (eds.), *Researching children's perspectives* (pp. 34–45). Buckingham: Open University Press.

Maxwell, J. A. 1996. *Qualitative research design: An interactive approach*. Thousand Oaks, CA: Sage.

McCammon, L. A. 1992. The story of Marty: A case study of teacher burnout. *Youth Theatre Journal* 7, no. 2: 17–22.

———. 1994. Teamwork is not just a word: Factors disrupting the development of a departmental group of theatre teachers. *Youth Theatre Journal* 8, no. 3: 3–9.

McVea, K. 2001. Collaborative qualitative research: Reflections for a quantitative researcher. Paper presented at the annual conference of the American Educational Research Association, April, Seattle, WA.

Meloy, J. M. 2001. *Writing the qualitative dissertation: Understanding by doing* (2nd ed.). Hillsdale, NJ: Lawrence Erlbaum.

Menard, S. 1991. *Longitudinal research*. Newbury Park, CA: Sage.

Mienczakowski, J. 1999. Emerging forms: Comments upon Johnny Saldaña's "Ethical issues in an ethnographic performance text: The 'dramatic impact' of 'juicy stuff.'" *Research in Drama Education* 4, no. 1: 97–100.

Miles, M. B., and Huberman, A. M. 1994. *Qualitative data analysis* (2nd ed.). Thousand Oaks, CA: Sage.

Millar, G. W. 2002. *The Torrance kids at mid-life: Selected case studies of creative behavior*. Westport, CT: Ablex.

Morse, J. M., and Richards, L. 2002. *Readme first for a user's guide to qualitative methods*. Thousand Oaks, CA: Sage.

Mouat, T. W. 1996. The timely emergence of social cartography. In R. Paulston (ed.), *Social cartography: Mapping ways of seeing social and educational change* (pp. 81–116). New York: Garland.

Murray, B. 1998. Nowhere to hide but together: A narrative case study of three classroom teachers, a drama specialist, and their supporters negotiating toward an artistic vision of teaching through drama in an urban elementary school. Ph.D. diss., Ohio State University.

Mussen, P. H., Conger, J. J., Kagan, J., and Huston, A. C. 1990. *Child development and personality* (7th ed.). New York: HarperCollins.

Naisbitt, J. 1982. *Megatrends: Ten new directions transforming our lives*. New York: Warner.

Nicholson, H. 1999. Research as confession. *Research in Drama Education* 4, no. 1: 100–3.

Nisbet, R. 1976. *Sociology as an art form*. New York: Oxford University Press.

Oakes, J., and Lipton, M. 1999. *Teaching to change the world*. Boston: McGraw-Hill College.

Oakley, M. W. 2000. Children and young people and care proceedings. In A. Lewis and G. Lindsay (eds.), *Researching children's perspectives* (pp. 73–85). Buckingham: Open University Press.

Ollerenshaw, J. A., and Creswell, J. W. 2002. Narrative research: A comparison of two restorying data analysis approaches. *Qualitative Inquiry* 8, no. 3: 329–47.

Patton, M. Q. 2002. *Qualitative research and evaluation methods* (3rd ed.). Thousand Oaks, CA: Sage.

Paulston, R. G., and Liebman, M. 1996. Social cartography: A new metaphor/tool for comparative studies. In R. Paulston (ed.), *Social cartography: Mapping ways of seeing social and educational change* (pp. 7–28). New York: Garland.

Petrocelli, J. V. 2002. Processes and stages of change: Counseling with the transtheoretical model of change. *Journal of Counseling and Development* 80, no. 1: 22–30.

Pettigrew, A. M. 1995. Longitudinal field research on change: Theory and practice. In G. P. Huber and A. H. Van de Ven (eds.), *Longitudinal field research methods* (pp. 91–125). Thousand Oaks, CA: Sage.

Pritchett, P., and Pound, R. n.d. *A survival guide to the stress of organizational change.* Plano, TX: Pritchett Rummler-Brache

Prochaska, J. O., DiClemente, C. C., and Norcross, J. C. 1992. In search of how people change: Applications to addictive behaviors. *American Psychologist* 47, no. 9: 1102–14.

Qvortrup, J. 2000. Macroanalysis of childhood. In P. Christensen and A. James (eds.), *Research with children: Perspectives and practices* (pp. 77–97). London: Falmer.

Researchers create formula to predict divorce. 2000. *Arizona Republic*, 17 September, p. J2.

Reutter, L., Field, P. A., Campbell, I. E., and Day, R. 1997. Socialization into nursing: Nursing students as learners. *Journal of Nursing Education* 36, no. 4: 149–55.

Rist, R. C. 1994. Influencing the policy process with qualitative research. In N. K. Denzin and Y. S. Lincoln (eds.), *Handbook of qualitative research* (pp. 545–57). Thousand Oaks, CA: Sage.

Rossman, G. B., and Rallis, S. F. 1998. *Learning in the field: An introduction to qualitative research.* Thousand Oaks, CA: Sage.

Royce, A. P. 2002. Learning to see, learning to listen: Thirty-five years of fieldwork with the Isthmus Zapotec. In R. V. Kemper and A. P. Royce (eds.), *Chronicling cultures: Long-term field research in anthropology* (pp. 8–33). Walnut Creek, CA: AltaMira.

Royce, A. P., and Kemper, R. V. 2002. Long-term field research: Metaphors, paradigms, and themes. In R. V. Kemper and A. P. Royce (eds.), *Chronicling cultures: Long-term field research in anthropology* (pp. xii–xxxviii). Walnut Creek, CA: AltaMira.

Ruspini, E. 1999. Longitudinal research and the analysis of social change. *Quality and Quantity* 33, no. 3: 219–27.

Rutter, M., Maughan, B., Pickles, A., and Simonoff, E. 1998. Retrospective recall recalled. In R. B. Cairns, L. R. Bergman, and J. Kagan (eds.), *Methods and models for studying the individual* (pp. 219–42). Thousand Oaks, CA: Sage.

Saldaña, J. 1989. A quantitative analysis of children's responses to theatre from probing questions: A pilot study. *Youth Theatre Journal* 3, no. 4: 7–17.

———. 1991. Drama, theatre and Hispanic youth: Interviews with selected teachers and artists. *Youth Theatre Journal* 5, no. 4: 3–8.

———. 1993. *The Arizona State University seven year longitudinal study of drama with and theatre for children: Qualitative analysis of data from the theatre for children component.* Unpublished manuscript.

———. 1995. "Is theatre necessary?" Final exit interviews with sixth grade participants from the ASU longitudinal study. *Youth Theatre Journal* 9: 14–30.

———. 1996. "Significant differences" in child audience response: Assertions from the ASU longitudinal study. *Youth Theatre Journal* 10: 67–83.

———. 1997. "Survival": A white teacher's conception of drama with inner-city Hispanic youth. *Youth Theatre Journal* 11: 25–46.

———. 1998a. Ethical issues in an ethnographic performance text: The "dramatic impact" of "juicy stuff." *Research in Drama Education* 3, no. 2: 181–196.

———. 1998b. "Maybe someday, if I'm famous. . .": An ethnographic performance text. In J. Saxton and C. Miller (eds), *Drama and theatre in education: The research of practice, the practice of research* (pp. 89–109). Brisbane: IDEA Publications.

———. 1999. Playwriting with data: Ethnographic performance texts. *Youth Theatre Journal* 13:60–71.

———. 2000. *Theatre of the oppressed with children.* Unpublished manuscript.

———. 2001a. *Finding my place: The Brad trilogy.* Unpublished manuscript.

———. 2001b. "If you ask tough questions . . ." *Research in Drama Education* 9, no. 1: 99–101.

———. In press. Dramatizing data: A primer. *Qualitative Inquiry.*

Saldaña, J., and McCammon, L. A. 2000. Finding the voice of the child: Strategies for interviewing children in arts education research. Paper presented at the annual conference of the International Drama in Education Research Institute, Columbus, OH.

Saldaña, J., and Otero, H. D. 1990. Experiments in assessing children's responses to theatre with the semantic differential. *Youth Theatre Journal* 5, no. 1: 11–19.

Saldaña, J., and Wright, L. 1996. An overview of experimental research principles for studies in drama and theatre for youth. In P. Taylor (ed.), *Researching drama and arts education: Paradigms and possibilities* (pp. 115–31). London: Falmer.

Sarason, S. B. 1999. *Teaching as a performing art.* New York: Teachers College Press.

Schofield, J. W. 2002. Increasing the generalizability of qualitative research. In A. M. Huberman and M. B. Miles (eds.), *The qualitative researcher's companion* (pp. 171–203). Thousand Oaks, CA: Sage.

Schwandt, T. A. 2001. *Dictionary of qualitative inquiry* (2nd ed.). Thousand Oaks, CA: Sage.

Scott, J. 2000. Children as respondents: The challenge for quantitative methods. In P. Christensen and A. James (eds.), *Research with children: Perspectives and practices* (pp. 98–119). London: Falmer.

Scudder, T., and Colson, E. 2002. Long-term research in Gwembe Valley, Zambia. In R. V. Kemper and A. P. Royce (eds.), *Chronicling cultures: Long-term field research in anthropology* (pp. 197–238). Walnut Creek, CA: AltaMira.

Shapiro, A. (prod. and dir.). 1999. *Scared straight! Twenty years later.* [Video]. (Available from AIMS Multimedia, 9710 DeSoto Avenue, Chatsworth, CA 91311.)

Sikula, J. 1996. Introduction. In J. Sikula (ed.), *Handbook of research on teacher education* (2nd ed.) (pp. xv–xxiii). New York: Macmillan.

Singer, B. (ed.). 1998. *42 up: "Give me the child until he is seven and I will show you the man."* New York: New Press.

Sleeter, C. E. 1996. *Multicultural education as social activism.* New York: SUNY Press.

Smith, F. C., and Abrahamson, B. (1999). Calendars and thinking logically. *Multicultural Perspectives* 7, no. 2: 29–34.

Smith, L. 2001. Research project focus. *Restructuring Public Education SIG Newsletter*, April: 2–3.

Spradley, J. P. 1980. *Participant observation*. Fort Worth: Harcourt Brace Jovanovich.

Stewart, A. 1998. *The ethnographer's method*. Thousand Oaks, CA: Sage.

Strauss, A., and Corbin, J. 1990. *Basics of qualitative research*. Thousand Oaks, CA: Sage.

———. 1998. *Basics of qualitative research* (2nd ed.). Thousand Oaks, CA: Sage.

Sztompka, P. 1993. *The sociology of social change*. Oxford: Blackwell.

Taris, T. 2000. *A primer in longitudinal data analysis*. London: Sage.

Tashakkori, A., and Teddlie, C. 1998. *Mixed methodology*. Thousand Oaks, CA: Sage.

Taylor, A. S. 2000. The UN convention on the rights of the child: Giving children a voice. In A. Lewis and G. Lindsay (eds.), *Researching children's perspectives* (pp. 21–34). Buckingham: Open University Press.

Troman, G., and Woods, P. 2000. Careers under stress: Teacher adaptations at a time of intensive reform. *Journal of Educational Change* 1: 253–75.

Tuchman, G. 1994. Historical social science: Methodologies, methods, and meanings. In N. K. Denzin and Y. S. Lincoln (eds.), *Handbook of qualitative research* (pp. 306–23). Thousand Oaks, CA: Sage.

U.S. unveils most accurate timepiece. 1999. *Arizona Republic*, 30 December, p. A7.

Vanover, C. 2002. Attunement. Paper presented at the annual conference of the American Educational Research Association, New Orleans, LA.

Vogt, W. P. 1999. *Dictionary of statistics and methodology: A nontechnical guide for the social sciences* (2nd ed.). Thousand Oaks, CA: Sage.

Wadsworth, Y. 1997. *Do it yourself social research* (2nd ed.). St. Leonards, Australia: Allen and Unwin.

Way, N. 1998. *Everyday courage: The lives and stories of urban teenagers*. New York: New York University Press.

Wenger, G. C. 1999. Advantages gained by combining qualitative and quantitative data in a longitudinal study. *Journal of Aging Studies* 13, no. 4: 369–76.

Who are the real movers and shakers? All along, it's been the young. 1999. *Arizona Republic*, 12 December, p. E24.

Willett, J. B., Singer, J. D., and Martin, N. C. 1998. The design and analysis of longitudinal studies of development and psychopathology in context: Statistical models and methodological recommendations. *Development and Psychopathology* 10: 395–426.

Winefield, A. H., Tiggemann, M., Winefield, H. R., and Goldney, R. D. 1993. *Growing up with unemployment: A longitudinal study of its psychological impact*. New York: Routledge.

Winkelman, M. 1994. Cultural shock and adaptation. *Journal of Counseling and Development* 73, no. 2: 121–26.

Wolcott, H. F. 1984. *The man in the principal's office: An ethnography*. Prospect Heights, IL: Waveland.

———. 1990. On seeking—and rejecting—validity in qualitative research. In E. W. Eisner and A. Peshkin (eds.), *Qualitative inquiry in education: The continuing debate* (pp. 121–52). New York: Teachers College Press.

———. 1994. *Transforming qualitative data: Description, analysis, and interpretation.* Thousand Oaks, CA: Sage.

———. 1995. *The art of fieldwork.* Walnut Creek, CA: AltaMira.

———. 1999. *Ethnography: A way of seeing.* Walnut Creek CA: AltaMira.

———. 2002. *Sneaky kid and its aftermath: Ethics and intimacy in fieldwork.* Walnut Creek, CA: AltaMira.

Yates, L., and McLeod, J. 1996. "And how would you describe yourself?" Researchers and researched in the first stages of a qualitative, longitudinal research project. *Australian Journal of Education* 40, no. 1: 88–103.

Young, C. H., Savola, K. L., and Phelps, E. (eds.). 1991. *Inventory of longitudinal studies in the social sciences.* Newbury Park, CA: Sage.

Zeitlin, M. A. 2002. *Mark Klett: Ideas about time.* Tempe: Arizona State University Art Museum.

Zwiers, M. L., and Morrissette, P. J. 1999. *Effective interviewing of children: A comprehensive guide for counselors and human service workers.* Philadelphia: Accelerated Development.

Index

difference, 68–77, 123, 144, 156–60
dimensions. *See* dynamics
direction, 49, 51, 85, 108, 118, 134, 140
divorce, 10, 29, 39–40, 87, 131–32
Divorced Dads, 10, 131–32
documents, 13, 19, 42, 59, 116
domain, 16, 106, 108, 135, 154
domestic violence, 145–46
duration: cultural, 7; of cycles, 146;
  dynamics of, 81, 90; individual, 7;
  observing, 32, 84; of phases and
  stages, 144, 148
dynamics, 88–92, 162–63; of change, 7,
  65; of contextual and intervening
  conditions, 157; in differences, 71,
  73, 123; in field notes, 53–54;
  idiosyncratic, 109, 121–22; language
  to describe, 88–90, 173n4; of phases
  and stages, 144; and time, 81–134

education, 4, 11, 89, 139, 140, 142–43.
  See also school
elegance, 141, 158
emergence, 99–103, 163–64; and
  absence, 124–25; of categories,
  69–70, 71, 112; of patterns, 121; in
  qualitative research, 34, 40, 43
emotion, 39–40, 84, 87, 91, 94–97, 132,
  151
emotional ambivalence, 136–37, 147
emotional intelligence, 31, 106–7
empathy, 103, 106
employment, 139
environment, 18, 78, 83, 89, 112
epiphanies, 107, 108–11, 164–65; and
  cycles, 146; as data, 51; vs. increase,
  101; observation of, 33, 80; and
  phases, 143; in *Scared Straight! 20
  Years Later*, 69; and stages, 145, 149.
  See also critical incidents
epistemological, xi
epochal, 6
Epstein, T. S., 2, 174n6

Erickson, F., 93, 94, 151
Erikson, E., 105
erode, erosion, 76, 113
escalation, 107. *See also* surge
essence, 151, 155
ethics, 22–29
ethnic, ethnicity: and adolescence,
  42–43, 122–23, 138–39; and
  development, 135, 136, 148–49; in
  education, 100, 109, 114, 137–38,
  152; ethos of, 124; identity, 84, 136,
  150; in NVivo, 56; researcher, 115;
  studies, x
ethnographic performance texts, x, 2,
  38
ethnography, ethnographer: and change,
  65, 77, 117; educational, ix–x, 2–3,
  4–5, 85, 120, 130–31; observations,
  17–18, 150; and time, 3–4, 18–19, 33
*Ethnography and Qualitative Design in
  Educational Research*, 16
*Everyday Courage: The Lives and Stories
  of Urban Teenagers*, 122–23, 138–39.
  See also Way, N.
evolve, evolution: and culture, 113, 117;
  and cumulative affects, 104, 106–7;
  and patterns, 148; process of, 7–8,
  50, 76, 128
experimental research, ix

family, families, 18, 26, 37, 78, 96, 140
field notes: constancy and consistency
  of, 114–15; contents of, 13, 36, 40,
  76; cumulative, 30–31, 41; decrease
  in quality, 112; dynamics in, 53–54;
  and ethics, 25; formatting of, 57, 77;
  language for, 89, 148; questions
  during, 158–59; sharing, 27–28, 31;
  and through-line, 152; time and
  change, 31–33, 58–59, 76, 80
fieldwork: and change, 17–18, 43, 113;
  entry, 86; and field notes, 80, 112,
  134; length of, 2–5, 13–14, 16,

About the Author

Johnny Saldaña is a professor of theatre at Arizona State University's Katherine K. Herberger College of Fine Arts, and his qualitative research studies range from ethnography to ethnotheatre. He has published numerous articles on theatre teachers' perceptions of their practice and young people's development as audiences and artists.